Witchcraft and a Life in the New South Africa

Witchcraft and a Life in the New South Africa reconstructs the biography of an ordinary South African, Jimmy Mohale. Born in 1964, Jimmy came of age in rural South Africa during apartheid, then studied at university and worked as a teacher during the anti-apartheid struggle. In 2005, Jimmy died from an undiagnosed sickness, probably related to AIDS. Jimmy gradually came to see the unanticipated misfortune he experienced as a result of his father's witchcraft and sought remedies from diviners rather than from biomedical doctors. This study casts new light on scholarly understandings of the connections between South African politics, witchcraft, and the AIDS pandemic.

Isak Niehaus is currently Lecturer in the Department of Anthropology at Brunel University. He is the author of *Witchcraft, Power and Politics: Exploring the Occult in the South African Lowveld* (2001) and *Magic! AIDS Review 2009* (2010) with Fraser G. McNeill. He is a member of the council of the Royal Anthropological Institute and has done extensive fieldwork in South African rural areas.

'Over its career religion has probably disturbed men as much as it has cheered them, forced them into a head-on, unblinking confrontation of the fact that they are born to trouble as often as it enabled them to avoid such a confrontation. . . .'

(Geertz 1973a: 103)

THE INTERNATIONAL AFRICAN LIBRARY

The International African Library is a major monograph series from the International African Institute and complements its quarterly periodical *Africa*, the premier journal in the field of African studies. Theoretically informed and culturally sensitive ethnographies and studies of social relations 'on the ground' have long been central to the Institute's publications programme. The IAL includes works focused on development, especially on the linkages between the local and national levels of society; studies in the social and environmental sciences; and historical studies with social, cultural, and interdisciplinary dimensions.

For a list of titles published in the series, please see end of book.

Witchcraft and a Life in the New South Africa

Isak Niehaus

Brunel University

International African Institute, London

and

CAMBRIDGE
UNIVERSITY PRESS

CAMBRIDGE
UNIVERSITY PRESS

University Printing House, Cambridge CB2 8BS, United Kingdom

One Liberty Plaza, 20th Floor, New York, NY 10006, USA

477 Williamstown Road, Port Melbourne, VIC 3207, Australia

4843/24, 2nd Floor, Ansari Road, Daryaganj, Delhi - 110002, India

79 Anson Road, #06-04/06, Singapore 079906

Cambridge University Press is part of the University of Cambridge.

It furthers the University's mission by disseminating knowledge in the pursuit of education, learning and research at the highest international levels of excellence.

www.cambridge.org
Information on this title: www.cambridge.org/9781108442695

First published 2013
First paperback edition 2017

A catalogue record for this publication is available from the British Library

Library of Congress Cataloging in Publication data
Niehaus, Isak A. (Isak Arnold)
Witchcraft and a life in the new South Africa / Isak Niehaus.
p. cm. (The international African library ; 43)
Includes bibliographical references and index.
ISBN 978-1-107-01628-6 (hardback)
1. Witchcraft – South Africa. 2. Mohale, Jimmy, 1964–2005.
3. South Africa – Social life and customs – 20th century. I. Title.
BF1584.S6N53 2012
133.4′30968–dc23 2011040991

ISBN 978-1-107-01628-6 Hardback
ISBN 978-1-108-44269-5 Paperback

Contents

List of Maps and Figures

Maps

Figures

Notes on Currency

Prices are expressed in pound sterling (£) until 1961, when the Union of South Africa became a Republic, and in South African rand (R) thereafter. The exchange rate has fluctuated throughout the 1970s, 1980s, and 1990s. In 2004 the exchange rate was approximately £ = R12.50 and US$1 = R7.00.

Central Characters

Jimmy Mohale. The biographical subject is a 41-year-old teacher and occasional ethnographic research assistant. He holds B.Ed and BA (Honours) degrees from the University of Limpopo. Jimmy is medium-built and serious, though he has an excellent sense of humour.

Luckson Mohale. Jimmy's father (71) is a retired truck driver with wide experience working in different South African cities. Although excitable and quickly angered, Luckson is usually an extroverted, warm, and talkative person. Luckson is exceptionally neat, knowledgeable about politics and tradition, and fairly similar to Jimmy in appearance. He always spoke to me in Afrikaans. We never discussed the topic of witchcraft.

Ngwa (née) **Ngobeni (Selina Mohale).** Jimmy's mother (about 68) is usually found selling fruit and vegetables at the Impalahoek market, near her home. She is a fairly stout woman, who loves her seven children with all her heart. Though emotional, she is soft-spoken, and renowned for extreme kindness. She has begun to suffer from respiratory problems in her old age.

***Ngwa* Usinga.** Luckson Mohale's second wife and Jimmy's younger mother (about 62). She is the mother of six children and has frequently experienced tension and strife with her co-wife in the past.

Moses Mohale. Jimmy's oldest sibling (49) is well-built, taller than Jimmy, and closely resembles his father. Though not well educated, Moses is decisive, somewhat intense, and serious. Like his father, he usually works as a truck driver in Johannesburg.

***Ngwa* Mohale (Jessie Thobela)** (46) is Jimmy's only sister. Like her mother, she works as a fruit and vegetable vendor. Jessie is soft-spoken and introverted, and has given birth to eight children.

Peter Mohale (37), Jimmy's brother, is a staunch member of the Zion Christian Church. Twice married, he works in Johannesburg, and is very seldom at home.

Henry Mohale. Though Jimmy's younger sibling (30), he is often treated as senior because he is named after his paternal grandfather. Henry is highly intelligent and hard-working. He holds BA and MA degrees in Information Studies, and works as a subject librarian at the University of Limpopo. Though a father, Henry is single. Of all the Mohale siblings, he was the least willing to believe that his father practised witchcraft.

Kagišo Mohale (27) is Jimmy's youngest sibling. Though he wishes to work as a policeman, Kagišo has been consistently unemployed since leaving school. He is tall, slender, and athletic. He was one of the first to suspect his father of witchcraft.

Kevin Mohale, Jimmy's younger sibling, died in 1984, shortly after he returned from initiation, at the tender age of thirteen. Though I never met Kevin, his death shook the Mohale family, and memories of Kevin were very much present in everyday discourse.

***Ngwa* Mashile (Lerato Mohale)** (39) is Jimmy's wife and mother of his three children. She is considerably taller than Jimmy, and suffers from asthma. A Zionist, she holds a PTC (primary teacher's certificate) and teaches in a local primary school. Though set in her ways, she is fairly introverted and soft-spoken. Separated from Jimmy after consistent quarrels over money and extramarital affairs, she is a caring and conscientious parent.

Kgopotšo Mohale (17), **Thandi Mohale** (15), and **Katlego Mohale** (5) are Jimmy and Lerato's children, who were attending school during the time of the events written about in this biography.

Andrew Mohale (34) was Jimmy's half-brother and one of the first to accuse their father of witchcraft. He was unemployed, separated from his wife, and renowned for smoking cannabis and for heavy drinking. Andrew was said to have died of AIDS-related diseases during 2005.

Iris Maluleke. As Jimmy's most important extramarital lover (27), she is widely blamed for destroying his family. From a poverty-stricken family, Iris is extremely attractive, and occasionally works as a hairdresser. She is known as being very assertive.

Duduzile Thobela (12) and **Rebecca Mohale** (27) are Jimmy's nieces. As Jessie's daughter, Duduzile was an industrious primary school pupil who died from a mysterious respiratory condition. Rebecca, who was Moses's daughter, worked as a chef at a holiday resort. She died, probably from AIDS-related diseases, in 2005. Relatives attributed their deaths to witchcraft.

***Ngwa* Chiloane (Nana Mohale)**, Luckson's mother, was also suspected of practising witchcraft. She lived in Luckson's home, and, despite her love for her son, was renowned for a quarrelsome nature and the dislike she expressed towards members of the Shangaan-speaking community.

Patrick Monna (35) and **Ace Ubisi** (39) are Jimmy's neighbours, friends, and occasional drinking mates. Patrick is a single mineworker of small stature, and Ace is a former security guard and first-division football player. Ace works as a photographer and occasional ethnographic research assistant. He is twice divorced and otherwise unemployed. Like Jimmy, both men have an excellent sense of humour.

***Ngwa* Mohale (Doris Mosoma)** (about 59 when she died in 1986), **Aaron Mohale** (about 74), and ***ngwa* Mohale (Basebele Mashile)** (about 65 when she died in 2001) are Luckson's siblings. Doris was accused of witchcraft and brutally executed by ANC Comrades in 1986. Aaron and Basebele both accused Luckson of witchcraft, and of being responsible for the multiple deaths in their families.

Isak (Sakkie) Niehaus (44), the author, a social anthropologist, has been doing ethnographic fieldwork in Bushbuckridge since 1990. Of Cape Afrikaans descent, he has taught at the Universities of Witwatersrand and Pretoria in South Africa, and currently works at Brunel University in the United Kingdom.

Preface

In 1990 I first started doing ethnographic research in Impalahoek[1] – a village of the South African lowveld populated by approximately 20,000 Northern Sotho and Tsonga speakers. At the time Impalahoek seemed to be on the brink of revolutionary change. Comrades (young political activists associated with the African National Congress) had rendered Lebowa – the Northern Sotho 'Bantustan' of apartheid South Africa – effectively ungovernable. A few years previously, Comrades had accused a number of elders of witchcraft and violently executed them. At the time there were ongoing battles between the youth and an organisation of adults called the Sofasonke ('We Die Together') Civic Union, which had resulted in three brutal murders.

As a white anthropologist, I soon realised the need to hire research assistants. I desperately required local helpers to steer me through the minefield of tumultuous and tense political situations. My research was also hampered by my poor command of the local languages – Northern Sotho and Tsonga. With this aim in mind I approached a teacher, Macbeth Shai, but he was unable to help me because he coached soccer each afternoon. Macbeth, a good judge of character, introduced me to some of his colleagues whom he said would make able assistants. I became great friends with many of those to whom he introduced me, and with them I formed the most productive working relationships of my professional career. I managed to complete 30 months of fieldwork that formed the basis of a monograph on witchcraft and political processes, and also a host of articles on topics such as dances, ethnicity, masculinity, politics, sexuality, taboos, and violence.

Throughout my fieldwork I involved my assistants as co-researchers rather than as mere guides, interpreters, and research subjects. They assisted me in identifying research problems, selecting informants, doing participant observation, and also in interpreting information. The last task often provoked fierce debates. Since I held full-time teaching positions throughout the period of my fieldwork, I could not secure prolonged

[1] The name of this village and of all persons in this monograph are pseudonyms. Unless otherwise specified all non-English terms are in Northern Sotho.

research leave. Instead of the conventional year in the field, I became a migrant, oscillating between the cities where I taught during term time, and Impalahoek, where I conducted research over vacations. Some of the most important tasks of my assistants were noting the details and dates of important events that happened in my absence.

I used several research assistants and sustained very different relationships with each of them. Jimmy Mohale, a teacher who was 27 years old in 1990, was one assistant whom I soon came to regard as my closest colleague and friend. Whereas some of my other assistants were better mentors and were more readily available for fieldwork, I tended to interact more easily with Jimmy on a social level. Jimmy and I both loved drinking beer, talking about history, cooking exotic dishes, and watching films. He regularly visited me at my homes in Johannesburg, Cape Town, Durban, and Pretoria. In Cape Town, Jimmy and my mother drew much attention when they scooped up ice-cold seawater in large plastic Coca-Cola bottles at Bloubergstrand. The water was later to be used for healing rituals in Impalahoek. As a fieldwork interlocutor, Jimmy increasingly occupied the role of a coeval, much as Al Muhammed had during Rabinow's Moroccan fieldwork (Rabinow 1977). The end of apartheid came in 1994, and friendships between white and black men were then easier and more commonplace than they had been in the past.

In 2002, Jimmy abruptly ceased working with me. There was never any overt argument between us, but I found it virtually impossible to locate him in the afternoons after school, or even on weekends. On the few occasions that I did meet him, he always offered some excuse. He either desperately had to go somewhere, or urgently had to attend to some family matter. I gained the impression that Jimmy purposefully avoided me: that he was no longer prepared to work for the small daily stipend I paid, or to continue assuming the subservient and stressful position of being a research assistant, described so aptly by van Binsbergen (2003: 51–74). However, Jimmy's kin and other friends told me a different story. Far from being too proud to work as a research assistant, they said that Jimmy was in a great predicament and was ashamed. He had deserted his wife and three children for a much younger woman, drank heavily, and became extremely short-tempered – even with the best of friends. Moreover, I learnt from Jimmy's brother that he now openly accused his own father of witchcraft, and that he had even gone so far as to consult diviners to kill the old man with vengeance magic (*letšwa*).

Perhaps Jimmy's strategy of avoiding me was wise. Through time I had become exceptionally fond of his children, was furious about what he had done to them, and openly sympathized with his wife. I also respected Jimmy's father, who had always treated me very courteously and kindly.

Jimmy was correct to assume that, despite his earnest attempts to educate me about witchcraft, I did not share his beliefs about his father's hidden malevolence.

As my anger receded, I began to fear that I might lose a friendship that still meant a great deal to me. I was therefore extremely happy, early in 2004, when Jimmy approached me and two other friends, as we were eating lunch and reading newspapers in my car, parked underneath the shade of a large tree. Jimmy greeted us, joined in, and began talking to us on the topic of local names that we were investigating at that time. A few months later he accompanied me to Pretoria and spent a pleasant week at my home. Jimmy now realised that I had already heard of his divorce and of his assertions about his father's witchcraft, but that I had not learnt about their details. Believing that a little knowledge is a dangerous thing, he vowed to tell me the full story of the events that had transpired in his life. His telling took the form of a biographical narrative told with enormous honesty and great narrative skill during the course of 21 sessions at my home in Pretoria, my small rondavel (round thatch-roofed house) at the Wits Rural Facility,[2] and at his home in Impalahoek.

On 11 June 2005, whilst we were still recording his biography, Jimmy unexpectedly suffered a serious attack of pneumonia. To Jimmy it was obvious that his sickness was the result of his father's witchcraft, and he consulted a range of diviners and Christian healers in his quest for a cure. He only once consulted a general practitioner. I suspected that Jimmy's sickness might well be AIDS-related, pleaded with him that he go to the hospital, and gave him money for this purpose. But Jimmy argued that biomedical practitioners cannot cure witchcraft, and proceeded to visit yet more diviners and Christian healers. His condition rapidly deteriorated, but he still defiantly refused biomedical treatment. I drove to Bushbuckridge to see Jimmy on the first weekend of September 2005, and was shocked to see how much weight he had lost and how shallow his breathing had become. I asked Jimmy whether there was anything that I could do for him. He suspected that I wanted to take him to the Nelspruit Mediclinic, and commanded me not to become involved in managing his sickness, but rather to complete his biography. On Friday 16 September, Jimmy's brother, Henry Mohale, phoned my office in Pretoria to tell me that Jimmy had died in the Mankweng Hospital outside Polokwane, at five o'clock the previous morning.

Even before then, I had realised that Jimmy's experiences could offer genuinely new insight into witchcraft beliefs in the contexts of South

[2] The Wits Rural Facility is operated by the University of the Witwatersrand and is used to accommodate researchers and to expose students to the realities of rural South Africa. It is located a few kilometers outside Impalahoek.

Africa's turbulent political transition from apartheid to democracy and the devastating HIV/AIDS pandemic. *Witchcraft and a Life in the New South Africa* is my attempt to tell this story to a broader scholarly community. His tragic death and his insistence that I record his last struggles added another crucial dimension to his biography.

Two very different influences have shaped the manner in which I wrote this biography – namely those represented by Charles van Onselen and by the late David Hammond-Tooke. I was extremely fortunate to work at the same universities as Charles, and I learnt enormously from his life stories of lesser known persons such as Nongoloza Mathebula, Kas Maine, and Joseph Silver (van Onselen 1984, 1996, and 2007). The doors of his office always stood open for me. As my former head of department at the University of the Witwatersrand, David's writings on cosmology and symbolism in Southern Africa added a crucial dimension to my understanding of historical processes and human experience. His monograph, *Boundaries and Belief: The Structure of a Sotho Worldview* (1981), was written especially for someone with my interests in mind. I hope that my eclectic use of their analytical insights does justice to them.

Other colleagues have also been extremely helpful – sometimes in less obvious ways. They include my numerous friends and research participants in Bushbuckridge, of whom I shall name only Kevin Mitchell, Eliazaar Mohlala, Sharon Pollard, and Eric Thobela; Nicolas Argenti, Harri Englund, Deborah James, Stephanie Kitchen, Adam Kuper, Patrick Pearson, and James Staples (in the United Kingdom, where I am based at the moment); Mary Crewe, Rehana Ebrahim-Vally, Anthony Goedhals, Zendré Lategan, Fraser McNeill, Jimmy Pieterse, John Sharp, Enos Sikhauli, and Natalie Swanepoel (in Pretoria); David Coplan, Conny Mathebula, Jonathan Stadler, and Robert Thornton (across the Jukskei River in Johannesburg); Susan Cook (Rustenburg); Leslie Bank (East London); Sven Ouzman and Ilana Van Wyk (Cape Town); Jens Andersson (Harare); Fred Golooba-Mutembi (Kampala); Nico Besnier and Peter Geschiere (Amsterdam); Erik Bähre (Leiden); Giorgia Tresca (Rome); Aleksandar Boskovic (Belgrade); Petr Skalnik (Prague); Don Handelman (Jerusalem); Adam Ashforth (Michigan); Graeme Reid, Hal Scheffler, and Jan Simpson (New Haven); Peta Katz (Charlotte, North Carolina); and Eirik Saethre (Hawaii). I especially wish to thank Florence Bernault (Wisconsin) for her support and guidance during the final stages of preparing this manuscript.

The fieldwork upon which this study is based was partly financed by extremely generous research grants by the Mellon Mentorship Programme, administered by the University of Pretoria. Despite my rather eccentric career choice, my parents, Anita and Hennie Niehaus, have always encouraged me in pursuing my endeavours. My mother has often asked me 'How is Jimmy doing these days?' I hope this biography provides an answer to some of her questions, at the same time as generating empathy for his adversities, conundrums, and choices (right and wrong) in social situations that were seldom of his own making.

Isak Niehaus
Uxbridge, Middlesex

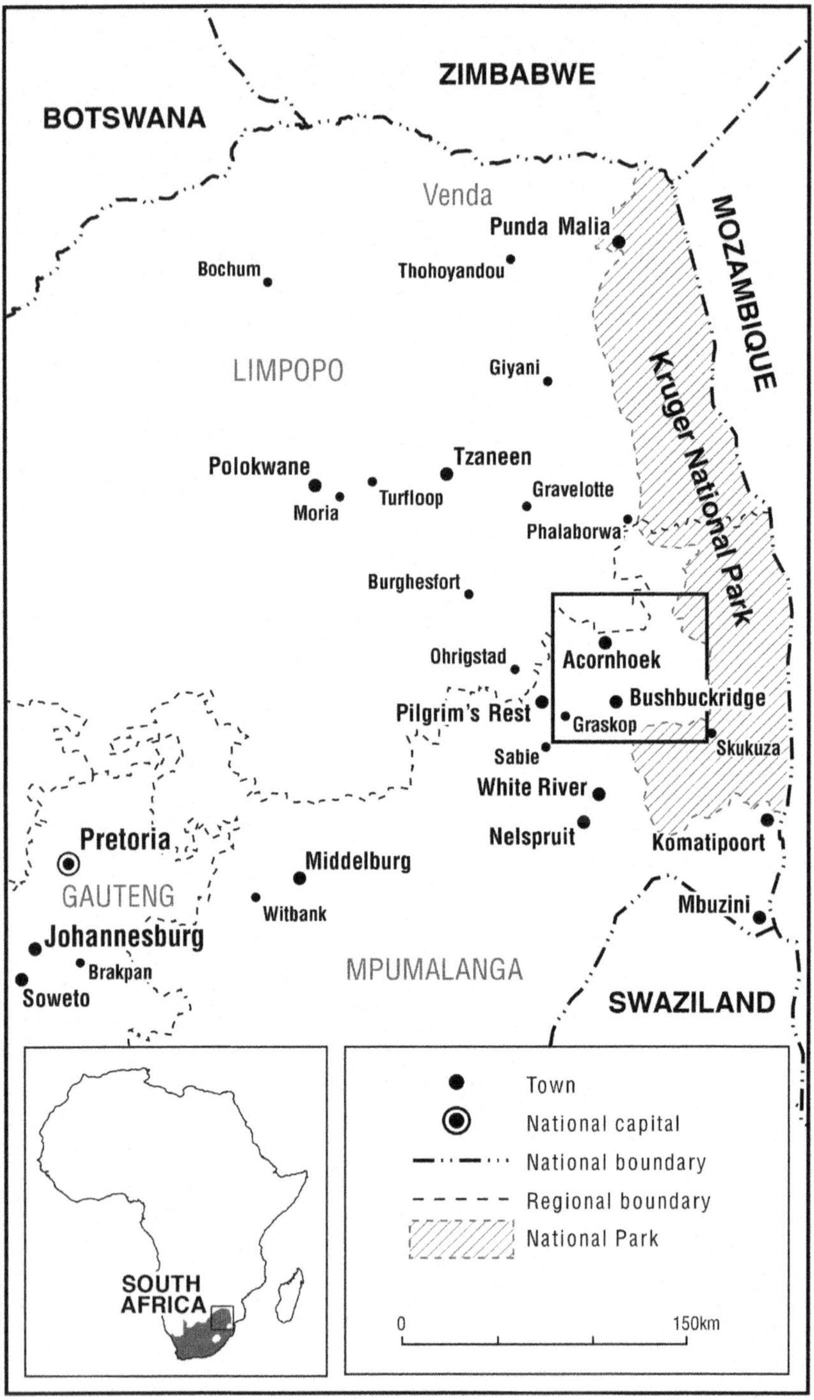

Map 1. North-eastern South Africa

Map 2. Bushbuckridge region, South Africa

1 Introduction

South Africans experienced 2004 and 2005, the years when I collected the bulk of information for this monograph, in very conflicted ways. A decade earlier former white supremacists and black freedom fighters had averted catastrophe by negotiating an end to racial conflict and establishing one of the most progressive constitutions on earth. Nelson Mandela had become the world's pre-eminent symbol of reconciliation. The country's constitution entrenched the right of freedom from discrimination on grounds of race, gender, ethnicity, religion, and sexual orientation. There was also growing confidence in South Africa's political system. The Independent Electoral Commission had supervised three successful elections and on each occasion the ruling ANC (African National Congress) had increased its majority. The international media touted South Africa's model of negotiation as a possible solution to seemingly insoluble crises elsewhere – in Israel, Sri Lanka, and the Sudan.

Tangible signs of 'development' abounded. Between 1994 and 2004, the country experienced sustained economic growth. The number of employed grew from 9.5 to 11.1 million; black directors of public companies increased from 14 (1 per cent) to 438 (13 per cent); the proportion of households with access to clean water rose from 60 to 85 per cent; and those getting electricity from 32 to 70 per cent. Six million citizens received housing, 1.8 million hectares of land had been transferred into black ownership, child-support grants were introduced, old-age pensions increased, and nutrition programmes reached 4.5 million school children (*The Sunday Independent*, 25 April 2004).

But another more disturbing side of South Africa's political transition was becoming apparent: one of unfulfilled promises and unmet expectations. In the wake of national reconciliation, South Africans began to experience the devastating effects of economic globalisation and de-industrialisation. Economists questioned government statistics about job creation. They pointed out that whilst the number of 'casual' workers had increased, there had been drastic job losses in the mining, manufacturing, and construction industries. Sources estimated that only 6.8 million of South Africa's economically active population of 15.5 million were 'formally' employed (Robinson 2004). Crime, domestic instability, violence, and HIV/AIDS emerged as issues of serious concern. In one survey, 23 per cent of all respondents indicated that they had been victims of crime (Leggett, Louw, Schönteich, and Sekhonyane 2003). In 1999 only 37 per cent of Africans in the 30 to 34 age group, and 51 per cent in the 35 to 39 age group, were married (Statistics South Africa 2000) and in 2002 fewer than 40 per cent of all African children under the age of 16 were reported as living with their fathers (Posel and Devey 2006: 38). Up to 48,000 rapes and 28,000 murders were reported to South African police annually (Jewkes and Abrahams 2002; SAIRR 2002), and an estimated five million South Africans were infected with the deadly HI virus (Walker, Reid, and Cornell 2004). These figures were amongst the highest for any country in the world. Whilst few South Africans held government directly accountable for these woes, alienation was mounting amongst the electorate. During the 2004 elections 44 per cent of South Africa's 27.5 million eligible voters shied away from the polls, and another 250,000 voters spoilt their ballots on purpose (*The Sunday Independent*, 18 April 2004).

Thus 2004 and 2005 were characterised by the paradoxical coexistence of enfranchisement and apathy, upward social mobility and unemployment, social welfare and increased mortality. Within this ambiguous context Ashforth (2005) discerns increased 'insecurity' and fears about 'witchcraft'. He contends that in Soweto,[1] South Africa's largest black township, the rapid rise of a black middle class, increased competition for jobs, declining fortunes of the poor, AIDS, the upsurge in crime, and dissipation of community solidarity have all contributed to increased distrust. Because misfortune can no longer credibly be explained with reference to the apartheid system as a form of structural evil, there has been a renewed emphasis on witchcraft. Ashforth claims that those who fail to achieve upward social mobility often see themselves as being held back by the malevolent powers of envious and jealous others. Many diviners reinforce and inflame these suspicions. In this social climate, witchcraft is nearly always a sub-text of what is spoken about kin and neighbours. Ashforth (2005) deploys the concept of 'spiritual insecurity' to capture the ethos of anxiety aroused by the indeterminacy of invisible forces, such as everyday threats of violence and of witchcraft.

Whereas Ashforth sticks to a strict division between an economy as empirical reality and spiritual beliefs and practices arising therefrom, Comaroff and Comaroff (1999a; 2000) transcend this division. They emphasise the perceived mystical basis of social inequality in post-apartheid South Africa, using the concept 'occult economies' to denote a situation in which individuals are imagined to deploy magical means

[1] Soweto is an acronym for Johannesburg's southwestern townships, and has a population of nearly two million people.

for material ends. They see these 'economies' in reports of elders who use witchcraft to abort the process of natural reproduction, businessmen who harvest human body parts to ensure good profits, and witches who conjure zombies as a vast army of ghost workers to fuel a vibrant immoral economy. These techniques are brutal forms of extraction, involving the destruction of others, but have the allure of making profits without ordinary production costs.[2] Comaroff and Comaroff contend that young men, for whom the promise of postcolonial prosperity is most obviously blocked, have taken it upon themselves to cleanse the country of witches and ritual murderers.

The aim of this monograph is to explore how the biography of one South African can inform our understanding of witchcraft in contemporary South Africa. I seek to tell the story of how one teacher, Jimmy Mohale, experienced the broader changes taking place in the country from 1964 to 2005, and came to interpret the misfortunes he encountered and his fatal illness as resulting from his father's witchcraft.

As a biographical study, this monograph complements Ashforth's lively *Madumo: a man bewitched* (1999), which focuses on a young man in Soweto who was accused of bewitching his own mother. The story tells how Madumo was robbed of his right to mourn her death, and was chased from home, having his blankets burnt. Madumo sees his experience of being labelled a witch as a sign that he himself is bewitched, and sets about to seek a cure by consulting a range of diviners and church-based healers. Though Madumo's attempts to reconcile with his siblings fail dismally, he visits his father's kin in a rural village near Mafikeng and hosts a feast for his paternal ancestors. When the ancestors are adjudged to be satisfied, Madumo is convinced that they are now behind him and that the witches have been defeated. He vows to stop smoking and drinking, to build a new home where his grandfather used to live, and to start selling second-hand clothes. Ashforth (1999) shows witchcraft accusations as arising from hostile struggles within the family, and from a reality of hatred that lies beneath the surface of togetherness.

Jimmy's story differs from that of Madumo in two crucial respects. First, it is set in a rural context. It takes place largely in Impalahoek, a village in the Bushbuckridge area of the South African lowveld populated by about 20,000 Northern Sotho and Shangaan people. During the era of apartheid, Impalahoek formed part of the Northern Sotho Bantustan, Lebowa. After the country's first democratic elections in

2 Comaroff and Comaroff (1999b) describe zombies as an 'army of spectral workers', who, like immigrants from elsewhere on the continent, usurp scarce jobs from young people and prevent them from establishing families. Through being in 'wandering exile', zombies bear testimony to the rupture of connections between people and place. As tools that are stored in a shed, zombies also highlight the mounting confusion of people and things.

1994, Impalahoek was incorporated into the newly established province of Limpopo, and then transferred to Mpumalanga Province in 2006. Second, whereas Madumo was unemployed and seen as draining household resources, Jimmy was an aspirant member of South Africa's new middle class. He was a brilliant pupil, obtained a Bachelor of Education degree, became a gifted teacher, married another professional, fathered three healthy children, and was an executive member of the local ANC branch. The misfortunes Jimmy attributed to witchcraft were therefore more unexpected, and more intimately related to his perception that something was subverting his life chances and preventing him from realising the middle-class life course he deserved.

Theoretical Concerns

The monograph focuses on Jimmy Mohale's narratives and recollections of very concrete experiences. But there are nonetheless a number of more abstract theoretical concerns that shape my understanding of the material. I adopt a 'pragmatic' approach, which seeks to understand the constitutive place of individuals and of events in social processes. Logically, this approach aims to transcend the oppositions between the abstract social system and the individual agent, and between history and event. It treats fieldwork as a matter of engaging and interpreting lived social worlds, rather than mapping out the nature of social systems (Ortner 1984; 1996; 2006; Hastrup 1995; 2005). I seek to narrate the interrelatedness of social contexts, historical processes, events, personal dispositions and states of mind. In so doing I aim to transcend the limitations of a purely interpretive and relativist approach, and I ask uncomfortable questions about anthropological interventions in times of fatal illness.

A foremost concern is to investigate the relationship between witchcraft beliefs and accusations, and the contexts in which they occur. In this respect, I see as untenable any strong formulation of Ashforth's (1999; 2005) and Comaroff and Comaroff's (1999a; 2000) arguments, which treat the proliferation of discourses about witchcraft as a 'response' to the ambiguities of the post-apartheid situation. At a seminar at the University of Chicago, during 2002, Sahlins made a telling criticism of the theory that witchcraft accusations are an index of political and economic inequalities. He pointed out that no witchcraft accusations are made in Polynesia, despite the salience of rank and hierarchy that prevails in that part of the world. Witchcraft, he suggested, has more to do with cosmology (personal communication).

Likewise, West (2007) argues that discourses about sorcery do not symbolise other realities. Muedan people in Mozambique were adamant that sorcery is not a metaphor of abstract things such as social predation. They insisted that sorcery is real! West (2007) contends that it makes greater sense to adopt a phenomenological approach, which engages with the Muedan world of sorcery from a particular space within it. This approach compels us to view sorcery practices as actual exercises in constructing, rather than merely representing, social realities. For him the reality of sorcery is built up through language and discourse, and is experienced through verbal constructs such as threats and accusations. 'People do not speak of sorcery: they actually speak sorcery' (West 2007: 53). As Muedans imagine sorcery, they experience their imaginings as real. In this conception, symbols stand for themselves and are an essential part of the world of which they speak. Hence sorcery or indeed witchcraft is an ever-present language, discourse, or sub-text in social encounters.

These critical interventions compel us to recognise a more complex relationship between beliefs and their contexts. Moreover, Ranger (2007) argues that the notion of occult economies wrongly aggregates different sorts of data, and does not connect the present to the past in any meaningfully documented way.[3] Evidence suggests that the post-apartheid context does not present a decisive rupture from earlier cosmologies. Witchcraft has a long historical presence in north-eastern South Africa, a presence that precedes the tumultuous events of the twentieth century (Delius 2001). It has been constantly reconfigured through time, outliving the institutions supporting it, and surviving to confront new situations of life (McCaskie 2000).

One can make a far more persuasive case for a somewhat weaker, less deterministic, formulation of the ideas of Ashforth (2005) and Comaroff and Comaroff (1999a; 2002). In the absence of accurate historical information, this formulation makes no assumptions about increased fears of malevolent mystical forces. I simply treat the sorts of frustrated expectations, social relations, and misfortunes encountered in contemporary South Africa as one possible context for witchcraft beliefs. As a cosmology, discourse, or language, witchcraft is never insular and inward-looking. Apologists of former apartheid policies, and also some proponents of African nationalism, mistakenly see witchcraft as a unique expression of African culture(s). But very similar beliefs are widespread in many non-African contexts.[4] Moreover, discourses of witchcraft are extremely open-ended, constantly allow for the incorporation of new

[3] Ranger's (2007) suggestions have sparked widespread scholarly debate. Ter Haar and Ellis (2009) advocate that we should discard the notion of the 'occult' altogether, and seek to understand phenomena such as witchcraft in the framework of 'religion' as a more neutral encompassing term. Meyer (2009) defends the theory of 'occult economies', suggesting that it might well be employed for the sake of detailed research. My sympathy in this debate lies with Ranger. His understanding of context incorporates a focus on the intersections between mystical beliefs and social domains, and also between local and trans-local forces. Unlike his critics, Ranger does not specify these contexts a priori.

[4] Witchcraft beliefs are encountered in contemporary France (Favret-Saada 1980), Russia (Worobec 1995), and India (Bailey 1998).

themes, and often link local realities to global forces. This capacity makes discourses of witchcraft eminently suitable for interpreting contemporary changes (Ardener 1970; Auslander 1993; Geschiere 1997; Ciekawy and Geschiere 1998; Moore and Sanders 2001; Green and Mesaki 2005).

At the same time, culture is not free-floating or autonomous. It seldom offers an adequate explanatory framework by itself (Kuper 1999). Classical theorists such as Evans-Pritchard (1937) and Marwick (1965) contended that Azande and Chewa only invoked witchcraft in certain situations. Witchcraft is not an epiphenomenon of other realities; it is essentially a discourse *about* things such as misfortune, profound social tensions, and grave interpersonal conflict (Evans-Pritchard 1937: 63–83).

A biography has all the drawbacks of a one-person survey, but it also offers new analytical insights. In my earlier monograph I ventured to suggest that witchcraft beliefs in Bushbuckridge have less to do with African identity than with people's unfortunate experiences in an overcrowded former Bantustan area (Niehaus 2001). In a provocative paper, Caplan (2004) questions my formulation. She draws an ambitious comparison between witchcraft in Africa and the imagery that informs the so-called 'war on terror' in the United States and United Kingdom. In both instances, she argues, those blamed for evil are excluded from the moral community and punished. This observation leads her to question whether 'marginalisation, misery, poverty and insecurity' are always the real issues, especially in the case of affluent Western countries. Caplan (2004) might well underestimate the different issues involved. But in reading her argument, I also realised how unsuited any conventional ethnographic monograph is to explore the conjunctions between misfortune and witchcraft. A biography is arguably a better vehicle for such an exploration.

The biographical narrative is credited for its syncretism and capacity to illuminate the interplay between the social, historical, and personal (Mills 1975; Ferrarotti 1981). It can show the influences of diverse discourses on people's lives and beliefs, and can reveal the discrepancy between conceptual models and concrete behaviour (Niehaus 2006a). A biography can also capture 'hidden historical processes' (van Onselen 1993). This diachronic temporality offers a more appropriate vantage point than conventional ethnographies for exploring how witchcraft is invoked to explain recurrent misfortune. Favret-Saada (1989) contends that farmers in the Brocage area of rural France only ask whether anyone wishes them ill when their farms become caught in a state of permanent crisis.

> The misfortunes that occur repeatedly and without reason on the farms are called 'spells'; animals and people become sterile, fall ill or die, cows abort or lose their milk, plantations rot or dry, buildings burn or collapse, machines break down, and sales drop drastically. (Favret-Saada 1989: 42)

In other words, we cannot explain witchcraft beliefs purely in terms of their systemic agency – that is, as the intended and patterned outcome of social processes and structures. This view excludes the possibility of unintended and unanticipated events – such as the sorts of misfortune that find expression in witchcraft – that are products of conjunctive agency (Sahlins 2004: 155). Whereas systemic agency calls for conventional social analysis, conjunctive agency exhibits an 'evenential' history that we can best capture through the narrative of storytelling (ibid: 157).[5] In other words, we can do so by mapping out the life course of specific persons through time.

A second, related, concern is to investigate the domestic contexts of witchcraft. This focus does not detract from my concern with broader political and economic processes. Cole and Durham (2007) observe that broader transformations provide new contexts for social reproduction and for intimate domestic relations. But reciprocally, they contend, practices associated with domestic relations mediate large-scale processes. Global processes, they assert, do not take place 'out there', but in decisions about specific relationships. A biography also offers an appropriate device for exploring the quality of social relationships as 'core sociological objects' (Bertaux 1981). I suggest that, in the post-apartheid era, witchcraft accusations have become increasingly private, and that witches have become increasingly masculine. These shifts may be partially due to the suppression of public witch-hunts by South Africa's ANC government, intent on pursuing a political modernist agenda (Niehaus 2010a). Significantly greater numbers of male cognates, such as fathers, are now identified as witches. I view this trend in the light of local experiences of de-industrialisation, which have made the status of the father extremely ambiguous. Discourses of social progress construct sons as improved versions of their fathers. Yet actual experiences of social and economic marginalisation of men in the new era contradict the subject positions that these discourses provide. Fathers, paradoxically, have achieved greater authority than their sons.

Impalahoek: The Reconfiguration of Witchcraft

I start with an account of the historical trajectory of witchcraft beliefs in the area presently known as Bushbuckridge, to provide the backdrop against which Jimmy's life story can be understood. It draws on archival records of South Africa's former Native Affairs Department, previously

[5] Malkki (1997) points to the conceptual distinction between repetitive, persistent, and normative cultural patterns as the domain of anthropologists; and transitory, non-repetitive, and anomalous news events as the domain of journalists. She questions the merits of this separation and suggests that anthropologists can learn a great deal from carefully considering the latter kind of phenomena.

published historical studies, and oral traditions and historical recollections gained from interviews with elderly village residents.

The earliest oral traditions refer to indigenous wars and to the migration of diverse Northern Sotho (Bakone, Baroka, Pulana) and Tsonga-speaking groups (Banwalungu, Hlanganu, Nxumalo) into the lowveld since the mid-nineteenth century. For example, the followers of the Pulana chief, Maripe, were said to have bewitched the Swazi invaders of Bushbuckridge, in the well-known battle of Mount Moholoholo in 1864 (Ziervogel 1954). Descendants of the spy, Malalathuleng Moekoena, proudly told me how their ancestor confronted a Swazi regiment by himself, became invisible, and laid a herbal compound called *sefolo* on the ground to cripple them. Malalathuleng also blew a pipe, made from the arm-bone of a deceased soldier, to make the enemy Swazi warriors tremble.[6]

The context of these beliefs changed as encroachment by whites altered the conditions under which Africans held land. In the late 1880s President Kruger's republican government surveyed and sold large tracts of land in the lowveld to speculators and mining companies. Kruger's government also granted former Afrikaner tenants 'occupation farms' in exchange for military service (Harries 1989: 91). The new landlords compelled Africans resident on their land to pay rent in labour, cash, and kind. After the South African War (1899–1902) the price of land rose and there was a transition from stock to arable farming, creating an acute labour shortage (Harries 1989: 93). The 1913 Native Land Act prohibited Africans from owning land outside defined Native Reserves, and thereby imposed a system of labour tenancy on the white-owned farms. The household head, or his sons, now worked for the white landlord for a period of three months each year, without remuneration. For the remainder of the year they cultivated their own fields and tended their own cattle (Harries 1989: 94).

The Land Act scheduled a number of farms for exclusive African occupation, but left intact a system of rent tenancy, whereby residents of the farms paid annual taxes to the African and European Investment Company, for residential, cultivation, and stock-keeping rights.[7] The settlement pattern was one of scattered hamlets (*metse*) comprising the homesteads, fields, gardens, and ancestral graves of co-resident agnatic clusters. During the early 1930s fields were still as large as a hamlet could cultivate and no stock limitations were imposed. Larger hamlets

[6] Delius (2001) argues that published and unpublished records of the Berlin Missionary Society suggest that beliefs in witchcraft and in 'zombies' were extremely pervasive in nineteenth-century Transvaal. However, at the same time, the missionary records show that the incidence of individuals being openly accused of, or punished for, witchcraft was low, and that large-scale and lethal witch-hunts were extremely rare.

[7] Valuation Lands Department, 25 October 1937, LDE 115/30, V 2328.

could harvest up to 90 bags of maize plus 30 bags of sorghum, and keep herds in excess of 150 cattle. By selling produce and stock to traders, hamlets could afford to pay rent. Men also worked intermittently at the Sabie forestry plantations or Pilgrim's Rest gold mines to obtain cash for clothes and other commodities (Niehaus 2001: 20).

However, with the creation of the Kruger National Park (a famous game reserve), the forestation of large tracts of land on Mount Moholoholo, and the expulsion of former rent tenants from the white-owned farms, numerous displaced households moved onto the company farms. This placed great strain on rural resources. By 1937 vast amounts of land had already been cleared, and in 1937, 1939, and 1941 plagues of locusts, commando worm, and drought regularly made agriculture a hazardous enterprise.[8] Faced with this crisis, large numbers of men signed contracts to work on the Witwatersrand.

In 1948, the year that apartheid became official government policy, the South African Native Trust purchased all company farms. Impalahoek now became part of the Bushbuckridge Native Reserve, administered by a white Assistant Native Commissioner (Niehaus 2001: 21). Impalahoek again served as a reception site for hundreds of households, displaced by the mechanisation of production operations on the surrounding white-owned farms (Harries 1989: 104). Having failed to acquire more land to accommodate the influx of additional households, the Native Affairs Department was compelled to alter the utilisation of land within the Reserve. Between 1952 and 1953 field officers demarcated three residential areas and several clearly defined arable areas. Whereas households had previously been allocated an average of 2.5 hectares of land, they were now allocated only 0.8 hectares for agriculture. Few households could produce more than six bags of maize on their reduced fields.[9] Moreover, in 1951 a foot-and-mouth epizootic decimated people's cattle herds.

Within Bushbuckridge, the term 'witch' (*moloi*, pl. *baloi*) came to denote a broad conceptual category. It referred to persons who inherited mystical malevolent power from their mothers, and also to those who deliberately set out to acquire harmful substances and skills. Witchcraft (*loya*) encompassed the diverse activities of poisoning, the use of potions (called *dihlare*), and also the deployment of familiars and of zombies. Women witches were said to skilfully use the lethal crocodile brain and

[8] Burns (2000: 14–19) writes that a food crisis and severe starvation prevailed in Bushbuckridge at the time of the Second World War. Whilst local people were unable to reap crops, the Maize Control Board was compelled by government to impose wartime restrictions and issued insufficient rations of maize and even seeds to sell in the general dealer stores. People fainted from hunger, and in a stampede by anxious buyers at a store a child was trampled to death.

[9] Reclamation and Resettlement Report, Native Affairs Department, Bushbuckridge 1957, NTS 17/423/1, V10226.

'slow poison' (*sejeso*). Once ingested, the former caused stomach cramps and headaches, and would eventually crack the victim's brain. The latter transformed into a reptile such as a frog, lizard, or snake that devoured the victim's body from inside.

Witches allegedly manufactured *dihlare* from herbs, roots, animal fats, and human bodily substances.[10] A potion called *sefolane* was placed on footpaths, entered the body through the soles of the feet, and caused paralysis of the legs. Another, *go kotola*, made from the victim's own nails, urine, faeces, hair, or footprints, was used to influence his or her behaviour. *Šibeka*, made from human blood, drove away rain-bearing clouds. Other kinds of potions caused friends to fight, cattle to trample their owners, and lightning to strike people's homes.

My informants readily associated witches with familiars (*dithuri*) and zombies (*ditlotlwane*). They alleged that witches sent their familiars – usually snakes, owls, hyenas, baboons, cats, and even lions – to attack and kill their victims. Witches allegedly changed their victims into zombies, by first capturing their aura or shadow (*seriti*) and then progressively taking hold of different parts of their bodies, until they possessed the entire person. But witches would deceive the victim's kin by leaving an image of him or her behind. The kin would believe that the victim was dead, but in reality they had buried the stem of a fern tree transformed into the victim's image by the witch. At home witches employed their zombies as servants to do domestic work, herd cattle, and cultivate fields. Hence, my informants conceptualised zombie-making as 'theft of persons' (Niehaus 2005a). The travails of zombies resonated with the actual experiences of young wives who left their natal hamlets for the unfamiliar ones of their affines, where they lived and worked under the constant surveillance of their mothers-in-law.

Drawing on the memories of informants I recorded 27 witchcraft accusations that occurred before 1960. In all cases witchcraft was said to have been motivated by feelings of envy, greed, and resentment. Thirteen accusations occurred between neighbours, ten between affines, and four between cognates. They took place in the contexts of unequal harvests, tensions between women and their daughters-in-law over domestic work, and disputes concerning the inheritance of cattle.

[10] The Northern Sotho word *dihlare* (sing. *sehlare*) is the equivalent of *murhi* in Tsonga and *muti* or *muthi* in the Nguni languages. These words all derive from the root 'tree'. It refers to any compound made by expert hand from mixtures of roots, leaves, barks, animal products, and even industrial chemicals. These substances are believed to have inherent agency. There are no limits to the uses of *dihlare* other than the skills or power of the persons making or using it. It can be used for healing, cleansing, strengthening, and protection: for the negative ends of witchcraft, bringing illness, misfortune, and death to others; or for gaining wealth and power at other people's expense. *Dihlare* also plays a part in communications between humans and spirits (Ashforth 2005: 41–4,133–7).

Throughout this period chiefs played a pivotal role in managing witchcraft accusations. In cases of drought, which threatened the livelihood of all villagers, chiefs sought out male witches who placed potions (*šibeka*) in the bush to drive away the rain clouds. The chief's assistants usually punished the accused person by tying him to a tree stump and by building a fire around him, making him feel the heat he caused others to endure. Hereafter, they would expel him from the chiefdom. Chiefs also encouraged commoners to report suspected witches to their court (*kgoro*). When they heard a witchcraft case, the chiefs required both the accuser and the accused to deposit a surety of five cattle at the capital for safekeeping. The chiefs and each party then elected representatives to accompany the accused to a witch-diviner (*mungoma*) in Phunda Maria, near Venda. (They walked the entire distance, about 200 kilometres each way.) These diviners were widely renowned for their ability to sniff out witches. If the diviner announced the accused to be a witch, he would cut holes in the culprit's clothes and would shave his hair in a rough manner. The accuser would then collect the cattle from the chief's kraal. If the accused was found not guilty, he or she would blow a goat's horn upon entering the village in a proclamation of innocence, and would be awarded the cattle in compensation for being wrongfully accused (Niehaus 2001: 133–9).

In 1959 the South African government introduced Bantu Authorities to Bushbuckridge. The local chiefdoms were now transformed into Tribal Authorities and their chiefs became accountable to a Bantu Affairs Commissioner. Consequently, chiefs lost their autonomy and assumed various unpopular tasks on behalf of government, such as collecting taxes, issuing arable plots, and controlling dipping and grazing operations.

To facilitate the influx of additional households, officials of the Bantu Trust implemented a comprehensive villagisation scheme in Impalahoek during 1960. They redivided all land into new residential settlements, arable fields, and grazing camps. The officials relocated all families onto stands in clearly demarcated village sections. Given the diminutive size of these residential stands, large agnatic clusters were fragmented into smaller households. As a result sons achieved greater independence from their fathers: they now paid their own taxes and kept their cattle in separate kraals, while their wives cultivated different gardens. Whereas the hamlet was previously an agnatic cluster, the new village sections became a diverse collection of unrelated households. Neighbours were often complete strangers. Although government conducted these relocations under the rubric of 'agricultural betterment', all households were prohibited from keeping more than ten head of cattle, and very few were able to secure access to arable fields (Niehaus 2001: 29–30). Thenceforth, migrant labour became a career.

During 1962 government divided the formerly ethnically heterogeneous Bushbuckridge Native Reserve along ethnic lines. The eastern side, designated as Mhala, was placed under control of a Shangaan Regional Authority, which became part of the Gazankulu Bantustan in 1969. The western side, in which Impalahoek was situated, was allocated to the Mapulaneng Regional Authority, and incorporated into the Northern Sotho Bantustan of Lebowa in 1973.

According to my informants, witchcraft attributions escalated as population removals brought about increased tensions and distrust between neighbours, and the system of oscillating migrant labour generated new forms of inequality that were fertile breeding grounds for envy and resentment. Moreover, villagers began to fear that migrants could purchase witchcraft substances as commodities in South Africa's urban marketplaces, and bring newer, ever-more dangerous technologies of malevolence into Impalahoek.

The ape-like *tokolotši* and snake-like *mamlambo* now became the most prominent witch-familiars. Villagers imagined the *tokolotši* to be a large ape with pronounced sexual features: the male had an enormous penis and the female huge breasts. Some informants described the witch and the *tokolotši* as separate entities. Others believed that witches could transform themselves into the *tokolotši* by smearing animal fat on their bodies. At night witches either sent this familiar – or assumed its form – to rape sexually desirable men and women in their neighbourhoods. The *tokolotši* allegedly caused infertility: it injected men with a syringe to make them impotent and sterile, and made women abort or give birth to horrible, deformed creatures.

The *mamlambo* (literally, 'mother of the river' in Xhosa) came in the form of a root or twig that seemed to be alive and to glow at night. But after some time it metamorphosed into the forms of a snake with awesome fangs and shiny eyes, and of a white lover with blond hair. The *mamlambo* predisposed its owner to luck in financial matters, or stole possessions or money for him or her. But the hedonistic pleasures derived from keeping the *mamlambo* bore great cost. The familiar soon expelled the witch's spouse, and demanded sacrifices of chicken, beef, and human blood.

Like the bizarre monsters of Ndembu initiation whose exaggerated features startle neophytes into thinking about features of their environment that they had hitherto taken for granted (Turner 1967a: 106), these familiars drew attention to new fears and subjectivities. The fear of the *tokolotši* as instigator of unwanted sexual intercourse became prominent in the context of a migrant labour system that separated husbands from their wives and undermined conjugal stability. The ape is an appropriate human double, seen as dangerous, strong, ugly, and unable to repress its desires (Niehaus 2001: 53). The *mamlambo*, in turn, resonates with people's selfish lust for money, which was potentially destructive of social relations. Snakes are seen as creatures from below the ground, and are associated with water – a basic source of prosperity – and precious metals. Its metamorphosis into the shape of a white person, too, is significant. A well-known Tsonga proverb states, 'White people have no kin. Their kin is money' ('*Mulungu a nga na xaka, xakara yena I mali*') (see Junod and Jaques 1939: 78).

The experience of working on distant mines and industries became a new allegorical vehicle for narratives about zombies. This is apparent in numerous idiomatic links. The tasks of zombies resembled those of unskilled workers. They, too, were treated harshly and fed only maize porridge (the staple diet of black workers). Their smallness evokes the diminutive status of black workers, their uniformity the perception that all workers were treated alike, and their speechlessness the inability of workers to question the dictates of their employers. Stories also arose of witches transporting zombies to irrigation farms by train, and deploying them to work in shifts, like mineworkers (Niehaus 2005a: 191–210).

Bantu Affairs Commissioners strictly upheld the Suppression of Witchcraft Act (No. 3 of 1957), and explicitly prohibited chiefs from intervening in witchcraft accusations. In terms of the Act anyone who indicated another person as a witch or approached 'witch-doctors' to 'sniff out' witches could be fined up to R2,000, or imprisoned for up to ten years. Should the person accused of witchcraft be killed, the perpetrators could be jailed for up to twenty years. Chiefs seldom defied the Commissioners. A perception now arose amongst villagers that chiefs were more inclined to shield the perpetrators than support the victims of witchcraft.

In isolated instances, villagers took justice into their own hands and violently took revenge against alleged witches. This happened when they were certain of the witches' identity, and could mobilise sufficient public support. For example, in 1977 Abel Dilebo visited home from Pretoria for Christmas. One morning he experienced excruciating stomach cramps. Abel claimed that his wife had poisoned his tea; he then died shortly after being taken to hospital. In the emotionally laden atmosphere of his funeral, Abel's siblings attacked his wife with shovels, beating her to death. The police arrested four of Abel's brothers and they were later imprisoned for periods of up to four years.

At this historical juncture, Zionist and Apostolic churches came to provide a new institutional context and space for managing witchcraft. These churches experienced phenomenal growth after the 1960s, their influence rapidly eclipsing that of the older Lutheran and Nazarene missions. A survey of all 26 churches in Impalahoek showed the Zion Christian Church (ZCC) to be the largest. Congregations of the church had 3,400 members. There were also 13 smaller Apostolic congregations, varying from about forty to a hundred members in size (Niehaus 2001: 32).

Formed in 1924 by Bishop Engenas Lekganyane, the ZCC comprised thousands of dispersed rural congregations throughout Southern Africa. Its structure resembled that of chiefly authority, descending from an archbishop to ministers (*baruti*), prophets, secretaries, and treasurers. During Easter, buses carried hundreds of thousands of worshippers to the ZCC headquarters at Zion City Moria in Limpopo Province, where the archbishop addresses the uniformed multitudes over an electronic sound system each year. Comaroff (1985: 238) describes Moria as 'a powerful central place' which 'administers a fund of spiritual, material and symbolic power'.

At the village level, the attraction of these churches stemmed from their emphasis on 'this-worldly' concerns. Rituals primarily aimed to harness the divine power of the Holy Spirit to heal the body and its immediate life-worlds (Comaroff 1985: 240). This is apparent in the practices of river baptism, divine healing, purification, the prohibition of drinking and smoking, uniformed dancing (*mokhukhu*), and night communion. Zionist prophets derived their gifts of divination and healing from an individual relationship with the Holy Spirit. The Holy Spirit revealed messages to prophets through visions, which only they could see, and voices, which only they could hear.

Unlike the leaders of mission churches who discouraged belief in witchcraft, Zionist prophets actively confronted the malevolent power of witches. Indeed, in Zionist cosmology, witches present a more immediate evil than Satan (Kiernan 1997). Prophets readily ascribed misfortune to witchcraft. But their response was nearly always defensive. The prophets used prescriptions from the Holy Spirit to protect church members and to fortify their homes against witchcraft. They also sought to heal witchcraft-related disease.

The issue of witchcraft made a brief incursion into the public political sphere during the anti-apartheid struggle of the 1980s. From April 1986, male youths, self-styled Comrades, aggressively confronted all institutions they associated with the apartheid system. Organising from local schools, they regularly enforced school boycotts, campaigning for free books, an end to corporal punishment, and for the introduction of student representative councils. The Comrades also launched a consumer boycott of white-owned supermarkets, and called upon villagers not to pay annual site taxes, service rents, and stock levies. They effectively brought the activities of Tribal Authorities to a halt.

During these campaigns the youth dedicated themselves to the complete eradication of evil.[11] Comrades called a series of meetings, at which

[11] See Ritchken (1995), Delius (1996: 26; 2001), Niehaus (2001: 146–54), Van Kessel (1993: 608–711), and Kirkaldy (2006) for historical and ethnographic accounts of the anti-witchcraft movements in the northern regions of South Africa.

they asked adult men to name those whom they suspected of witchcraft. They then formed disciplinary squads to punish the accused. Between April and May, Comrades burnt hundreds of homes throughout Bushbuckridge and attacked more than 150 suspected witches, killing at least 36 (SAIRR 1988: 907). They thus challenged the authority of chiefs and magistrates, who were unable to punish witches. In reaction, an organisation called the Sofasonke Civic Union was formed to re-impose adult control. For a period of more than a year there was great political tension and conflict between the Comrades and Sofasonke, marked by several violent attacks and counter-attacks.

After the ANC was legalised in February 1990, adults again assumed political authority. Former Bantustan leaders, chiefs, businessmen, and school principals were elected to lead the ANC branches that mushroomed throughout Bushbuckridge. Women – previously excluded from political participation – joined the ANC Women's League in large numbers. But the youth, who previously formed the vanguard of the anti-apartheid movement, were increasingly marginalised and youth activism was confined to the ANC Youth League (Niehaus 2001: 156–82).

The management of witchcraft became a contentious political issue. From 1990, the ANC national executive strictly forbade ANC members from acting against witches. Van Kessel (1993: 611) writes: 'With hindsight, the leading activists saw witch-burnings as a serious mistake, which diverted the struggle from the real enemy.' But there has been a continued popular demand that ANC leaders should act against witches.

The largest public witch-hunt in Impalahoek occurred in December 1990, and involved considerable contestation between the youth and ANC leaders. After a series of inexplicable deaths, Comrades apprehended about ninety suspected witches, and transported them by bus to a witch-diviner in Mbuzini (near the Swaziland border). The diviner sniffed out 34 of the suspects as witches, and proceeded to 'kill' them symbolically. He beat them behind the neck with a switch, shaved their hair in a rough manner, commanded them to undress, and smeared their bodies with black oil.[12] When the buses returned, the Comrades entrusted the accused to the nearest local police station for safekeeping.

On 7 January 1991, ANC leaders asked the station commander to hand over the accused to them, and assured him that they would protect them. They took the accused to a nearby sports ground, where well over

[12] Residents of Bushbuckridge generally consider the back of the neck, where they stab oxen when slaughtering them, as the most vulnerable part of the body. The haircut is an essential part of funeral rites. At night relatives of the deceased shave the corpse's hair and place it in the coffin. Corpses are buried naked, wrapped only in white linen. By smearing them with black oil, the witch-diviner tainted the accused with the colour of death (Niehaus 2001: 165). Amongst the Poroporo communities in Tanzania ritual specialists shaved the body hair of alleged witches to suppress their power (Green 1994).

a thousand people had gathered to see them. Here the ANC leaders asked the accused to fetch their witchcraft potions from their homes and to burn these in public. However, the youth became so antagonistic that the ANC leaders had to transport the accused back to the police station by bus, and police eventually dispersed the crowd. The ANC leaders did not halt the witch-hunt, but rather sought to minimise its terror. Many villagers were glad that there had been no killings. Some young men, however, described their leaders as misguided, saying that mild forms of punishment would not deter 'witches by birth'.

The ANC won a dramatic victory during South Africa's first democratic elections of 1994 – claiming 92 per cent of all votes cast in Limpopo Province. By voting in the elections villagers sought to achieve political representation in national centres of power. They saw African nationalism propagated by the ANC as eminently suited for this purpose.

The first decade of democratic rule did not bring an end to either political contestation or economic inequality. In 1995 local residents complained about inadequate service delivery in Limpopo Province and demanded that Bushbuckridge should be incorporated into the province of Mpumalanga, instead. But government announced that the border would not shift. In response, residents of Bushbuckridge constituted a Border Crisis Committee and launched a 'rolling mass action' campaign. They organised protest marches and embarked upon a prolonged school boycott and strike. The protesters laid burning tyres on all major roads, stoned police vehicles and post-office vans, and burnt down several government buildings, causing millions of rands' worth of damage. The police fatally wounded two protesters (*City Press*, 15 June 1997). President Nelson Mandela appointed a task team to improve service delivery, and in 2005 Bushbuckridge was transferred to Mpumalanga.

A new, albeit small, local elite has emerged, obtaining well-paid government positions, and securing lucrative construction and service delivery contracts from government. But during the same period de-industrialisation has brought increased hardship for many other villagers. In 1990/1 my research assistants and I conducted a survey of 87 households in Impalahoek, and in 2003/4 we revisited all previously sampled households. Over this period, unemployment increased from 40 to 56 per cent (see Appendices 1 and 2). The greatest job losses occurred in mining, Pretoria's steel factories, the military, and teaching. The only increases were amongst taxi drivers, security guards, shop assistants, game lodge employees, and seasonal farm workers. Over this 13-year period, the welfare recipients in the sampled households doubled. They no longer included only old-age and disability pensioners, but also women receiving monthly child maintenance grants from government.

The HIV/AIDS pandemic started rather late in Impalahoek. Only in 1997 did my informants identify the first AIDS-related deaths.[13] But since then the death rate has escalated rapidly and by 2005 nearly all families had lost loved ones to AIDS. Initiatives to stem the spread of HIV have been slow, and have emphasised prevention rather than cure. Numerous non-governmental organisations propagated the virtues of safe sex amongst the youth. But medical services provided by a network of three public hospitals, health centres, and clinics have been woefully inadequate. Only in 2004 did these health care facilities start making antiretroviral therapies available.

Political discontent, economic inequality, and increased mortality rates have all contributed towards continued fears of witchcraft. For example, bereaved families frequently contested the opinion that their loved ones had died of AIDS-related diseases, claiming instead that they had been the victims of witchcraft. This deflected responsibility and blame from the deceased.

Provincial commissions have advocated that witchcraft be recognised as a reality by the law, and that legal reforms be implemented to punish the practise of witchcraft more harshly than the accusation of others as witches (Niehaus 2010a). Government, however, has continued to oppose public witch-hunts. For example, in 1994 Seth Nthai, the newly appointed head of Safety and Security in Limpopo Province, addressed a public meeting in Bushbuckridge. He said that he was horrified by witch-killings and called upon the police to arrest anyone who accused others of witchcraft. Nthai also issued a firm warning: should the local police fail in their duty, he would take disciplinary measures against them and send police from elsewhere to arrest the witch-hunters (*Weekend Argus*, 18/19 March 1995).

In the past decade, witchcraft accusations have become increasingly internalised. Witchcraft has also retreated from spaces of public political debate, and now exists more as 'deep knowledge', confined to hidden, safeguarded spaces where formal orthodoxies can be re-evaluated, subverted, and contested (Apter 2007b). This is evident in the resurgence of mystical vengeance. Members of bereaved families, who believe that a witch might be responsible for the death of their loved ones, might ask diviners to treat the corpse with a potion called *letšwa*. This potion is believed to make witchcraft rebound, causing the killer to die in a similar

[13] Whilst the attributions of our informants are not an accurate gauge of AIDS-related deaths, they often used criteria similar to those employed by fieldworkers of the Agincourt Verbal Autopsy Survey to describe the symptoms of AIDS. Our informants spoke of drastic slimming, persistent diarrhoea, hair loss, coughing, black sores and discolouring of the mouth. They also mentioned signs of dementia in the final stages of sickness, and said that the victims' lovers or spouses also suffered illness and death.

manner to the victim. In this manner, villagers now used mystical means to combat mystical crimes.

There have also been important shifts in patterns of witchcraft accusation. During fieldwork I recorded details of 279 witchcraft accusations that were made in Impalahoek between 1960 and 1995: in 47 per cent (130 cases) the accused person and the victims were non-kin such as neighbours, and in 24 per cent (66) they were cognates. During ongoing fieldwork I learnt of 198 additional accusations that were made between 1996 and 2008. These patterns were now reversed: in 47 per cent (93 cases) the accused and their victims were members of the same cognatic kinship networks; and in only 22 per cent (44) they were non-kin. During this time period the percentage of male accused increased from 44 per cent (125) to 62 per cent (108). Such evidence suggests that in more recent years it is mainly male insiders who are accused of witchcraft.

Capturing Witchcraft Biographically

My primary aim in writing about witchcraft through the genre of biography is analytical rather than ethnographic experimentation (Clifford and Marcus 1986). A self-reflexive concern with modes of ethnographic representation is, nonetheless, integral to my aim of capturing aspects of witchcraft that have thus far evaded intellectual scrutiny. In this respect, biographies that draw on oral testimony offer us the possibility of transcending conventional monological modes of ethnographic writing based upon 'I-witnessing' (Clifford 1988: 28–34). Biography moves into the realms of more polyphonic and collaborative models of writing, where ethnographic texts are constructed through processes of dialogue and negotiation between anthropologists and key informants.[14]

Throughout the research process Jimmy himself put forward topics for discussion and I carefully listened to and recorded his accounts of his own life experiences, with as little prompting and questioning as possible. In the texts I seek to capture Jimmy's point of view through the use of lengthy quotations, reconstructed from notes taken during interviews. Like most other research participants in Bushbuckridge, he found the use of cassette recorders obstructive.

Jimmy's narrative intentions and skills were thus crucial in directing this work. In telling me his story, Jimmy's aim was not purely to make chronological sense of the events that had shaped his life. He had already

[14] Well-known examples that come to mind are Mintz's *Worker in the Cane* (1972), Crapanzano's *Tuhami: portrait of a Moroccan* (1980), Werbner's *Tears of the Dead: the social biography of an African Family* (1991), Gudeman and Rivera's *Conversations in Colombia* (1992), Brown's *Mama Lola: a vodou priestess in Brooklyn* (2001), Hoskins's *Biographical Objects: how things tell the stories of people's lives* (1998), and Chernoff's *Hustling Is Not Stealing: stories of an African bar girl* (2003).

diagnosed the source of his misfortune, and spoke with the explicit intention of convincing me that he had been the victim of his father's witchcraft. This explains the pessimistic tone of his narrative, and also the theme of successive miseries, and an elusive quest for happiness and security. Throughout the production of his biography, Jimmy was extremely sociable and displayed a fine sense of humour. But I gained the impression that his joking was 'laughter out of place', defining frustration in a general context of tragedy (Goldstein 2003). At times, Jimmy appeared somewhat anxious and paranoid. He sometimes mistakenly believed that others harboured negative intentions towards him, and often sought to escape rather than confront tense social situations. Whilst these personal dispositions do not, by themselves, explain his beliefs, they are congruent with his self-representation as a victim of witchcraft.

As a university graduate, Jimmy had studied History and Religious Studies and wrote a short dissertation on the concept of salvation in black theology. He also helped me collect and interpret ethnographic information over the course of fifteen years, listened to lectures I gave, and read many of the papers I wrote. He clearly understood an ethnographic attitude towards culture and took pride in his English vocabulary. Jimmy's narrative would have been significantly different had this not been the case.

Apart from these idiosyncratic factors, broader conventions of storytelling and cultural constructs of personhood also shaped this biography. Jimmy's narratives seem to shift between progressive and regressive meta-understandings of history. Anti-apartheid movements such as the Comrades, in a manner similar to South Africa's new government, posited an optimistic, linear vision of time. In their vision, political struggles were a precursor to liberation, and development initiatives a vehicle for social improvement (Ferguson 2006). But, in direct contrast, elder villagers frequently understood history in terms of a 'myth of a golden past'. They never spoke favourably about apartheid, but nonetheless contrasted earlier prosperity, social order, unity, and physical strength to present-day poverty, disorder, strife, and weakness (Niehaus and Stadler 2004).[15] Elders portrayed agriculture as a better livelihood than wage labour, and spoke nostalgically about earlier times in which jobs were easier to come by, there was less crime, and people generally lived longer lives. Dystopic fears of AIDS, the uncontrolled influx of foreigners into South Africa, and of natural calamities such as floods, drought, and forest fires coloured their visions of the future. Jimmy was different from his elders in that he did not idealise the past, nor did he hesitate to tell me about the violence

[15] Elders would, for example, argue that the segregationist policies of Jan Smuts were less oppressive than those of the later apartheid regime, and that in the era of democracy Nelson Mandela was a better political leader than Thabo Mbeki.

and insecurity of his childhood. But he was greatly distressed that all his investments in future projects had failed to pay dividends.

Jimmy's accounts of the events in his life frequently resembled gossip and assumed a narrative form best described as 'episodic melodrama'. Gossip occurs amongst people in networks and in groups, protects individual interests, projects guilt onto others, and cannot easily be verified by other means (White 1994; Steward and Strathern 2004). As episodic melodramas, his accounts were emotional and forthright in their moral lessons; they often centred on the subjects of witchcraft, sex, money, and violence; and they were seldom related to broader social changes (Abu-Lughod 2005: 82, 113). Such narratives regularly appear in the local tabloid newspaper, *The African Sun*, under captivating headings such as 'Businessman in court for murder!', 'Dead man's skull, leg missing', 'Border war ends', 'Teacher arrested for alleged rape', 'Lions on the prowl in villages', and 'Civic aids witch hunt'.

Anthropologists often discern less psychologised concepts of personhood in non-Western, non-middle-class contexts. For example, Hoskins (1998) demonstrates how Kodi people of Indonesia construct identities around certain objects. Kodi people's lives are so intertwined with ritually important domestic objects that they cannot disentangle their concept of self from the things they value. Hoskins could therefore use the history of objects as metaphors to elicit indirect accounts of her informants' personal experiences. In contrast, residents of Bushbuckridge – with the possible exception of diviners, who have an extraordinarily rich material culture (Rodgers 1993) – construct personhood in relation to others rather than around objects.

Contrary to some theorists, I do not think there is much merit in contrasting the 'individual' of the capitalist West with the 'dividual' of other societies, once characterised by greater gift giving. Whereas the individual is autonomous, self-directing, defined by internal qualities, and insulated from material influences, the dividual is permeable and partable, incomplete, and continuously involved in processes of being built by the gifts of others, and of reproducing others through gifts. Dividuals are compound sites of the relations that define them, and embody society in their dispositions.[16] This dichotomy is unnecessary. LiPuma (1998) shows that both individual and dividual (or relational) modalities of personhood are universally recognised. All languages, for example, presuppose an 'I' as well as a 'you'. The emphasis on these modalities is thus a matter of context and degree. One might add that social class is a crucial component of this context, as wealthier and more powerful persons presumably have greater opportunity to be self-directing.

[16] See Dumont (1965) and Marriot (1976) on India; Wagner (1986) and Strathern (1988) on Melanesia; and Taylor (1990; 1992) and Piot (1999) on Africa.

In Bushbuckridge people commonly have as many as six or seven different names given to them by their fathers, other kin, diviners, birth attendants, teachers, friends, fellow football players, and also by themselves. These names refer to events at the time of a birth, to a particular ancestor, to famous football players, and to personality traits. One's position in broader kinship structures (that is, in relation to paternal kin, maternal kin, and affines) is also vital to the construction of personhood. Despite the demise of the hamlet as a corporate and co-residential group, a model of it has continued to exist as a sort of virtual reality – removed in time from the social contexts in which it was originally encountered (van Binsbergen 2001). But kinship relations are now more ego-centred and are mobilised only in specific situations. This tendency is exemplified in Jimmy's narrative, which frequently depicts the self as constituted in interactions with others, rather than in terms of enduring personal attributes. During interviews Jimmy referred to his encounters with hundreds of kin, friends, colleagues, and acquaintances. The proliferation of others in Jimmy's narrative might tax the reader.

Clifford (1988) reminds us that all speech is inter-subjective and located on the borderlines of the self and others: life stories are structured by the listener's presence; by his or her questions, expectations, and attributes; and also by the nature of the interactions between the storyteller and listener. Hoskins (1998: 2) calls these encounters the 'shadow' relationship of biographical texts. The similarities between Jimmy and me, in terms of gender, age, and profession (both male, in our thirties when we did the bulk of fieldwork, and teachers), and the differences in our ethnicity, colour, class, and marital status (Jimmy was Northern-Sotho from a working class background, and married; I am Afrikaans, middle-class, and single) created possibilities and at the same time constrained the subjects we discussed.

Through working together for a period of 15 years, Jimmy and I grew to trust one another to such an extent that we could without fear discuss intimate personal information. Under such conditions one would expect an incremental progression in both the quality and quantity of data (van Onselen 1993: 507). This is especially true in the case of witchcraft. Residents of Bushbuckridge are hesitant to discuss this topic with outsiders, partly because it is a criminal offence under the Suppression of Witchcraft Act to accuse others of practising witchcraft. Hence, one can only learn about this topic through long-term, intensive, participant observation. In gradually acquiring knowledge of these beliefs, I generally adopted an attitude of 'critical sympathy'. Unlike some anthropologists, I was never caught up in witchcraft to such an extent that I came to accept its existence as an empirical reality (Favret-Saada 1980; Stoller and Olkes 1987). Neither did I hide my opinion that witchcraft beliefs are mistaken. Yet I do not think that believing is a prerequisite to understanding. Debates – such as the famous one between Livingstone and a Tswana rain-doctor (Kuper 1987: 150–4) – can provide insight into unquestioned assumptions, and reveal similarities and differences in worldviews.

Initially, Jimmy's talk about his father's witchcraft assumed the convivial form of good, malicious gossip. But as he came to see himself as a victim thereof, our discussions became deadly serious. Ashforth (2005: 14, 122, 127) observes that, when lives are at stake, residents of Soweto resist the pull of worrying about witchcraft by not speaking about it. If faith enhances the power of potions, one might reduce their malevolence by refusing to acknowledge that one had been bewitched. Jimmy no longer spoke freely about witchcraft in public. He feared that his father had uncanny power to overhear spoken words at great distances, and might use others as secret agents of witchcraft. Under these conditions, Jimmy closely confided in me and preferred me to interview him at my home. He believed that it was fairly safe to speak about his problems to a white person such as myself, who was sceptical of mystical beliefs, and possessed neither the inclination, nor the power, to practise witchcraft.[17] But there are also drawbacks to a long relationship of friendship and trust. Under these conditions the storyteller is likely to assume that the listener has intimate knowledge of the subject under discussion, which leads to less elaborate, more impatient, and sometimes unclear explanations (van Onselen 1993: 507).

Other aspects of my research persona also shaped the stories Jimmy told and the manner of their telling. In my interactions with Jimmy, I never hid my disdain for apartheid and freely criticised the inadequacies of South Africa's post-apartheid government. Yet I always portrayed myself as an academic and 'learner of culture' rather than as a political activist. However, I soon discovered that in economically deprived areas, where education is highly valued, an academic persona is an intensely political position. Jimmy identified education as the only legitimate path to social mobility and personal progress, and constantly argued that as a university graduate he deserved greater recognition in life. He was also, at times, extremely critical of government, and he often portrayed less-educated members of the new elite as undeserving of their status.

This identity was reinforced by our use of language. During fieldwork we nearly always communicated in English. This practical arrangement also had an important symbolic component. The language of fieldwork has political loadings (van Onselen 1993: 508). Throughout Southern Africa, English is the *lingua franca* of higher education.

[17] Residents of Bushbuckridge generally see white South Africans as wealthier outsiders, who are antithetical to the position of the poorer, envious insiders who are witches (Niehaus 2001: 63–82).

The economic disparity between us was also significant. Despite living extremely modestly, I earned much more than Jimmy, and paid him and my other research assistants a small daily stipend from my research account. I was also able to help them out whenever they were financially desperate, and to act as a taxi-driver. Given the nature of this relationship, it made a great deal more sense for Jimmy to highlight, rather than conceal, his financial difficulties.

At times my bachelor status was another sub-text of our dialogue. In Bushbuckridge, single men are viewed extremely ambivalently, and are often stigmatised for not having fathered children. Jimmy was also surprised to learn that some of my male colleagues who visited me during fieldwork were gay. But as Jimmy began to experience marital problems, he concluded that my avoidance of marriage must have been because I viewed women as 'troublesome'. Jimmy also appreciated the company of my gay friends and admired their intellects. He later proclaimed that although he was still 'straight', he was no longer homophobic. Some men were gay, he said, because they were intelligent enough to realise how difficult heterosexual relations were. These contexts facilitated lengthy open discussions of Jimmy's own marital problems, in which I nonetheless found it difficult to suspend judgement. I vocally disapproved of marital violence and of cheating; he sometimes spoke of women with a misogynistic undertone.

Even though Jimmy made an enormous contribution to this telling of his life story, I remain the sole author of his biography. I include my own discussion of broader social changes to contextualise Jimmy's narrative, and interpret many of his statements for the reader. In addition, I have structured Jimmy's much shorter stories into a book-length narrative, selectively including, ordering, and omitting parts of the interview material. Unfortunately, Jimmy only lived long enough to read and give feedback on draft versions of three chapters. I also liberally edited Jimmy's narrative to correct his grammar and render it more readable. In some cases I give his original expressions in brackets for the benefit of South African readers.

Van Onselen (1993: 498–501) warns of the risk that biographers might slip into various forms of psychological reductionism. To overcome this tendency, he suggests, we should pay close attention to the primary groups surrounding the principal subject. These might include members of his or her family, peers and colleagues of the same age group, and employers. This biography is more subjectively oriented than van Onselen's (1996) account of the life of a South African sharecropper. Due to my anthropological concern with meaning and intention, I play Jimmy's own perspectives in a louder key. Nonetheless, I also draw on interviews that I conducted – with Jimmy's father and his two brothers, Henry and Kagišo Mohale, and with some of his neighbours, colleagues, and drinking mates – and also on the results of fieldwork that we conducted in Impalahoek during the previous fifteen years.[18] I use this material to cross-check the accuracy of Jimmy's statements and render his biography more sociologically significant.

How This Biography Is Organised

Contrary to a conventional historical narrative and to the advice I regularly give graduate students, this biography is not always chronologically ordered. Instead, the discussion is organised around key themes in Jimmy's life story.

The next five chapters relate how Jimmy gradually came to the realisation that his personal problems were due to witchcraft, and how he moved through time from a state of initial disbelief to a passionate conviction that his father was bewitching him. Chapter 2 focuses on his experiences of growing up and attending school from 1964 to 1982. I highlight his accounts of the everyday violence he encountered at home, in the inadequately resourced schools, and on the village streets. I also show how Jimmy sought security in the close bonds he forged with his siblings and with maternal kin, and sought to attain respect through his educational achievements. I suggest that the violence and mistrust characterising these social relations are mirrored in Jimmy's early fears of witchcraft.

In Chapter 3 I focus on Jimmy's experiences of being circumcised, getting married, attending university, becoming a father, and working as a teacher in Bushbuckridge. Contrary to his own expectations, Jimmy did not experience his path towards adult manhood as one of unimpeded progress. He was circumcised late in life. Political struggles disrupted his university studies and he failed to secure a promotion after teaching for more than sixteen years. Jimmy initially thought that the source of his misfortune lay in his inability to form appropriate political connections, but later started believing that more sinister and unseen forces might be subverting his life course.

Chapters 4, 5, and 6 shift focus to examine Jimmy's changing relations with his father, Luckson Mohale. Luckson's own siblings first accused him of practising witchcraft during the early 1960s, after disputes over the inheritance of cattle. Following a spate of misfortunes in Luckson's own household – sickness, motor vehicle accidents, and divorce – some

[18] Gudeman (2006) has recently commented upon the controversy surrounding Burgos-Debray's biography of the Guatemalan activist Rigoberta Menchú (see Burgos-Debray 1996; Stoll 1999). He sees one of the central shortcomings of the biography as the author's lack of ethnographic knowledge. Burgos-Debray did ethnography from a distance by interviewing Rigoberta Menchú in Paris, not checking the informants' claims, not checking the tapes of the interviews. and not discussing her own political positioning.

of his own children, too, started to believe rumours about his witchcraft. But Jimmy vehemently defended his father. Jimmy's change of mind occurred as the result of further misfortune in his personal life, including the painful experiences of marital disharmony and a situation of financial ruin. But it was, ultimately, the disturbing revelations of diviners and Christian prophets, following the deaths of his niece and half-brother, that convinced Jimmy of his father's culpability. In Chapter 7 I discuss the attempts by Jimmy and his siblings to use vengeance magic against their father.

Chapter 8 documents the devastating impact of the AIDS pandemic in the neighbourhood where Jimmy resided, and then discusses his belief that many deaths that seemed to be AIDS-related were actually the result of witchcraft. I then relate the advent of Jimmy's own illness, its stigma, his decision to consult diviners and Christian prophets rather than biomedical doctors, his final struggle, and his death.

The final ethnographic chapter describes how mourners at his funeral selectively fashioned a contrived biography of Jimmy as a middle-class professional. They suppressed all tensions from public view, and buried Jimmy from his parents' home. During the service different speakers extolled Jimmy's virtues as a father, husband, kinsman, educator, research assistant, political activist, and Christian. I account for the disjuncture between the actualities of Jimmy's life story and the biography presented at his funeral by suggesting that mourners purposefully constructed an operational model of what Jimmy's life 'ought to have been'.

Drawing on incidents from Jimmy's biography, the concluding chapter addresses questions about witchcraft, paternity, and anthropology in post-apartheid South Africa. In addition to noting the salience of witchcraft in situations of inequality and misfortune, I show how witchcraft addresses questions of morality. Like 'conscience', it confronts people with the moral significance of their own choices. I highlight the limitations of cultural relativism, and outline the need to balance empathy with critical engagement.

Jimmy's biography is an extremely disconcerting story that reveals intimate personal details, discusses gruesome deaths in the most graphic manner, and sometimes portrays his teachers, neighbours, colleagues, kin, father, and also the ANC in an extremely negative light. It also poses questions about the appropriateness of divination as a response to AIDS. Certain anthropologists might well see these representations as an 'invasion of privacy', 'sensationalism', or even as 'pornographic'.[19] After much soul-searching and anguish about whether to write this biography

[19] See, for example, the controversies surrounding Turnbull's portrayal of the impoverished Ik (Wilson et al. 1975); Crapanzano's work on white South Africans (Crapanzano 1985; Boonzaier et al. 1990; Hugo 1990; and Whisson 1990); and Scheper-Hughes's analysis of schizophrenia in rural Ireland (Scheper-Hughes 2000; 2001).

at all, I made three decisions. I decided first, to shield the identity of my informants by using pseudonyms and changing minor details of the story-line; second, to write the biography in the style of an anthropological treatise rather than in the style of a popularly accessible, journalistic, account; and, third, to tell Jimmy's full story with very little censorship of its disturbing details. This is partially in deference to Jimmy's own wishes.

In the face of severe crises – failed development, domestic violence, way too many early deaths, and inappropriate coping strategies – silence is a far more serious abuse of intellectual freedom than the revelation of unpalatable truths. The alternatives – selectively reporting on the achievements of South Africa's post-apartheid government, constructing contrived realities about humane sociality (*ubuntu*) (van Binsbergen 2003: 427–58), and ethnographic romanticism – are infinitely worse options.

Whilst it is true that our research subjects, most notably political leaders, strategically present idealised realities of themselves to outsiders, they also complain about their misfortune. In these situations of crisis, I believe ethnographic realism and the 'mapping of misery' are still appropriate goals (Coplan 1998). Jimmy definitely saw value in telling me the miserable details of his life story. Eleven days before his death, I asked Jimmy whether there was anything that I could do to help. 'Yes,' he said. 'Go to your car! Take your notebook! Write what I tell you! We must finish the story!'

2 Early Experiences, Initial Suspicions

During the course of my fieldwork I have had numerous conversations with Jimmy's father, Luckson (misspelt as Luxon in his identity document) Mohale. He has always been most keen to tell me of the past, particularly about the profound differences between the times when his paternal uncles were adults and those when he became a grown man. Whereas the working lives of his uncles were characterised by a desperate struggle to retain access to agricultural resources, Luckson's own adulthood was almost entirely consumed by migrant labour.

Luckson was born in Impalahoek in 1934, as the fifth of Nana Mashile's seven children. Though recognised as Rexon Mohale's son, he was actually born a few years after his father's death. In Bushbuckridge, biological descent alone does not dictate social paternity. Whereas Trobriand islanders deny paternity to affirm the sacred principle of matrilineal descent (Malinowski 1927; Leach 1966), Northern Sotho and Shangaan people sometimes creatively invent fatherhood to protect their mother's reputation as a chaste widow and to affirm the 'equivalence' and 'unity' of sibling groups (Radcliffe-Brown 1965).[1]

Luckson's grandfather, Malathole, came to Bushbuckridge from Bokgaga – a tiny Northern Sotho chiefdom, situated near the present-day town of Tzaneen (see Hammond-Tooke 1981). The Mohale totems are both the impala and the *mokolokoto* nut, and their members still recite the following family praise poem:

Age Mohale, wa o je mokolokoto	Thanks Mohale, who ate *mokolokoto*
le Rakgabati le Motsela.	with Rakgabati and Motsela.
Tsa motsela mosengwane,	With their short tails,
di eta maloka.	they walk in a row.
Makhubedi a bo rita,	With their red backsides,
di eta maloka.	they walk in a row.
Phala tsa mona marula dia tloga.	The impala ate marula and left.

While the middle section clearly refers to the attributes and behaviour of impala antelope, as in most praise songs the actual meaning of other

[1] See Bothma's (1978) analysis of sociological and biological paternity amongst Northern Sotho speakers.

words is obscure. Luckson suggested that the eating of the *mokolokoto* nut and marula fruit might actually be metaphorical references to sexual intercourse. The exclamation '*Mokolokoto*!' is still used as a word of praise by Mohale's descendants. Despite this genealogical and performative heritage, in genealogical terms, Luckson could not have been more junior: both his paternal grandmother and his mother were third wives. The marginality of this small Northern Sotho group was accentuated in Bushbuckridge, an area dominated by large lineages of Sotho-speakers (Pulana and Baroka) and Tsonga-speakers (such as Hlanganu).

Luckson's first name was Samanisi ('one who is summoned', derived from English). This name is a mimetic reference to an event on the day of his birth, when the magistrate summoned his father's brother to court, and sent policemen to repossess items from his home to settle unpaid debts. A teacher at the Nazarene Mission School in Acornhoek, where he attended classes as the only Sotho-speaking boy from 1942 to 1947, gave him the name Luckson. He himself chose a third name, Kelebotse ('I am handsome'), after he returned from the circumcision lodge in 1952.

From Subsistence Agriculture to Wage Labour

In 1934 Impalahoek still fell under the jurisdiction of the Pulana chief (*kgoši*) Setlhare Mashile, but the chiefdom had already lost its autonomy. Five years previously, the African and European Investment Company purchased the farm, and all households on it had become rent tenants.

Luckson, nonetheless, idealised the 1930s and 1940s as a golden era of prosperity. During his childhood, he lived as a member of a large extended household (*motse*), comprising his father's brothers and their kin. Collectively, they kept approximately 54 cattle (including two stubborn Afrikaner bulls) and cultivated maize, pumpkin, and melon on a large field. Luckson recalled that in the 1940s annual rent was set at 10*s* for a residential stand, 4*s* 6*d* per cow, 1*s* for dipping, and 2*s* for grazing. Yet the Mohale household easily met these costs. Each year they sold one cow – for £5 – to pay for the grass and the dip of the remaining cattle.

He never mentioned any of the adversities that cultivators and pastoralists encountered in this part of South Africa, such as overcrowding that placed great strain on rural resources, or the droughts and plagues of commando worm (*sefenefene*) that periodically wrecked people's entire harvests.

Though they had abundant food, they lacked many facilities and commodities that even the poorest households now take for granted:

We lived in a thatch-roofed house with no beds. We slept on reed mats. Until 1949, when I was fifteen years old, I never wore shoes, pants, or shirts – only leather thongs. We also did not know tea – we only drank it at Christmas.

There were no taps. We dug for water with spades or we fetched it from the wells and from the fountains.

When Luckson was a child, men only engaged in wage labour periodically, when it was absolutely necessary to earn money for purchasing clothes and commodities such as soap and candles. Luckson boasted to me that his father was only once employed as a road construction worker. His mother, Nana, never engaged in wage labour, but brewed and sold sorghum beer to the men who built the railway line passing by their compound and to work-seekers from Mozambique, who travelled through Bushbuckridge on foot, en route to the Pilgrim's Rest gold mines.[2]

For Luckson, 1948 signalled the most crucial turning point in the transition from a livelihood based upon subsistence agriculture to one based upon the remittances of migrant labourers. In that year, Chief Setlhare died, D. F. Malan's National Party defeated Jan Smuts's United Party at the polls, apartheid became the government's official policy, and the South African Native Trust purchased all the farms in Bushbuckridge.

The new National Party government increased rents and imposed additional taxes for residential stands. It also established an extensive and repressive system of policing in the newly constituted Native Reserve. White agricultural officers of the Native Trust took stringent measures to ensure that households promptly paid all rents and taxes, ploughed only their allotted fields, chopped only dry firewood, and kept licences for all bicycles and dogs. The agricultural officers and their assistants regularly inspected homes, imposed hefty fines, and even went so far as to order boys to hang their unlicensed dogs. Nature conservation officials, based near the Klaserie railway station, sought to prevent unlicensed fishing, poaching, the felling of protected trees, and veld fires. They ensured that nobody kept snares or fishing lines at their homes.[3] The South African Police (called *mpša wa mmuso*, literally, 'dogs of government') were supposed to prevent crime, but, according to Luckson, mainly arrested people for frivolous offences such as illegally eating venison or brewing beer with sugar. In addition, the railway police (*mapodiša a sitemela*) and traffic officials patrolled rail lines and roads. At the same time, chiefs and headmen still ensured the maintenance of traditional agricultural taboos, and judged cases of divorce and fighting in their courts.

2 See Bonner and Shapiro (1993) for an analysis of gold mining in Pilgrim's Rest during the early 1900s.

3 Carruthers (1995: 89–102) argues that white domination and racial segregation were the underlying principles of nature conservation in the South African lowveld. The South African state enforced stringent measures of wildlife protection in the areas adjacent to the Kruger National Park during the 1930s and 1940s. These included restrictions on trespassing and on firearm and dog ownership, and a ban on all trapping of wildlife. Impoverished communities 'on the other side of the fence' were widely seen as intruders in an environment which deserved European custodianship.

Luckson's mother, Nana, was twice arrested: once for chopping wet wood, and once for selling dough cakes (*makwenya*) in front of a general dealer store. In the 1950s the police arrested twenty men (including Luckson's paternal uncle) for killing a buffalo, which had wandered near the dipping tank, with axes and assegais. They were taken to Bushbuckridge by van, found guilty in court, and sentenced to six months' imprisonment in Barberton.

Luckson described the manner in which government responded to the foot-and-mouth epizootic of 1951, and implemented the 'agricultural betterment scheme' in 1960, as cynical attempts to deprive people of their cattle and crops, and to force them to work for whites as migrant labourers. He claimed that during the epizootic, the field officers did not heal people's sick cattle, but killed them. The officers placed Impalahoek under quarantine, inoculated all cattle, and burnt the carcasses of dead animals to ensure that nobody ate the meat or used the hides:

Those whites [the agricultural officers] made a nuisance of themselves everywhere they went. They came here with a different method. They pulled out the tongues of our cows and injected them. I really don't understand these people. Their method killed many cows and at the time meat was already very expensive.

During the implementation of 'agricultural betterment' in 1960 – when land was subdivided into distinct residential, arable, and grazing zones – the Mohale hamlet (*motse*) was fragmented into smaller households. White agricultural officers moved Luckson and his brothers to different village sections. Luckson, his wives, and their children were allocated a stand in a residential zone called Kgapa Madi (literally, 'scooping blood': the place earned its name from a series of murders which took place there). Here, they did not have a single field to plough.

In retrospect, Luckson was surprised that people complied and moved without offering any overt resistance:

In those days we could not refuse. We still listened to white people. If you saw a white person in a shop you would take off your hat for him. Then, the government could send one policeman to arrest a hundred men. Quarrelling is something new. The thing of refusing is something of today.

However, Luckson was not nostalgic about acquiescence: he has supported Nelson Mandela and the ANC from his youth onwards.

Unlike his father and paternal uncles, Luckson worked as a wage labourer for his entire adult life – from 1949 (when he was only 15 years old) until 1995 (when he retired at the age of 61). For 46 years he worked continuously, without spending a single year at home. Luckson began to work as a child labourer on two white-owned citrus farms for 10*s* per month. He then worked as a 'kitchen boy' at the home of Mr Roberts

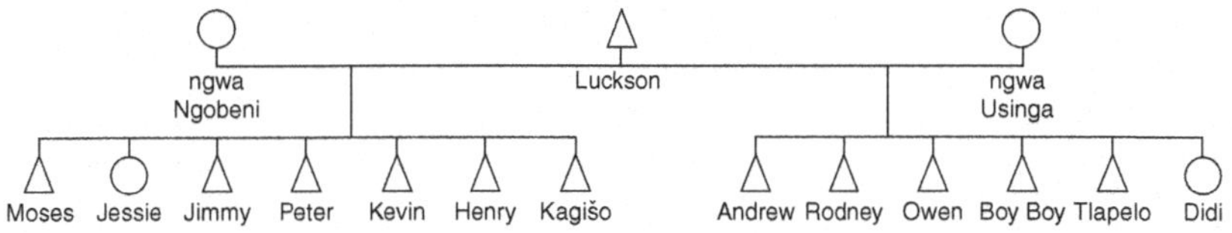

Figure 2.1. Luckson Mohale's descendants

in the town of Graskop, as a general labourer at the Watson and Jones saw mill in White River (from 1953 to 1956), at the Vlakfontein mine in Brakpan (for four months in 1957), at the Modderfontein dynamite factory in Johannesburg (for six months in 1958), for the Native Resettlement Board in Meadowlands, Soweto (from 1959 to 1963), for the South African Railways in Koedoespoort, Pretoria (from 1964 to 1974), and finally as a truck driver at Louw Transport in Phalaborwa and in Nelspruit (from 1975 to 1995). Luckson tried to visit home each month and remarked that at Louw Transport all workers from Bushbuckridge were permitted to travel home in a company van each fortnight. Despite becoming a highly skilled driver and a foreman in his later years at work, Luckson always perceived wage labour as a less favourable option than farming would have been.

Luckson's Descendants

Luckson married two Shangaan wives. *Ngwa* ('from') Ngobeni, whom he wed in 1954, had seven children, and *ngwa* Usinga, whom he married in 1969, had six (see Figure 2.1). Luckson was also renowned for having fathered many children outside his marriages. Yet Jimmy accepted these extramarital affairs as unexceptional.

Our father had many paramours [dinyatši] *in the places where he worked and he fathered children from women in Pretoria, Nelspruit, Phalaborwa, and even here in Impalahoek. When I was a child many of our stepbrothers and stepsisters came to see my father. . . . But we were not worried about this. What our father did was what everyone was doing. This is exactly what his peers did.*

Jimmy Mohale was born in 1964, the third child (second son) of Luckson's senior wife, *ngwa* Ngobeni. Though he later acquired six other names, he always preferred to be addressed as 'Jimmy':

My father named me after his supervisor at work in Pretoria – an Afrikaans man. Maybe my father liked him. I heard that this supervisor was a strict guy and a racist. He used to beat [black] people, utter rude statements, and call people derogatory names such as 'kaffir'. I am the opposite. But I like that name the most. It is easy to pronounce.

Jimmy's other names are Bernard (after a male nurse at the hospital where he was born), Jazzman (after a ferocious defender in the Orlando Pirates football team), Lepara ('walking stick', someone on whom you can rely), Badzy (a 'cousin' to everyone), Mtomeng ('lover'), Duma (a talkative person), Dubuka (someone who assists people), and Ramadimabe. Of these secondary names, Ramadimabe was the most significant for Jimmy. Elders often perceive a baby's incessant crying as a sign that a forgotten ancestor wants to manifest himself or herself in the child. The crying will stop only once a diviner has identified the responsible ancestor, and parents have appeased the ancestor by naming the baby after him or her (Mönnig 1988: 102–7). Ramadimabe literally means 'father of misfortune' and was Jimmy's maternal great-grandfather's mother. He could not, however, explain to me why a woman was called 'father'. But he was adamant that Ramadimabe has been the most helpful of all his ancestors, and that she has constantly protected him:

We don't just take her name in a negative sense. She was not only a person who was prone to misfortune, but also a person who was very resilient and strong and who could contain misfortune. Like her, my life has also been a life of long suffering, but I am also resilient and tough. This woman has really helped me. She sometimes comes to me in dreams and warns me of the bad things that can befall me. If it had not been for her, I would have died a long time ago. She protects me against evil.

The Mohale Household, 1964–81

Jimmy's relationship with his father was always extremely ambiguous; it was marked, he told me, by deep respect and admiration, by uncertain love, but also by fear and resentment:

Of all his thirteen children, my father loved me the most. There was nobody more important in my life. I did not love my father. I worshipped him. He was everything to me. I would not have chosen anyone else as a father. He was always clean and he was very strict as a father. This was very good. He would see to it that his children did not smoke. He used to tell us, 'If I see you smoking I'll beat you up.' Also, he did not drink and I admired that. Most of the elderly men around here drink too much and are unclean. I would not have been proud to show others that such a man is my father. My father can also advise people very well. He will tell you about things such as taboos [diila] *and rituals. He has great knowledge about them. That he knows very well. My father also has good leadership skills and can speak well in public.*

Here Jimmy referred to Luckson's role as a founder member, organiser, and spokesperson of the Mapulaneng Burial Society. On the negative side, however, Jimmy remarked that his father never supported his

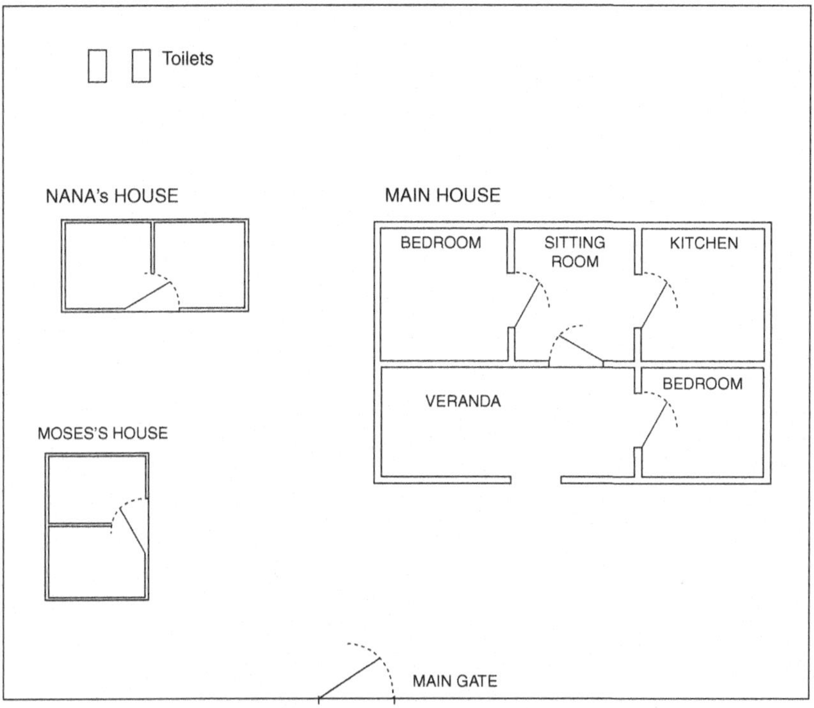

Figure 2.2. Sketch map of the Mohale home, 1976

descendants properly, seldom reciprocated their love, and was always extremely short-tempered.

As elsewhere in Southern Africa (Solway 1990), relations between co-wives in Bushbuckridge are nearly always extremely competitive and tense. It is therefore deemed appropriate for a polygamous man to provide each of his wives with her own home, on separate residential stands (Niehaus 2001: 105–6). Against this expectation, Luckson required his two wives and thirteen children to share a single four-roomed house. He bought each wife a single bed and made all his children sleep on thin reed mats on the cement floors of the bedrooms and sitting room. Luckson also expected his wives to care for his aged mother, Nana, for whom he built a small two-roomed house elsewhere on his stand.

Jimmy sketched the flow plan (see Figure 2.2) of their home and domestic arrangements. He noted that after Moses (his eldest brother) married in 1976, Moses too built a small two-roomed house on the site.

This domestic setting was characterised by persistent paternal neglect and everyday violence, by enormous tensions between Luckson's mother and his co-wives, and by grave social insecurity. Yet the very same setting was also conducive to bonds of extreme loyalty and affection between mothers and their own children, and of intense solidarity between siblings.

According to Jimmy, Luckson was always impartial in his dealings with his two wives. However, his mother, *ngwa* Ngobeni, and *ngwa* Usinga, whom he called younger mother, despised one another:

My father would either sleep with ngwa *Ngobeni or with* ngwa *Usinga. It did not seem to matter to him. He did not have a favourite. It was not obvious which of his wives he loved. I really don't know if he loved any wife – perhaps he just owned them. . . . But the relations between my mothers were not good – not at all. At times they were not speaking to each other. It was very bad to stay in the same house. Just imagine such a situation.*

My mother tried to sell fruit, vegetables, and small dough cakes at the market to make us live, and she also gave us bread to sell to the other kids at school. At one stage my mother even traded cannabis [dagga]. *She would employ another youngster to sell it for her. When I was 14 or so, I also had to help my mother sell moonshine* [tototo]. *People call it keys for the mortuary'.*

My mother had a very good heart. She never left a child crying, without giving it food. She provided for all of us. But our younger mother had a terrible heart. When she cooked, she only gave the food to her own children. She never gave us anything – not even when we were hungry. We would be very angry when our half-brothers ate, whilst we had no food. She [ngwa *Usinga*] *would also swear at us. We were not her children, so she thought it would be fine for her to use vulgar language when speaking to us.*

Once it became so bad that they started accusing each other of witchcraft. In 1981, ngwa *Usinga gave my mother relish* [meroho], *but my mother did not eat it and threw it away. She thought that it had been poisoned. When my father arrived he had to take them to Gumede, a witch-diviner* [mungoma] *in Manyelethi. But Gumede said that this woman* [ngwa *Usinga*] *was not a witch.*

In addition to these tensions, Luckson's mother, Nana, was constantly involved in disputes with her daughters-in-law and even with her own grandchildren. These were partly based on ethnic and linguistic discrimination: a surprising fact when we recall the initial marginality of the lineage into which she had married.

My grandmother loved my father, but she disliked our mothers and even us. She was troublesome and she was fond of shouting at my mother and younger mother. The problem with her was that she was an extreme tribalist. She hated all Shangaans and she had wanted my father to marry a Mosotho woman from her own family [that is, a cross-cousin, usually the mother's brother's daughter (MBD)]. She did not want to see some of our family members – such as our cousins [who were Shangaans] – at our site. She was just as nasty to our neighbours. The Ndlovu family, who used to live next to us, even moved away to live in Rooiboklaagte because of her. The only grandchildren whom she liked were those of her last-born-daughter, who was married to Mashile [the Pulana royal family].

We did not like our grandmother because she was nasty and she used to boss us around. She told us that she did not want children to play near her house or to go into her rooms. She kept her rooms locked at all times.

Luckson was nearly always at work, and his absence from home did little to ease the strife. During his fleeting visits he, nonetheless, violently asserted his authority within the household.

My father could be a very violent man. He used to beat up his wives right in front of us. Then we were still young. One morning he beat my mother with a porridge stirrer [lefeto]. *He hit her so hard that the stick broke and the metal wire stuck in her head. We had to take my mother to hospital and ask the doctors to remove the wire.*

Luckson also beat his sons. In 1977, Andrew accused Jimmy of burning him whilst the boys sat around a fire, and Luckson severely assaulted Jimmy, beating him with a belt so fiercely that he caused head injuries. A year later, Kagišo fought with another boy at primary school and broke the boy's nose. In retaliation, Luckson lashed Kagišo with the belt, over his entire body.

Such violence has been seen as having a deep impact. Psychological research suggests that men who are exposed to violence as children are likely to perpetrate violence themselves, later in their lives, as adults (Cameron and Fraser 1987). This is particularly so in contexts where popular ideas about gender permit the use of violence to maintain male authority. However, Sideris (2005) contends that, in the Nkomasi area of Mpumalanga, exposure to violence led some men to question dominant masculinity and negotiate more caring and equal relations with their wives and children. Male employees of the Masisukumeni Women's Crisis Centre, which assists survivors of rape and domestic violence, harboured bitter memories of how their own fathers had treated their mothers and them. They were emotional when they recalled financial deprivation, insults, beatings, material deprivations, and incidents such as being thrown against coal stoves (Sideris 2005: 125). Fieldwork in Impalahoek, however, paints a more complex picture. Violence was patterned, but also unpredictable (Niehaus 2009), and it would be futile to divide male informants into 'violent' and 'non-violent' men. Exposure to the violence left Jimmy feeling deeply ambivalent about his father, and led him to identify strongly with his mother. But the pervasiveness of violence made it hard to transcend. If we see violence as a language, then Jimmy could not escape from the 'prison house' of that language.

In stark contrast to the disharmonious relations existing between the adult members of the Mohale household, unity prevailed between the Mohale siblings and half-siblings. In an extremely perceptive essay, written nearly eighty years ago, Radcliffe-Brown (1965) highlights the importance of sibling-ship as a principle of cooperation in Shangaan and Northern Sotho kinship systems.[4] He suggests that the sibling group is characterised by the structural principles of internal solidarity and equivalence 'in relation to a person outside it and connected with it by a specific relation to one of its members' (1965: 65). For Radcliffe-Brown, these principles explain practices such as the sororate, in which a wife's sister replaces her in cases of death or infertility, or the levirate, in which a deceased husband's brother takes care of his wife and children.

Labour migration enhanced the importance of sibling-ship. Wage-earning parents often dispersed their children to relatives, asked neighbours to care for them, and on some occasions even left them at home without adult care. These experiences often compelled siblings living together to develop mutually supportive social bonds, independent of those with their parents (Niehaus 1994: 118, 119).[5] Moreover, there is little evidence of sibling rivalry over inheritance. James (1988) writes that an extreme shortage of land and cattle in Bantustan areas, such as in Lebowa, brought about a new system of inheritance. Whereas older brothers now moved away from the family home, the younger son inherited the residential stand, home, and fields. This, James argues, did not amount to preferential treatment of the youngest son, but saddled him and his wife with the arduous responsibility of caring for his aged parents.

Jimmy recalled that the relations between the Mohale siblings were extremely supportive. They formed the nucleus of the groups that built wire cars and played games such as *tsheretshere* (with blocks and stones), *kgašu* (with a tennis ball), and football. Moses once bought Jimmy a hard plastic ball, which he used to recruit his own football team. These street games were prone to violence, and boys regularly fought to establish a hierarchy, with status being based on physical strength.

[4] Radcliffe-Brown's discussion draws on Junod (1966). It is important to recognise that Junod collected much of his material, which was subsequently published in *The Life of a South African Tribe*, whilst he was stationed at the Shulivane Mission, near the town of Tzaneen, between 1899 and 1907. This area is known for its ethnic diversity, and much of Junod's ethnographic discussion also pertains to Northern Sotho-speakers, like the Kgaga (see Harries 1981; Hammond-Tooke 1981: 3–4).

[5] Philip and Iona Mayer (1970) highlight the extremely important roles that siblings and peers play in the socialisation of individuals amongst Xhosa-speakers in the Eastern Cape. I would argue that their notion of 'socialisation by peers' describes what happens in most rural areas of the country.

In these fights the Mohale siblings could always rely upon each other's assistance.

As children we did not understand why the adults would quarrel. We never had problems with each other. There was a lot of interconnectedness between the brothers and the sisters.

The other boys all believed that Kevin and Andrew were twins: and did not know that they were really half-brothers. If you fought with one of them, both would fight you. Whenever the other boys troubled Kevin and Andrew, Peter would search for them and beat them up.

Household Fission (1981)

In 1981, after *ngwa* Ngobeni had accused *ngwa* Usinga of witchcraft, Luckson attempted to resolve the tensions between them by building *ngwa* Usinga her own three-roomed house, on a stand in another section of Impalahoek. Whilst the two co-wives enjoyed living separately, this new arrangement did not entirely eliminate social stress.

Jimmy recalled that he was extremely sad when his half-brothers left their home:

My father realised that our house was too small to accommodate all the children. But we kids were definitely not happy [to be separated] because we were used to our half-brothers. They had been part of our lives for a very long time.

The members of Luckson's two houses now began to accuse him of favouritism, and the formerly supportive relations between half-siblings gradually became disharmonious. Initially, Luckson spent most of his time in Impalahoek with his younger wife, in her new home. Luckson's mother Nana accompanied him, also preferring to reside at the place of *ngwa* Usinga, her younger daughter-in-law. Kagišo (the last-born son of the first house) told me that his father actively discriminated against the senior wife, *ngwa* Ngobeni, and sent her hardly any remittances:

When I was young I could see how my father handled my mother. He earned money every fortnight, but he gave her only R50 and with this she had to buy maize meal and pay our school fees. In 1993 I wanted money for a school trip, but my father told me he had already given the money to my mother. He referred to the R50. But he gave the sons of his second wife money to go on the very same trip. They also wore expensive clothes.

But the members of Luckson's second house complained of paternal neglect in a different register. Jimmy observed that whereas all the children of the first house were fairly well educated, Tlapelo was the only child of the second house to have passed her Grade Twelve (matric) exams:

My half-brothers disliked my father. They were under the impression that we went to school because he paid our school fees. This was not true. I could not stand those things. It now became very difficult to make them understand that we – as brothers and as sisters – had to stay close.

Whenever Luckson lost his temper and swore, Andrew (the eldest son of Luckson's second wife, *ngwa* Usinga) retaliated and swore back at him. Andrew eventually expelled his father from his mother's home. Luckson now returned to the house of his senior wife, *ngwa* Ngobeni, and henceforth spent nearly all his leisure time with her and her children.

Being Dispersed

In 1976 *ngwa* Ngobeni temporarily separated from Luckson, and she took Jimmy and his younger brother, Peter, to live with her parents in another village section, called Tsakani. Jimmy reflected on the reasons for the separation:

My father was mad. For no apparent reason he said that he no longer wished to see my mother and chased her from his home. My mother later reconciled with him and returned to his homestead, but Peter and I chose to remain with our maternal relatives.

From then onwards, Jimmy would alternate between sleeping at the homes of his maternal grandparents, his maternal uncles, and later also the home of his elder brother, Moses. Jimmy remarked that he no longer had a particular place to stay at night. He nonetheless spent most days with his siblings. These flexible arrangements enabled him to flee from the overcrowding, hunger, and violence at his parental household and to seek greater comfort and security at the households of his maternal kin. Being dispersed to the homes of more fortunate relatives enabled Jimmy to secure access to the necessities of life that he would not otherwise have had.[6]

In Bushbuckridge Ngobeni is a more prestigious lineage than Mohale. *Ngwa* Ngobeni's grandfather, Dumase, was originally a Swazi, but was orphaned and raised by Mnisi, who was a member of a royal Shangaan lineage. As an adult, Dumase enjoyed considerable wealth and influence.

[6] Spiegel (1986) draws attention to the dispersal of dependants in the Matatiele area of the Eastern Cape. He sees this practice as a response to the exigencies of labour migration. When a worker's children have no adult at home to care for them they must be placed with others in a foster relationship. Children are also dispersed to other kin when remittances are unreliable or when their parents are unemployed. In an extended sample of 48 households, he documented no fewer than 35 children who had moved from home to home between 1982 and 1984.

He owned numerous cattle, cultivated very large fields, and established a circumcision lodge for Shangaan boys. The local Pulana chief (*kgoši*), Setlhare, appointed Dumase as headman of all Shangaans in his chiefdom. Chief Setlhare even asked Dumase to act as regent, when he left for Europe to participate in the First World War. This was a clever strategy. As the only non-Sotho headman it was impossible for Dumase to usurp the chief's position. After Dumase's death, he was succeeded as headman first by his brother, and then by his grandson, Paulus Ngobeni.

And so Jimmy preferred sleeping at the homes of his maternal kin:[7]

I went to live with my grannies because it was full everywhere else. My mother's family were a little bit better off than my father's family. It was also more peaceful there. The people were friendly, there was food galore, and there was no violence.

He was particularly fond of his mother's brothers. Both Junod (1966) and Radcliffe-Brown (1965) observed generally supportive relations operating between the mother's brother (*malume*) and sister's son, in Shangaan and Northern Sotho kinship networks. They described the *malume* as a 'male mother' and guardian of his sister's children. In Bushbuckridge the mother's brother was expected to listen to their problems, undertake responsibility for their initiation, advise his nephews about sex, ensure that no foul play was involved when they died, and assist in carrying their coffins. If the mother's brother died without progeny, his sister's children would inherit from him, sharing with his brother's children (Niehaus 2001: 95, 96).

At his maternal relatives' place in Tsakani, Jimmy assisted in herding the forty cows from the Ngobeni family kraal, both after school and during school vacations:

This was not my kind of work. On weekends we would take the cattle into the veld and catch locusts, make snares for the birds, and go fishing. I was never successful. Only the other boys were. I was not really a rural boy. I would go through things only for the sake of association, but not effectively or efficiently. Many times we lost the cattle and they [his mother's brothers] denied us food.

This residential flexibility thus afforded certain privileges, but the life was by no means an easy one. By 1978, Jimmy's eldest brother, Moses, had divorced and remarried. Luckson Mohale now asked Moses to leave the parental homestead, as the eldest son was expected to do. Moses

[7] In his analysis of kinship amongst the Chopi of Mozambique, Webster (1977) found that lineages were shallow, if not non-existent, and that there was a strong bilaterality that gave a father's and mother's kin almost equal importance in the life of the individual. There was also an emphasis upon lateral rather than on lineal kin, and great flexibility in the way in which rules were applied. Through this 'plasticity' Chopi kinship 'spread the risk' of impoverishment. Many of Webster's comments are also applicable to kinship relations amongst Tsonga- and Northern Sotho-speakers in the South African lowveld.

also obtained a site in Tsakani, but could only afford to build a two-roomed shanty from planks that had been discarded by a local saw mill. While Moses was working as a migrant labourer at the Saratoga Timber Company in Johannesburg, he asked Jimmy, who was then only fourteen years old, to reside with, and assist, his wife:

I attended high school from Moses's home. Here money was always in short supply. I had to go to school without shoes, even in Grade Eight when I was already in high school. This was terrible. In the winter months it was very cold.

Schooling

In 1953, the South African government closed down all mission schools and introduced a state-sponsored system of Bantu Education. Though the new system did provide a rudimentary form of education for masses of African children, African schools have always received considerably less funding than white schools. This inequity was amongst the most glaring injustices of the apartheid system.[8]

Jimmy attended Impalahoek Primary School from 1972 to 1977, and Mashile High School from 1978 to 1982. He described the unsatisfactory conditions at these schools in great detail:

There was a drastic shortage of classrooms at the primary school. In Grades One and Two we attended class in shanties manufactured from planks, and in Grade Three our class sat in the shade of a large marula tree [scerocarya birrea]. *How can you study under a tree? It was very dusty and whenever a car passed all the eyes would be on the car. This was a major distraction. There were also no taps or toilets. We kids used to shit in the blue gum forest. I am sure that this was a health hazard because there was shit all over the place. Most of my primary school teachers were underqualified: some senior teachers had only a Grade Eight certificate. Conditions at Mashile High School were slightly better. Only Grade Eight classes studied underneath trees. There were plenty of taps and toilets, and all our teachers had at least passed their Grade Twelve exams.*

In both schools textbooks were virtually unheard of and pupils were expected to copy notes from their teachers, in exercise books purchased by their parents. Only in Grade Eleven were textbooks introduced, but these, too, had to be purchased. School fees amounted to about R40 per year – a substantial amount of money for impoverished rural

[8] One of the most blatant forms of discrimination during the era of apartheid was the differential state expenditure on education for different categories of the South African population. Between 1978 and 1979 the South African government's per capita expenditure on a white child was R724.00 and on an African child in a 'white area' only R71.28. The pupil–teacher ratios in white schools were 1:18.6 and in African schools 1:45.9 (SAIRR 1980: 450).

households – and pupils whose parents could not afford to pay were sent home. These recollections prompted Jimmy to remark:

The kids are complaining now. They are mommy's babies who don't want to work.

Draconian disciplinary measures prevailed in the local schools. These were, in part, a product of the authoritarian educational ideology of Christian nationalism (Ashley 1989: 7–28). But local factors were also involved. Migrant labourer fathers seem to have transferred the responsibility of disciplining their children, and of policing their sexuality, to teachers (Morrell 1998: 7). In this respect, the dictatorial rule of the teacher in the school mirrored that of the father in the domestic domain.

Teachers established discipline by enforcing a host of rules, and by upholding these through corporal punishment. By monitoring the clothing, physical appearance, and conduct of pupils, teachers aimed to preserve the immaturity of adolescence, and to exorcise sex from the schools. Teachers prohibited primary school boys from wearing long pants, and only permitted secondary school boys to wear long grey flannels. The skirts and dresses of schoolgirls had to cover their knees. Boys were also prohibited from wearing certain popular hairstyles, and girls were not allowed to dye, straighten, or lengthen their hair. The girls were not allowed to have long, painted nails, nor to wear earrings and stockings. Students always had to adopt the appropriate posture. Boys were not permitted to stand with their hands in their pockets, and girls were forbidden to sit with their legs open. Boys and girls always sat on different sides of the class, played in separate areas of the school, and were not permitted to talk to each other during break (siblings and cousins were the only exemptions). Love affairs could not be countenanced, and it was a very serious offence to write any love letter, to kiss, or to hold hands. Other misdemeanours included swearing, arriving late, not doing homework, not answering the questions posed by teachers, and failing tests.

Jimmy described corporal punishment in the schools as pervasive, unjust, and humiliating:[9]

These beatings were terrible. They were more like killings. At primary school the teachers even beat our football team for losing matches. In those years

[9] Corporal punishment was pervasive in South African schools during the 1980s. A survey of 300 male and female first-year students in Johannesburg found that 267 (89 per cent) had been physically punished at some stage or other of their school career. The reported incidence of physical punishment was significantly higher in schools for black children. Thirty per cent of black students reported being hit on a daily basis (Rakitzis 1987). Holdstock (1990) shows that corporal punishment causes physical injury and psychological harm, impairs scholarly performance, breeds violence and aggression as learnt responses, acts as an incitement to rebellion, disempowers pupils, and drives out love, trust, and intimacy from adult–child relationships.

I was also a football player.... Our coach never appreciated defeat. Each time we lost he would whip [sjambok] *the whole squad.*[10] *One day Impalahoek played against Setlhare [a neighbouring school]. We were trailing 0–3 at half-time and that meant we were going to be whipped on the Monday. Nearly half of the players started crying during the game. They were weeping, knowing what would happen to them on the Monday at school. I did not cry – I was only scared. In the second half there was a miracle. We equalised by scoring three goals. But this was not enough for the principal. On the Monday he called the whole squad [into his office] and warned us severely.*

Teachers vigilantly patrolled the schools, looking for signs of illicit love affairs, and on a few occasions their efforts were rewarded. During 1977, a primary school teacher found a love letter in a girl's exercise book:

The teacher announced in our Monday assembly that Harold had written a love letter and that Sofi was the recipient. Everyone said 'Shhhh!'. The teachers then questioned Harold and Sofi in the staff room. He was fifteen and she was only thirteen. Harold admitted that he had written the letter, but he denied ever having screwed Sofi. The teachers said that by accepting his letter, Sofi had accepted his proposal. But she denied that she loved Harold. The teachers then forced Harold to lie down on the table in the principal's office and beat him more than fifty strokes. Harold started crying even before the teachers could torture him. He yelled so loudly: the whole school could hear that he was being killed. Afterwards, Harold ran home and wanted to quit school. But the teachers persuaded his father that he should return. From that day we school kids saw Harold as a criminal. We were scared to associate with him. When we looked at him we saw trauma.

Jimmy himself only fell foul of his teachers when he was in high school. In 1981 his Northern Sotho teacher assaulted him in class, and only one year later the school principal punished him severely for getting drunk on a school outing to Pretoria:

When I was in Grade Eleven, I desired a certain girl in our class. She was older than me and she would tell me everything about screwing. She would even demonstrate how guys shiver when they are about to release [ejaculate]. By then I was still young and I had not screwed. When she told me these stories I could feel my machine [penis] rise. Unfortunately for me, I learnt that a teacher called Mr Sibotse also desperately wanted her. One day Sibotse wrote a letter to the girl, telling her how much he loved her. She showed me the letter

[10] '*Sjambok*' is Afrikaans for 'whip' (noun and verb). A *sjambok* is usually manufactured from hippopotamus hide or from very strong plastic.

and told me that no matter how badly Sibotse pleaded, he would never win her love. This guy learnt that I knew of the letter and then started hating me.

One day Sibotse gave us a test for Northern Sotho and I scored 96 per cent. When he distributed the scripts, he accused me of copying. He asked me, 'How come you got 96 per cent and the next student only 72 per cent?' The other pupils told him that I was bright, but he never expected anyone in the class to get such a high mark. Sibotse called me to the front and, notwithstanding my pleas, started lashing me on the hands. He wanted to lash me again, but I withdrew my hands. That is when he hit me with his fists – right there in class. I was so angry. I started retaliating. Sibotse beat me and I fell on the floor. But I grabbed him by the foot and pulled. He also nearly fell. Then I let go of his foot and ran outside. Sibotse followed me, but I picked up stones and threw them at him. He then reported me to the principal's office.

Fortunately, the principal decided in my favour. When he summoned me, I told him that the teacher had physically assaulted me, and I said that I would report the teacher to my parents. The principal then arranged for us to meet and the guy apologised to me. He cried and said that I had degraded him. I forgave him and afterwards I even cleaned his car. In those days we saw the teachers as demigods.

After this incident, Jimmy was increasingly drawn into participating in the 'underlife' (Goffman 1961), or 'counterculture' (Willis 1977) of Mashile High School. In his final year at school, he befriended Sidney Mokgope, the son of a wealthy businessman. Sidney regularly sent Jimmy to call his girlfriend and, in exchange, bought Jimmy food.

In September 1982, Jimmy went on an outing of senior pupils from Mashile High School to the Reserve Bank, the zoo, and Kruger Square in Pretoria, and also to Hartebeestpoort Dam:

There were three buses: each had 65 kids and only three teachers. Our bus had to be serviced along the way, in White River, and Sidney bought us food in town. After we had eaten, he asked us whether we wanted something to drink and bought us Guards of London [a popular brand of gin] and a bottle of tonic. We started drinking, knowing that the lady teachers would not bother us. On the way to Pretoria I sat in the back of the bus. Many of the boys were drunk, but I was the most conspicuous. I was totally cooked. At Witbank I threw up in the bus and the driver had to stop. He made me sit on the steps at the entrance to get fresh air. Those 'born again' [Christian] teachers never thought that they would ever see me drunk! In Pretoria we stayed at a service training centre for teachers. We played Beach Boy songs the whole night through and we did not sleep much. Sidney asked me to call his girlfriend. They slept together in the corridor and I slept in the male dormitory. Unfortunately we overslept.

Jimmy clearly saw the school trip as a very significant event in his early socialisation and spoke about it with great excitement, perhaps because it captured the theme of transgression. He was proud of being a good student, whilst at the same time, challenging injustice at the school, and defying the arbitrary authority of teachers. Jimmy elaborated upon the punishment he received:

On Monday the buses returned to Impalahoek; on Wednesday the principal called 17 of us to his office. The teachers divided us according to the crimes we had committed: five couples for having sex; six boys for being drunk; and one boy for being a bully and for beating up the other kids. The teachers also accused me of facilitating sex. They beat me twenty shots on the buttocks with a cane. Those who screwed received more. Even the girls were beaten. The principal threatened to expel us, but he allowed us to stay after we had pleaded with him and agreed to water the school's trees and flowers for an entire week.

Violence was extremely pervasive at school. It established a hierarchy between teachers and pupils, and also between students themselves. Jimmy recalled one incident in 1980, when a pupil called Patrick Monna and his mates severely beat Sello Mashego, who had come to Impalahoek from Johannesburg during the national uprisings of 1976, for propositioning a young woman in their neighbourhood. Sello was so badly injured that he refrained from attending school for several days. Then Sello and his friends retaliated. They entered the schoolyard, whilst the other pupils were writing their exams, bearing knives and even a revolver. Patrick Monna tried to flee, but Sello's friends caught him and dragged him into the central quad, where they knifed him. A woman teacher bandaged Patrick and the principal took him to hospital in his van. Fortunately Patrick survived. The police subsequently arrested his assailants.

Even within an environment marked by inadequate resources and laced with violence, Jimmy earned the reputation of being an excellent pupil:

I loved school and I never failed. Not once in my life did I fail! I always attained position one or position two [in class]. It was only in maths that I was not so good.

In 1982, Jimmy graduated as the top Grade Twelve student from Mashile High School. He took all subjects in his matriculation exams on the higher grade and obtained a B symbol for History; C symbols for Northern Sotho, English, and Agriculture; a D for Afrikaans; and an E for Biology. Jimmy passed with full university exemption. His B was the highest mark awarded for History in the entire Mapulaneng circuit:

There is still a trophy at the Mashile School – the one that I won in 1982. In that year there was no C for History in the whole circuit. The next students obtained Ds. Then we wrote four essays in a single history paper. It is not like now. With those symbols you could get far.

Jimmy's achievement should be seen in the context of the generally shocking exam performances in the former Lebowa Bantustan. In 1982, only 4,795 (48 per cent) of the 9,990 pupils who wrote their Grade Twelve exams in Lebowa passed, and only 975 (10 per cent) attained university exemptions (Ritchken 1990).

Learning about Witchcraft

Jimmy encountered witchcraft from a relatively young age. He did not exactly understand what his mother meant when she accused her co-wife, *ngwa* Usinga, of attempting to poison her. But as a child, he came to suspect that his paternal grandmother, Nana, practised witchcraft. Nana was excessively private and possessed expert knowledge of potions (*dihlare*). Jimmy learnt that Nana assisted initiation masters with potions to fortify their circumcision lodges, and that neighbours once asked her to give them potions to 'finish off' an elderly woman who was terminally ill (that is, to assist them to perpetrate euthanasia). 'Is this not witchcraft?' Jimmy asked me.

Moreover, Jimmy recalled how he and his mother once observed Nana running with the speed of a teenager:

I saw this with the naked eye. We were at home that evening and in the dark my grandmother ran incredibly fast towards the toilet. She did not know that others were watching her. My mother said this was witchcraft. It also seemed as though my grandmother dug in the ground. The next day we went to the spot, but we saw no signs of any tampering.

It thus came as no surprise to Jimmy when their neighbours accused Nana of sending witch-familiars to steal their relish (*meroho*):

I remember how our neighbour, Mrs Mathebula, once came to our home at six o'clock in the morning and greeted my parents. I could see that she was terribly angry. Mrs Mathebula said to my mother, 'I'm here to lodge a complaint! Your mother-in-law troubles us. She comes to our house at night to pick relish to feed her zombies. I really don't like this. Each morning she passes by my yard naked, carrying my relish.' My mother did not respond.

Jimmy also listened to how his mother, *ngwa* Ngobeni, attributed the sickness and misfortune her children suffered at home to witchcraft. In 1977, when he was thirteen years old and residing with his maternal kin, Jimmy suffered terrible headaches and profuse nosebleeds. His mother took him to an apostolic healer, who revealed that witches were responsible for this condition. The witches had apparently placed a type of potion called *sporiani* – that causes incurable headaches – on the footpath that he used to walk to school.

The next year, Jimmy had an uncanny experience, one that he subsequently interpreted as a direct encounter with witch-familiars:

When I did Grade Nine, I lived in a two-roomed shanty, with Moses's wife in Tsakani. Moses built the shanty from planks, cardboard and corrugated iron that had been discarded by the saw mill. My brother's shanty was poorly constructed and had many holes. From inside the shanty you could see outside, and from outside you could throw a stone that could hit a person inside his house.

Late one night I heard donkeys making a terrible noise in the field across from Moses's site. There were about six donkeys forming a circle, with their heads to the ground. They made the sound "rhuuuurhuuu" and they seemed to be eating the jogo beans [dinthlu]. *I woke my sister-in-law and asked her,* 'Squeeza *[daughter-in-law]! Can you hear something?' She replied, 'Yes. I can hear the donkeys.' I wanted to be a hero so I went outside and took a plank, with a nail protruding from it, to beat the donkeys. I wanted to nail them and make them pay for disturbing my sleep. My sister-in-law followed me. The heads of all the donkeys faced towards the centre. I hit the first donkey on the thigh with all my might and also the second one. I did not know that it was possible for a living creature to endure so much pain from being pierced by the nail. But the donkeys did not respond and did not even try to run away. It was as if I had hit a child and the child laughed at me.*

Then, when I raised the plank for the fourth time, all the donkeys reversed. A huge monster emerged from the centre. I became paralysed. I was terrified. I was so terrified that the plank fell from my hand and my mind said 'Run for your life!' I screamed, 'Squeeza*! Run into the house!' We locked the corrugated-iron door, but the thing came after us and pushed against the door. It went, 'Kajank! Kajank!' Then the thing moved around the shanty. I could feel its fury. That night I was shit-scared and I prayed to God to take the thing away. My sister-in-law cried. Then, finally, at about five o'clock in the morning, it left. But we were still too scared to go outside.*

The next day we inspected the place where the donkeys were, but there were no signs that they had disturbed anything. All the beans were still fresh. I think that we experienced witchcraft. Those donkeys were familiars. Real donkeys feel pain and don't eat jogo beans. I really don't know what the monster was – but it looked like the tokolotši, *with large arms and with a huge upper torso. At that time I suspected that neighbours had tried to bewitch me. They were envious that I was intelligent at school.*

It is unclear precisely what Jimmy encountered that evening. But this invocation of witchcraft served to advance his own interests. It justified his move, soon after the event, from his brother's poorly constructed shanty to his maternal uncle's more secure home.

In 1984, only two years after Jimmy had completed school, a tragic event occurred in the Mohale household. At the start of the year, Jimmy's brother, Kevin, developed severe ear-ache and spent some time in hospital. Jimmy heard somewhere that witches had planted cockroaches in his ears. But, despite his sickness, Luckson sent Kevin to the circumcision lodge. It was winter and Kevin became seriously ill after he was circumcised. From the lodge Kevin was taken straight to hospital, where he died from an acute respiratory disorder.

Everyone believed that Kevin was a victim of witchcraft:

After Kevin's death we consulted a diviner in Casteel. The diviner threw the bones [divination lots] and told us that someone had doctored the presents we gave Kevin when we welcomed him home from the lodge – his handkerchiefs and money – with potions. The diviner said that two witches were responsible: one of them lived within our house, and the other was a neighbour who lived behind us. My mother suspected three people: my younger mother [ngwa *Usinga*], *my grandmother, Nana, and a family of renowned poisoners who lived within our neighbourhood. Although my mother had warned us about this family, Kevin regularly played with their children.*

The fingers pointed to my grandmother, Nana. People complained about her all around Impalahoek. The situation became so tense, after Kevin's death, that my grandmother even left my father's house to stay with my aunt. My grandmother said that she, herself, was sick and that the Shangaans were bewitching her. My grandmother passed away one year later. I thought that she might have been trapped and that her own witchcraft bounced back onto her.

For two years after Kevin's death, I used to see him in my dreams. I used to see Kevin playing football and attending school. I told my mother about these dreams. She called a prophet and the two of them took me to Kevin's grave. Here they took soil from the grave and hit me on my chest and on my back with it. They also made an invocation [phasa], *saying, 'Kevin! Please don't trouble your brother.' After that, I stopped dreaming about him. But I still thought about him when I was awake. I loved that guy.*

Kevin's death shook Jimmy, and it also had a deep impact upon all the members of his household. In retrospect, Jimmy was surprised that his father, Luckson, seemed to be unconcerned about Kevin's death. At the time, however, his conviction was that by not shedding any tears his father was demonstrating his status as a proper man.

Jimmy's encounters are by no means exceptional. Scholars of Southern Africa have often been surprised to discover how actively children participate in creating discourses of witchcraft. In the domestic domain children are frequently seen as victims of witchcraft, and in Pentecostal church services children have publicly confessed to practising witchcraft themselves (Badsteubner 2003; de Boeck 2005). Children of Impalahoek often imagined witches as a powerful and malevolent source of sickness. Boys and girls between the ages of 8 and 13 drew pictures of witches with powerful muscles; witches possessing beast-like attributes such as horns; witches who set zombies to work; and others who consumed copious amounts of alcohol and knifed their coevals (see Lategan 2006).

Jimmy's narratives about distrust and fear that characterized his childhood, and also about his experiences of violence on the streets and in school, and of death, provide some insight into why children might find witchcraft discourses so compelling. In the context of these insecure life-worlds, the malevolence of witchcraft possesses a unique vividness and 'aura of factuality' (Geertz 1973a: 119). This shows the futility of viewing discourses of witchcraft in terms of the metaphor of a mirror, or of a reflective surface, which shows social life in an inverted form, as some scholars do (Mayer 1954; Crehan 1997). In Impalahoek witchcraft does not show the world in reverse, but is continuous with social life. It is not that the world is peaceful and that witches are violent; rather, people and witches are equally violent.

3 Becoming a Man

After completing school in December 1982, Jimmy returned to his parents' home. From here he went to visit his brother, Moses, in Johannesburg, and began the difficult task of seeking employment and of building a career:

I thought of becoming a policeman or a clerk. We did not know of other professions. I said that I wanted to protect the community against crime. In 1983 I applied for admission [to the South African Police]. But my height was a problem – they said that I was too short. At that time I was extremely disappointed. But this was actually a blessing in disguise. I could have died working as a policeman during those riots of the 1980s. Then I thought of being a clerk, but I did not apply anywhere. I registered for a diploma in computer science in De Korte Street in Johannesburg, but I could not study there because nobody would pay my fees.

Then, when I returned to visit my family at home, Marumo [the principal of Impalahoek Primary School] invited me to join his teaching staff. He said that they could hire me as a private [unqualified] teacher at the school for 1983 and 1984. In 1983 I was paid R172.52. It was the very first time in my life that I earned a salary. At that time it was a lot of money. Today we can equate it with about R6,000. I would say I earned more than my father. That was a hell of a lot of money. My parents did not want money from me. But I used to buy them groceries and things such as a bed, a wardrobe, a hifi, a stove, lamps and a television. I really enjoyed teaching at the school. This was the happiest that I ever was in teaching.

Love, Circumcision, and Marriage

In Bushbuckridge merely having a job was a less important criterion of adult masculinity than being married, and in this respect Jimmy lagged behind. Though already nineteen years old, Jimmy had not yet been circumcised, nor had he ever engaged in penetrative sexual intercourse. In this respect Jimmy was somewhat out of kilter with group-orientated practices. Northern Sotho boys are usually sent to circumcision lodges between the ages of eleven and fourteen, and have their first sexual encounters shortly thereafter. The reason for this delay in Jimmy's socialisation is not clear to me. From what I could ascertain Jimmy felt anxious and lacked confidence in matters of love when he was a young man. Moreover, he had invested in a modern life course, in which schools played a more prominent role than 'traditional' institutions such as initiation lodges.

Jimmy explained the events that led to his becoming a husband and a father as follows:

When I was small we used to play a game we called mantlwantlwane *with the other kids. They would say, 'This is your wife'. Then you and the girl disappeared into the maize field and you had mock sex. The boy lay on top of the girl, but he did not take his pants off. When you are fourteen years old you might take out your penis and put it between her thighs, but this was not real sex. We called it* matanyola *[thigh sex]. For me real penetration started with Lerato.*

Jimmy met Lerato Mashile, who eventually became his wife, at a sports day for schools at a technical college in Tzaneen:

It is here that I proposed love to her.[1] *I was 18 years old and she was sixteen. We had a relationship for two years without having sex. At times we slept in the same bed at my brother's house. But we did nothing. I wanted sex, but I was scared of impregnating her. I was also scared that if I screwed her she would discover that I was not circumcised, and she would leave me.*

Though Jimmy was ashamed of being uncircumcised he had, until then, refused to go to the circumcision lodge:

All the time, I was not interested in initiation [ngoma]. *I was interested in school. But I decided to go because I realised that an uncircumcised youngster cannot propose to any girl of his choice. I went to the lodge in June 1983 – when I was already a teacher. I informed Lerato that I was going to be circumcised and I asked her to wait for me.*

Jimmy decided to attend the lodge of Joshua Malathole, the best-known Baroka initiation master. Throughout Bushbuckridge the Baroka style of initiation is highly sought after, even amongst Shangaans who have no tradition of initiation. The Baroka are seen as the autochthons of Bushbuckridge, and this endows their initiation lodges with great prestige.

Upon his arrival, Joshua greeted Jimmy, handed him a club, and instructed him to walk along a certain footpath until he encountered a sheep, and then to beat the sheep to death. But Jimmy discovered that

[1] In local idiom 'to propose love' means to tell a woman that you love her, and request sex from her.

Joshua had deceived him. At a bend in the footpath, three strong adult men leaped from the bushes, grabbed Jimmy from behind, pinned him to the ground, and pulled down his pants. Joshua then arrived with a sharp knife and circumcised Jimmy in the middle of the path. From here, the men led Jimmy to a clearing in the bushes. Nearly fifty boys – all considerably younger than Jimmy – were sitting in the clearing, trying to nurse their circumcision wounds. Many cried from the excruciating pain. At the lodge the boys had to undergo further hardship:

For all the time that we were at the lodge [about seven weeks in total] we were naked. We did not sleep in huts, but in the open bush. Remember – this was in winter. In the evening the initiation master put some logs on a constantly burning fire and we could sit next to the fire in a long line.[2] *To keep warm we also dug holes like small graves, filled the bottom of the holes with grass, lay in the holes, and put a blanket of grass on top of our bodies. This was next to a river. Some nights we could sleep, but other nights this was impossible because of the cold.*

The regime at the lodge was as harsh as that of Jimmy's father at home and that of his teachers at school. Here, too, seemingly arbitrary rules and institutionalised violence were the most crucial components of discipline:

We were not allowed to argue or to fight and we were not allowed to refuse any of the food they [the initiation master and his assistants] gave us. It was usually porridge and cabbage, to which they would not add salt. They [the initiation master and his assistants] said that if they added salt our wounds would not heal. You were also prohibited from eating before they told you. They punished us by beating us with small sticks. They would start by beating you on the buttocks, and would then beat you on the back. But they were never allowed to beat you on the head – else your parents would complain. Another rule of the lodge was that you were not allowed to wash. During the days they told us to go and hunt buffalo and zebra, but nobody ever saw these animals in the bush.

According to Jimmy, initiates received only the most rudimentary instructions:

They used to say that we were guinea fowls [gaka] *in the forest. They also told us that we had to respect our seniors and anyone who was elderly at all times. We were also forced to learn and memorise many recitations and songs – some were lengthy, others were short.*

[2] The structure of Baroka initiation in Bushbuckridge closely approximates Hammond-Tooke's (1981) descriptive account of Bokgaga initiation in the Tzaneen area, about a hundred kilometres further north. However, men in Impalahoek tended to speak about their experiences at the circumcision lodges in less prudish terms. Hammond-Tooke seems to de-emphasise the theme of sexual instruction and also the lewd manner in which seniors speak about sex in the presence of the initiates.

Yet he observed that much of the talk and many of the songs learned at the lodge were about sexual matters. In contrast to the teachers at school, the initiation master and his assistants actively incited the boys' sexuality:

They used to tell us that with our foreskins removed our penises were like arrows and that we would encounter no problems when screwing.

The only song lyrics that he could still recall encouraged boys to have sexual intercourse, but warned them about some of the dangers of sex, notably that of incest:

Ndi elile ndi hlehla no mnabo,	I walked along the river stream,
ndha thi di bonani.	between the two valleys.
Ndha thi, 'Di bona o muri mnduna?'	I asked, 'What wonderful tree is this?'
Ndha thi tlwa.	Then I entered.
Bana! Baka le lahle lenyogo!	Boys! Don't indulge in sex!
Le tlo nyoba le di kgatšedi.	You'll end up screwing your sisters.
Dikgaetšedi ke tša bagwe.	Your sisters are for brothers-in-law.
Joo! Nna. Joo!	Joo! Please. Joo!

Midway through their ordeal in the bush, the initiation master forced all the initiates to drink beer containing a dark powdery substance. Jimmy later discovered this powder was actually ash that the initiation master had manufactured by roasting the circumcised foreskins of all his initiates. By drinking this powder the initiates allegedly immunised themselves against each others' bodily fluids and germs. This enabled them to have sex with the same women safely.

Being the oldest boy at the circumcision lodge, Jimmy constantly rebelled against the initiation master's instructions:

They never trusted me because I was cheeky. I did not want to sing their bullshit songs and I refused to eat their food. I also told them that I wanted salt on my food. Once they called the boys to go collect wood in the bush and to search for buffalo and zebra. But I did not go. Instead, I decided to crawl underneath the thicket and I slept there for the entire day. The initiation master even blew his kudu horn [phalaphala] *and told his assistants that one of the initiates had fled. They held roll-call and went to search for me. I then came out of the thickets and told them that I had been asleep and had not heard anything. That evening they did not feed me. Another time I again defied them and decided to wash myself underneath the bridge. They found me on a rock and asked, 'What are you doing?' I told them that I had washed because an itchy tree had scratched my body.*

Despite such punitive attitudes, Jimmy found that the principle of seniority, so valorised by the lodge, worked directly in his favour. As the oldest initiate, Jimmy as a rule escaped punishment. He also commanded the respect of his younger companions, who respectfully called him *rangwane* (older paternal uncle):

Towards the end of the initiation, Joshua Malathole employed me as his treasurer. The parents had to pay the initiation fees to me, and I ran the finances of the lodge. He also employed me as a monitor of some sort. I had to cut the meat they grilled into parts and divide these amongst the boys. I also had to distribute oranges.

In July, Jimmy graduated from the circumcision lodge and resumed teaching at Impalahoek Primary School.

Recent studies view circumcision as a necessary, rather than sufficient, 'rite of passage' from boyhood to adult masculinity.[3] In Bushbuckridge a circumcised boy of thirteen is definitely not a man. From a post-Freudian perspective, Gilmore (1990: 26–8) sees circumcision as, rather, a great 'deed', whereby boys dramatically renounce the bond with the mother, and move into the realm of men. He argues that boys experience the process of psychic separation from her as particularly problematic. This is because all infants establish a primary sense of identity and unity with the mother as nurturing parent. But, for boys, individuation involves the acquisition of a different gender identity, which is the opposite of hers: 'The struggle for masculinity is a battle against the regressive wishes and fantasies of return to primeval maternal symbiosis' (Gilmore 1990: 28). It is telling that initiation masters constantly degrade the mother, using phrases like 'your mother's arse' ('*mosona mmago*') and 'your mother's vagina' ('*nyo mago*') when swearing at the initiates. Initiates are brought to stand in a new relationship to women: previously they were nurtured by their mothers; now they were expected to dominate women sexually.

The process of initiation does not idealise masculinity, but represents the masculine domain as one of exceptional hardship and even of suffering. Here Heald's (1996) analysis of Gisu initiation in Uganda provides valuable comparative insight. She argues that initiation is aimed at 'battle-proofing' rather than 'catharsis' (turning negative emotions into positive ones) or 'trauma' (an aspect of repressive socialisation). For her, battle-proofing consists of desensitisation: of enacting situations of danger, and allowing initiates to become accustomed to, and inured against, fear. The bravery that boys display during the circumcision ritual provokes force of character, which is an essential attribute in a violent society. In short, the

[3] See van Gennep (1961), Gluckman (1962), and Turner (1967a) for the earlier view that initiation constitutes a 'rite of passage'. Despite the other shortcomings of their analysis, I believe that their idea of 'liminality' still offers extremely valuable insight into the process and structure of male circumcision rites.

ordeal allows men to develop confidence in their ability to face danger. Heald's (1996) theory captures a central aspect of Baroka circumcision rituals, but fails to capture the highly sexualised character of masculine capacity that the local rituals establish.

Jimmy did not explicitly mention the themes of transition from the female to male domain, or that of battle-proofing. Of greater significance for him seemed to be the necessity of conforming to outdated, sometimes even brutal, social dictates that granted him a licence to legitimately engage in sexual intercourse. In a somewhat ironic tone, he told me: 'I was now a man.'

Once this barrier had been crossed, Jimmy and his girlfriend, Lerato, had full penetrative intercourse. For the next four years they had an almost completely monogamous relationship. In 1987, Lerato became pregnant, and Jimmy decided to pay her parents an initial instalment of R700 as bridewealth. By accepting this payment, Lerato's parents indicated that they considered their daughter to be fully married. Lerato now moved to the household of Jimmy's parents, and began to work as daughter-in-law (*makoti*) for his mother, *ngwa* Ngobeni.

Jimmy told me that he could not have wished for a better wife. Lerato gave birth to three healthy children: the elder daughter, Kgopotšo, in 1987; another daughter, Thandi, in 1989; and a son, Katlego, ten years later, in 1999. As a wage earner, Lerato also made a substantial contribution towards the household income. She studied at a local College of Education from 1990 to 1992, earned a teaching diploma, and obtained a teaching position at Malapane Primary School, in a nearby village, where she still teaches.

Long after his wedding, Jimmy felt compelled to tell me:

There is no woman who can compare with Lerato. She is humble, she is not talkative, and she is not too sophisticated. But she is resilient and she is a good mother. She has disciplined our children very well. You can see how well-behaved they are. She also helps them with their schoolwork. I like women who are quiet. Lerato is not someone who gossips and washes our dirty laundry in public. Like me, she is also not a fashion-monger. She has an ear to listen. Although she was not gifted at school, she listened to me when I told her to study. She made no excuses with her studies.

University of the North and the Anti-Apartheid Struggle, 1985–94

Whilst Jimmy worked as an unqualified teacher in 1984, he successfully applied to the South African Student Educational Trust (SASET) for a bursary to study at university. Like most other youngsters from Bushbuckridge who went on to higher education at the time, Jimmy enrolled at the University of the North (now called the University of Limpopo) in Turfloop, in a rural township thirty kilometres from Polokwane.

South Africa's apartheid government established this university in 1959 to cater specifically for students from Lebowa and Gazankulu, and produce graduates that could be absorbed into the administration of these Bantustans (Oxlund 2010: 33). From its inception, the university was under the control of conservative Afrikaans professors allied to the Broederbond (lit. 'brotherhood', an extremely powerful secret society),[4] and black lecturers who were largely supportive of the Bantustan system.

However, the university soon became renowned for student activism. In a well-known incident during 1972, the student leader, Abram Tiro, criticised the Bantu Education system at a graduation ceremony and was summarily expelled. Mass protests across the country followed his expulsion (Oxlund 2010: 34). The University of the North subsequently became a bastion of the Black Consciousness Movement (BCM). Steve Biko's Azanian Student Movement (AZASM), which had remained true to this ideology, was a dominant force on campus. However, by the time Jimmy arrived at Turfloop, important changes were under way. The balance of power was shifting towards the newly established United Democratic Front (UDF) and towards the 'non-racial' ideology of the Freedom Charter. The university had become the single most important site of the anti-apartheid struggle in the northern Transvaal (van Kessel 2000).

Jimmy was overwhelmed by the size of the institution and by the array of subject choices.

I had no concept of university. I was stupid. I thought it was just like another [teachers'] college. But on my arrival I discovered that it was a huge institution. The lifestyle was radically different from what I was used to. I found it very hard to decide on a course [of study]. I wanted to be a lawyer, but in those days the students associated doing a law degree with political activism, and I did not want to be identified with those ones. I had experienced teaching and this influenced my career choice. Therefore I decided to study education.

Jimmy studied at the University of the North in 1985, 1986, and 1988, obtained a Bachelor of Education degree, and then returned to Turfloop in 1994 to complete a Bachelor of Arts (Honours) degree in Religious Studies. In 1987 he took a break from his studies and again worked at Impalahoek Primary School as an unqualified teacher. Lerato was

4 In their daring exposition of the inner workings of the Afrikaner Broederbond, Wilkins and Strydom (1980: 250–85) highlight the prominent role that this influential secret society played in university governance, particularly of the Afrikaans-medium and Bantustan campuses. They list several prominent professors at the University of the North as Broederbond members.

pregnant and he had insufficient money to pay registration fees. Throughout Jimmy's studies, his brother, Moses, paid all his pocket money.

He quickly overcame his initial bewilderment and enrolled to study Education, History, English, and Religious Studies. Though Jimmy's favourite subject was History, he obtained his best marks for Religious Studies. His most intriguing teacher was Professor van Zyl (Chair of the Polokwane branch of the National Party, who openly defended apartheid in class), his favourite lecturer Gareth Shapiro (a young left-wing history graduate from the University of Natal), and his most supportive teacher Professor Matthews Kgope (who chaired the Religious Studies Department).

Jimmy's dissertation in Religious Studies examined the concept of salvation in black theology, and he was awarded the degree *cum laude*. In 2000 I met Matthews Kgope at the Quinquennial World Congress of the International Association for the History of Religions, in Durban, and spoke to him about my research assistant. Matthews described Jimmy as one of the very best students he had ever taught.

But Jimmy found studying academic subjects easier than engaging with the politics of resistance, and experienced his political socialisation as particularly problematic. By the 1980s, AZASO (the Azanian Student's Organisation, later called SANSCO, see Badat 1999), which was aligned to the UDF and ANC, had gained control of the student representative council. This enabled a central core of UDF activists to establish themselves at the university. Louis Mnguni, a philosophy lecturer, became the new chair of the Northern Transvaal region of the UDF, while Joyce Mabundafhasi, a library assistant, became its secretary; and Peter Mokaba, a student, became president of SAYCO (the South African Youth Congress). These leaders had a militant profile and used Turfloop as an 'engine for building the struggle' – as a centre for ideological direction, communication, and coordination of anti-apartheid activism (van Kessel 2000: 167–71).

The AZASO/UDF activists of Turfloop promoted student involvement in community affairs, formed political organisations in their home villages, launched trade unions, and assisted high school pupils to establish student representative councils. They regularly held conferences at the university to organise the non-student youth.

Until 1985, the University rector, Professor Pontius Mokgokong, allowed students to organise relatively freely on campus. But the administration became increasingly unable to deal with student complaints and protests about conditions at the university, including accommodation, the food served at residences, and semester marks for readmission. In 1985, Jimmy's first year at Turfloop, the rector was hospitalised to receive treatment for leukaemia. The newly established post of vice-rector had not been filled, the registrar for academic affairs had retired, and the term of the university council had expired (Odendaal 1988: 14).

Students demonstrated about the poor quality of food and threw stones at the administration buildings on campus, and the police responded by detaining student leaders. This, in turn, provoked fiercer student demonstrations and harsher police repression. According to one journalist, what started with complaints about food nearly resulted in a 'bloodbath' (Odendaal 1988: 14). At one stage the police went as far as to detain all the students in the great hall, and only allowed those attending classes to leave. Many students decided to prepare their own food. But new university rules banned stoves, hot plates, refrigerators, and perishable foodstuffs in the residences. Students found guilty of contravening these rules could face expulsion (SAIRR 1989: 307).

The political situation at Turfloop worsened considerably after P. W. Botha's National Party government declared a national 'state of emergency' on 12 June 1986. Police conducted intermittent raids on campus and detained several members of the student representative council. Serious divisions also arose among the students. Whilst some students called for a total boycott of the mid-year exams, others wanted to write the exams. Professor Mokgokong, who had now resumed his duties, eventually called upon the South African Defence Force to restore order. The military sealed the perimeters of the campus with razor wire, expelled about four hundred students who attempted to disrupt the exams, and escorted the remaining students to their residences. Movement was now strictly controlled, and only 'approved students' were allowed to enter the campus. For the next two years the University of the North was literally under siege. Military tents were pitched on the football field, military patrols marched past the lecture halls, and convoys of military vehicles circled the campus twice a day. Yet, the political protests continued.

Jimmy found books more appealing than politics, and was more successful at attaining good exam grades than at building political connections. Before coming to university he had learnt about 'black power' from pupils such as Sello Mashego who fled from Soweto during the 1976 uprising to complete their schooling in Bushbuckridge. But Jimmy was rather sceptical of these pupils, whom he regarded as slick township youths and womanisers:

In those days I had scant knowledge of politics. I had only heard about Mandela's fight for the freedom of black people.

As Jimmy learnt more about politics on campus and became more aware of the injustices of apartheid, he began to admire Nelson Mandela, and decided to vote for AZASO during the student representative council elections. Occasionally, he also attended political meetings:

We used to listen to Peter Mokaba – the man with the big voice – and also those other politicians. I used to agree with them. I enjoyed toyi toying *[protest dancing] and singing songs, although the lyrics were not always about liberation. We also lit candles at Solomon Mahlangu's death.*[5]

But Jimmy's views were ambivalent, and he was unable to identify completely with the student activists. Over time, he became increasingly sceptical about the manner in which AZASO operated and about campus politics in general. He resented the constant disruption of classes, the manner in which student activists elevated food to a life-and-death issue, the militancy and violence of some students, the destruction of property, and the division of students into different political factions. In addition, he believed that the students naïvely underestimated the capacity of the apartheid state:

In 1985 we missed about a quarter of all classes and in 1986 the classes were so disrupted that the police and the soldiers came onto the campus. I did not like this. I suffered at university because I did not have enough money. I even had to drop out [in 1987] because I did not have enough funds. I lived in residence and I ate from the hostel, but I struggled to get money for toiletries. Beer was a luxury for me. The other students complained that the food was too little, stale, contaminated, and badly prepared. But as a rural boy I found nothing wrong with the food. I wanted anything that was food. I was not fussy about how it was prepared or whether or not it was fresh. I ate it. As long as there was food on the table I was content. I did not agree when they threw stones about the food. To me it did not matter. I only wanted to see a lecturer teaching.

There were many political organisations at the university and I sympathised with all of them. All of the student organisations fought for liberation, so I could not understand why they were fighting each other. What I did not like was black people labelling other black people as police spies. The big rivals were AZASO and AZASM. There was no tolerance. At one stage all the AZASM students had to leave our residence because their lives were being threatened. There were about six of them. AZASM then tried to kill my floor-mate – Andrew Dipela – who was a member of AZASO. The AZASM members came one night to attack Andrew. They broke his door and he had to flee. I did not understand this in-fighting. That is why I never wore a T-shirt of any organisation.

[5] Solomon Mahlangu was trained as a guerrilla fighter of the ANC's military wing, *Umkhonto We Siswe*, in Tanzania. Although he successfully infiltrated South Africa, he was soon apprehended by the security police, sentenced for terrorism, and executed. Mahlangu has the status of a martyr in the South African liberation struggle.

I don't think many students understood liberation. They thought that it was blacks against whites, and said that whites were the enemy. But they were contradictory. They would sing songs about Joe Slovo [a white leader of the South African Communist Party]. But they had not met Joe Slovo and they did not know what he looked like. If they had met him in town they might even have burnt him. They were crazy – for them the freedom of Mandela was not real freedom. In the liberation they fought for the whites should go to Europe. For them the ideal state was a state where everyone grabbed everything for himself. There would be total lawlessness. I think Winnie Mandela was behind this mentality.[6]

Each and every time they went on strike, some of the students destroyed university property. The damage was huge. They once set fire to a lecture hall and the entire E Block burnt down. . . . They even burnt university cars. If they believed that the state was the enemy, why did they not go to Pretoria and destroy state property? Why should university property be destroyed? I did not understand this.

Jimmy was also appalled by other instances of violence. He recalled that after one demonstration a student activist stabbed his own cousin to death. This happened on the very same floor of the residence in which Jimmy lived:

During the day students were boycotting [classes], protesting and toyi-toying. *At night they looted the cafeteria. They ransacked the whole place, stealing meat, alcohol, cold drinks, plates, tumblers, glasses and cigarettes. This is when the two cousins started fighting over a packet of twenty cigarettes. The one was a second-year pharmacy student, the other a third-year law student. The pharmacy student took a knife and stabbed the law student on his chest. The injured student then ran down the corridor, tried to open the door of my room, but fell on the steps opposite and died. His friends came to fetch him and took him to Dr Lelaku [in town], but he was certified 'dead upon arrival'. The police arrested the pharmacy student who had stabbed him. He screamed as they took him away. That is because he felt so guilty. The other students said something about witchcraft. They said that someone had bewitched the pharmacy student to kill his own cousin. I felt very bad and I was scared. Imagine how the*

[6] In more sedate circles of the ANC, Nelson Mandela's former wife, Winnie Madikizela-Mandela, is known for inflammatory, sometimes irresponsible, populist rhetoric. In 1986 she screamed at a political meeting: 'With these necklaces and with these matches we shall liberate this land.' The episode caused great embarrassment for her husband, even whilst he was still a political prisoner. Winnie Madikizela-Mandela was later found guilty of being complicit in the kidnapping of the young activist, Stompie Sepei (who was later murdered), and also of perpetrating fraud. She was given suspended sentences on both counts (Mandela 1995). Jimmy contrasted Winnie's feminine irresponsibility in the public domain with her husband's masculine reason. Such binary oppositions are fairly pervasive in a range of societies and often crop up in the mythologies surrounding female politicians such as Eva Peron (Taylor 1979).

parents of the deceased would have felt after they had paid so much money [for his studies].

Jimmy also criticised the widespread intimidation that characterised consumer boycotts:

The students used inappropriate strategies that undermined their moral integrity. There was lots of opportunism. During the consumer boycott, the Comrades would beat up people who bought groceries from the shops. They made them eat powdered soap and confiscated the other goods. The students even did this on campus. In 1994, when I was doing my Honours degree, I once came to visit you in Johannesburg and you gave me some money to buy a duvet. Then I accompanied those two black American women to Turfloop by mini-bus [combi] taxi. Only in the taxi did I hear that the students were boycotting the shops. Everyone looked at me and I knew that I might lose my duvet. The stupid Comrades could ask me, 'Where did you buy this?' and take it from me as tax. After we arrived at Turfloop, I had to wait till dark before I could take the duvet onto the campus. I used the rear gate and I only felt safe once I was in my room. I immediately tore off the labels, burnt the boxes and put the duvet on my bed. That time I had a narrow escape.

Moreover, the student movements seemed to be unperturbed by serious crime, such as gang rape, perpetrated by the students themselves:

Women were not allowed into the male residences, but they still intruded. Many of the women who came into the residences illegally were raped. I think that place was bewitched. The students used to have gigis – this is the name for a street party – and then women came to drink with the men in their rooms. Many times I heard how the men dragged drunken women into the toilets to rape them – the one after the other. This happened with animal lust. It was a weekly thing. Sometimes it even happened in the rooms.[7] *It did not matter how hard the authorities warned them – the advice fell on deaf ears.*

The alcohol business flourished on campus. Some of the students had fridges in their rooms and they sold beers. Cannabis [dagga] *was also common – even amongst the women students. The residences were very noisy and there was music all the time. You had to acclimatise to extreme moral decay.*

Jimmy recalled vividly how the South African Defence Force invaded the University of the North:

[7] Gang rapes are by no means unique to South African universities. Sanday (1990) notes that 'chain pulling' occurs with alarming frequency in the male college fraternities of the United States. She suggests that this kind of rape violently enforces masculine domination over women. It enacts male bonding, in which young men, who compete for women in other contexts, collaborate and share the same woman as sexual object. Voyeurism and the opportunity of publicly demonstrating one's heterosexual virility to one's peers are important components of such rapes.

The problem started with the 1986 exams. Because of all the disruptions we missed many classes. Some of the SRC [student representative council] members spent the entire year in jail. That's why some students did not want to write their exams. The students also complained about rule A19. This rule stated that if you failed your major subject, you would be excluded [from the university] the following year. . . . Those of us who attended class and studied hard wanted to write the exams. I was one of them. Most students wanted to write and there was nearly a confrontation.

The army came in September 1986. They protected us and escorted the students to class. The army even sent us 'Good Luck for the Exams' cards, and the soldiers monitored the exams. There was an ambiguity. I wanted them there [on campus] because I wanted my degree. I wanted them to protect us.

However, it soon became apparent to Jimmy that the presence of the security forces – particularly of the police – was exacerbating the problems on campus:

The police caused more shit and they added fuel to the fire. They came onto the campus to shoot people, not to police crime. The situation was almost like a concentration camp. There were many well-known police officers. Even Gideon Nieuwoudt – the security policeman who murdered so many [political] activists at Vlakplaas.[8] *We knew Sergeant van Dijk as the most brutal police officer. There was also a certain Hechler. The police deployed all those killers at Turfloop. We knew them all. Van Dijk used to drive around the hostels in a police sedan with aerials. Then the students would shout, 'Hey! Van Dijk is here! Go for cover!' The police once dispersed a gathering of students and randomly started firing at the students. They shot and killed one student, as he was mounting the fire escape steps of our residence. I heard that he was a leader of the Modjadji College student representative council, who was visiting Turfloop for a conference. When he died I wondered why the life of a black person should be so cheap. I could not understand why the campus security allowed the police onto our campus.*

The police killed another student, Josephine Mashobane, in Polokwane. She was pregnant and the police arrested her when she went to town for a medical check-up. They interrogated her, and beat her till she died. She was not even an SRC member: Josephine was only studying at Turfloop. This made her a victim of apartheid and she became a hero. The police held black life in disdain. A number of other students were maimed. One student was reading in his hostel

[8] Gideon Nieuwoudt was one of the apartheid regime's most notorious assassins, and was responsible for the killing of numerous anti-apartheid activists, including Matthews Goniwe. Refused amnesty by South Africa's Truth and Reconciliation Commission, Nieuwoudt died of cancer in 2005. I could find no evidence to corroborate Jimmy's assertion that Nieuwoudt was deployed to suppress the uprisings at the University of the North.

room. The police shot outside, a bullet ricocheted from the wall and hit him. Because of this he lost an eye. But nobody compensated him.

Jimmy believed that the student activists could not match the might of government and security forces:

I did not think that the students could [successfully] challenge the apartheid government. I did not believe that liberation and freedom were possible. I thought the government was invincible. The soldiers and the police had dogs, guns, tanks,[9] *and the legislation on their side. The left wing claimed that they ran the university structures, such as the senate and council. But this was just pure tokenism. The people who really ran the university were the white professors who supported the National Party. I thought that if people could not transform the university, they would never be able to transform P. W. [Botha – then South Africa's president].*

He, nonetheless, admired the fearlessness of the student activists, and commended the courage with which they confronted the security forces, and their single-minded dedication to their cause.

I was awe-struck by their bravery. They were bare-handed, but they confronted the police and soldiers, who had guns and dogs. Perhaps it was the singing and the dancing that made them feel invincible. The students would take buses into town to cause shit. There they would go to the police station and provoke the police by throwing stones at them. The police unleashed their dogs to bite the students, and countless students would be taken to hospital. I heard that once the police shot six students with rubber bullets. I don't know of a single instance in which the students won. But they always forgot the past.

When [Desmond] Tutu preached against apartheid in London and called for sanctions, I thought he was wasting his time. I believed that it would be much better for him to preach the word of God. I thought that with sanctions we would lose our jobs, have no money for school, and that we would not eat. The odds were against black people. Each day we were told that the police killed students. . . . The students said that the blood of the martyrs paves the way for liberation. But I thought that there was too much blood and that the path to liberation was over-paved with blood. I thought that the struggle was futile. I started wondering whether black people could run this country. That's why I subscribed to negotiation.

[9] Struggle mythology sometimes intimates that South African security forces used 'tanks' to suppress political uprisings in the townships during the 1980s. For instance, tanks feature prominently amongst the stage props of Bongani Ngema's musical, *Sarafina*. In fact, the apartheid regime's security forces used a far less imposing kind of armoured vehicle which fired only teargas, called the 'Hippo'. The iconography of tanks creates the emotional effect of military battle, and invokes parallels with the brutal repression of pro-democracy demonstrators in Tiananmen Square in Beijing.

Jimmy's experiences of university studies at Turfloop reinforced his marginal position relative to his peers, a position already apparent during the circumcision ritual. His views of politics were extremely ambivalent. At the same time that he condemned the coercive practices of the student movement, he also deplored the treatment of students by the government's security forces. It was increasingly apparent that Jimmy was an individualist. He invested in his future by dedicating himself to his studies, but failed to build appropriate political attributes and connections.

Returning to a Transformed Bushbuckridge

In 1989, when Jimmy returned to Bushbuckridge from Turfloop, the political situation had been irretrievably transformed. Matsikitsane Mashile and his brother, Segopela Mashile, were the first political activists in Bushbuckridge. In the 1950s they joined the ANC and led tenant struggles against the use of child labour by Hall and Sons, a giant farming enterprise. With the banning of the ANC they were initially jailed on charges of sabotage, and then banished to the Transkei and Ciskei, respectively (Ritchken 1995: 290). Only in 1980 did ANC underground networks again become operative in the area. Matsikitsane and Segopela Mashile were both elected to the Lebowa Legislative Assembly. By taking local issues to the highest authorities, they effectively used their prominent positions in the Bantustan government to further popular political causes (Ritchken 1995: 299–301).

In April 1986, the Mashile brothers and UDF activists from Shatale township launched the Setlhare Crisis Committee and the Brooklyn Youth Organisation at a public meeting in Impalahoek. Twelve adults (including a telephone exchange operator, a bank teller, and six teachers) were elected to the Crisis Committee. But police soon detained all active committee members. This thrust the youth into the forefront of the political struggle (Ritchken 1995: 310).

The Youth Organisation attracted a large following amongst local male school students, henceforth known as Comrades. Their initial campaigns focused upon schooling. By the late 1980s the conditions in the local schools had become critical. The principal of Mashile High School in Impalahoek imposed a levy of R16 per student to build five classrooms. Although the classrooms were completed in 1987, the levy was still charged in 1988 and in 1989. There was a serious shortage of textbooks. The pupil–teacher ratio was 68 to 1, and teachers regularly missed classes. Since 1982, when Jimmy studied at Mashile, the school's examination results had deteriorated considerably. In 1989, only 60 (18 per cent) of the 330 pupils who took their final Grade Twelve exams passed. Only one pupil passed Physical Science and all 17 students who took mathematics failed (Ritchken 1990: 12).

There were also widespread complaints about male teachers having sex with schoolgirls. Some of these teachers came from faraway places such as Polokwane, and resided in the school's singles' quarters. They allegedly called girls to their quarters, asked them to fetch water, clean their rooms, or cook, and to have sex with them. According to gossip the head teacher impregnated an eighteen-year-old student and gave her a concoction to induce an abortion. In another reported incident, a schoolgirl fainted when she had sex with the harshest disciplinarian in the school. Schoolboys gossiped that this was because his 'machine' (penis) was too large (Niehaus 2000b: 395). These narratives should not be taken at face value, and truth is not necessarily their most relevant aspect. Their telling nonetheless expresses profound resentment of excessive patriarchy, at the historical juncture when discourses of rights became prominent (Niehaus 2010b: 838–41). But, at the same time, there is much evidence of actual sexual harassment and of rape in South African schools.[10]

The Comrades enforced a series of class boycotts, demanding that 'school building fees' and corporal punishment be abolished, and that a student representative council be established. Once these demands had been met, they placed placards at the school, warning that teachers who participated in reactionary politics or had sex with schoolgirls would be 'necklaced'. In the vocabulary of struggle politics this meant that Comrades would execute them by placing a burning tyre that had been doused with petrol around their necks. These protests led to a drastic reversal of power. Three prominent Comrades, who carried guns at all times, virtually ran the school. They regularly interjected when the principal spoke in the school assembly, virtually suspended all school rules, and carefully scrutinised the behaviour of teachers. Comrades whipped one teacher who had sexual relations with a married woman student, and they left him for dead. He and six other teachers left the school.

The schools provided a base for wider community participation. Comrades organised a 'stay away' on May Day and, as in Turfloop, they launched a consumer boycott of all white-owned supermarkets. They laid concrete slabs on the roads to force workers to stay at home, and confiscated consumer goods. Comrades also called on villagers not to pay annual site taxes (R1), service rents (R15, for water and graveyard maintenance), and stock levies (85c per head of large stock, 40c per head

[10] In a study of women in three South African provinces, 2 per cent of those who had been to school disclosed that they had been threatened with exam failure or bad marks if they refused to have sex with their teacher (Jewkes and Abrahams 2002: 1238). The 1998 South African Demographic and Health Survey assessed the frequency of rape in a nationally representative sample of 11,735 women aged between 15 and 49 years. Of the women interviewed, 153 (1.6 per cent) reported having been raped before the age of 15 years. The largest group of perpetrators (33 per cent), were school teachers (Jewkes et al. 2002: 319–20).

of small stock). In this manner Comrades effectively brought all activities of the Tribal Authority to a halt.

Through some of their campaigns the Comrades explicitly aimed to win approval amongst adults. For example, Comrades confronted a notorious criminal gang, which had maintained a reign of terror in Bushbuckridge, and burnt the homes of gang members. Comrades also formed squads to escort commuter-labourers home at night. They regularly organised marches to the police station to demand more effective provision of piped water, roads, and electricity. In 1989 more than ten thousand people participated in such a march. Catholic priests walked in front of the procession, and adult women marched along carrying empty water canisters. The Comrades also engaged themselves in the morally ambiguous field of witchcraft, but we shall examine these interventions in the next chapter.

There is something reminiscent of *Animal Farm* (1945) – Orwell's satirical novel about pigs who lead a revolt against a farmer only to be corrupted by the absolute power they hold – in the status of the Comrade leaders. Whilst condemning the exploitation of schoolgirls by teachers, the political activists claimed the most attractive schoolgirls for themselves. In Impalahoek, Comrades even launched a campaign called 'building soldiers' during which they sought to impregnate young women and replace the youth activists killed during the freedom struggle. Parents complained that Comrades would force the young women to attend political meetings at night, and afterwards have sex with them in the forest.[11]

Towards the end of 1989, adults formed the Sofasonke (lit. 'together we die') Civic Union to reimpose their authority in all villages. Sofasonke's executive committee comprised two high school principals, a teacher, and a minister of the Nazarene Church. On 26 November, a group of eight hundred Sofasonke supporters, mostly women, burnt down the homes of twelve prominent Comrades. Armed Sofasonke groups patrolled the villages at night, ensuring that there were no youths on the streets. On Christmas Eve Sofasonke members waylaid the van of Matsikitsane Mashile's burial society, killing one of his political associates and wounding another in the thigh.

Early in January 1990, Nelson Ramodike, Lebowa's Chief Minister, with representatives of the South African Council of Churches (SACC) and the UDF, met Comrade and Sofasonke leaders in an attempt to end the violence. However, the very next night several houses and cattle were burnt. On 30 January, Comrades killed Chocate Mashile, a leader of the Sofasonke Civic Union who was also a school

[11] See Lodge (1991: 120), Van Kessel (1993: 607), and Ritchken (1995: 343, 401) for descriptions of this campaign in other areas of rural South Africa.

principal: they brutally 'necklaced' him in broad daylight. In retaliation, Sofasonke members butchered to death a fifteen-year-old schoolgirl, who was the sister of a Comrade. Only after the Lebowa police arrested twenty Comrades and five Sofasonke members did the violence subside.

Already critical of the student movements at Turfloop, Jimmy condemned many of the strategies employed by the Comrades in Bushbuckridge. His perceptions were not only shaped by his university experience: they were also coloured by the experiences of his younger brother, Henry Mohale, who was a pupil at Mashile High School at the time. Henry claimed that marshals regularly forced youths to attend political meetings at night. Before adjourning, the marshals whipped all 'non-liberated' boys who did not come to the meetings voluntarily, and took all 'beautiful girls' to their homes. Comrades once arrived at his aunt's home, sang freedom songs at the gate, and demanded to see his girl cousins. The Comrades whipped Henry when he tried to obstruct them. On another occasion, Henry told his mates that Gunman Ubisi was a thug who knew nothing about politics,[12] but Gunman's girlfriend overheard these remarks. That afternoon Gunman and three other men abducted Henry from a softball match, and again beat him severely. Henry eventually became a member of the rival Pan African Congress (PAC). 'After I was indiscriminately whipped,' Henry told me, 'I had to find a new political shelter.'

The patriarchal violence that Jimmy encountered at home and in school found a clear parallel in the political domain. Jimmy perceived the 'majoritarianism' practiced by the student activists in Turfloop and by the Comrades movement in Bushbuckridge as essentially coercive, and as relying upon physical force rather than intellectual persuasion. At times he even sympathised with Sofasonke. Contrary to overwhelming evidence, he did not really believe that Sofasonke agents had murdered Matsikitsane Mashile's employee. Jimmy wondered how Sofasonke knew precisely when the two men would arrive, and why they were shot outside their own vehicle. Jimmy speculated that perhaps the husbands of their extramarital lovers had hired someone to kill them. Alternatively, he said, their employers might have murdered them because they had stolen money from the burial society. Yet unlike his brother Henry, and despite condemning the political strategy of local Comrades, Jimmy still supported national ANC leaders such as Nelson Mandela.

[12] In 1986 Gunman Ubisi was the leader of the notorious *psyianga* ('rebel' in Tsonga) gang which operated from the village of Cottondale. At first there were fierce battles between *psyianga* and the Comrades, and the Comrades went so far as to burn the homes of several *psyianga* members. But Gunman later joined the Comrades and became a member of the ANC Youth League. Despite this change of heart, there were persistent rumours that Gunman worked as an assassin for taxi associations.

Moletele High School, 1990–3

In 1990 Jimmy joined the staff of Moletele, a well-known local high school, as a history teacher. However, over the next 16 years, he learnt that his academic qualifications and work performance were insufficient guarantees of progress in the teaching profession.

One of the reasons why Jimmy chose to teach at Moletele was that he greatly admired the school principal, Caswell Shubane. Jimmy, however, did not know that Caswell had fallen foul of the Comrades:

On the first day I arrived at Moletele as a new teacher, the students were on strike. This happened just after the Comrades had killed Chocate Mashile. As we sat on stage at the school assembly and the principal introduced us as new teachers, the kids began throwing stones at us. The kids were opposed to all the teachers whom Caswell appointed. They demanded that the principal be dismissed. This is because he belonged to TAWATA [a conservative teacher's union], was against Jacques Modipane [leader of the Brooklyn Youth Organisation], and because he had the slogan, 'Education First! Liberation Later!'

In February, the Comrades made an attempt on Caswell Shubane's life. They came to the school in a sedan with shades [tinted windows]. Gunman Ubisi [the well-known 'hit man'] was inside. Fortunately, Caswell's in-laws had phoned him and told him to flee from school. . . . Caswell fled to Polokwane and that was the last time I saw him. . . . Caswell is very talented and today he is the Dean of Students at the Tshwane University of Technology.

For reasons that had less to do with these complex political alignments than with local nepotistic practices, Jimmy's ambitions of securing early promotion were soon frustrated:

I enjoyed teaching, but I made no progress. The classes were large – with more than seventy-five kids per class. I taught three classes and this made teaching very difficult. The Department [of Education] appointed Ketebotse Mosoma from Cottondale as our caretaker [principal]. I thought that he would promote me because I was highly qualified. But during the school recess Ketebotse appointed his half-brother as Head of Department. His half-brother had only a one-year teaching certificate. He did not even have a diploma.[13] *I could see that Ketebotse wanted to surround himself with unqualified people who*

[13] In the past the vast majority of teachers in Bushbuckridge did not hold degrees, but rather 'certificates' or 'diplomas'. The certificate was the lesser qualification and involved only two years of study at a teacher's training college: a diploma involved three or four years of study at a college or university. To register for a certificate one needed to have only a Form Three qualification, whereas one needed to have passed Form Five with a conditional exemption to enrol for a diploma. In 1998, teaching certificates were officially phased out in South Africa.

could only say, 'Yes boss'. This showed that there was no prospect of promotion for me.

For me the last straw was when they [the Department of Education] appointed George Thlou as the new principal. George taught me at Mashile and he was very dishonest and extremely biased. He thought that he was a good teacher, but he was not. I'm sure the Department only appointed him as a subject specialist in History because I obtained a B when he taught me History at Mashile. When George came to Moletele he had just completed a degree at Venda [University]. This is not a good degree. You know Venda. You know how they give away degrees there.[14] *George was a self-installed Apostolic minister and he only associated himself with the 'born-again' Christians at Moletele. He took advice only from them and he tried to transform Moletele into a Christian school. George hated teachers who smoked, teachers who belonged to the other churches, and those of us who did traditional things. He was also a womaniser who screwed schoolgirls wherever he went. He would call the girls into his office, and would then make appointments to screw them at the motels after school hours. The other teachers caught him many times. I realised that George did not like me and that I could not work for him.*

Tlasede High School, 1993–2005

In 1993, Ben Chiloane, the principal of Tlasede High School, informed Jimmy that there was a vacancy on his teaching staff. Jimmy said that he preferred to work for Ben Chiloane, and that Tlasede was located much closer to his parents' home. So he applied for a transfer to Tlasede.

By now South African schooling had entered a new era. In 1990, the ANC was unbanned and immediately broadened its support base. Van Kessel (1993) shows how 'former adversaries of the youth' began to see ANC membership as an insurance policy for the future. Businessmen and teachers were soon elected to lead ANC branches, and youth, previously hailed as 'shock troops' of the revolution, were now 'cast aside and marginalised' (p. 613). Teachers gradually re-established their authority over local schools. In 1992, the National Education Crisis Committee (NECC) launched a 'back-to-school campaign'. Disciplinary squads were formed to punish latecomers and to escort pupils found loitering en route during school hours into the classroom.

In April 1994 the ANC won an overwhelming victory in South Africa's first democratic elections, gaining about 97 per cent of all votes in Bushbuckridge (Niehaus 2006b: 540). Education now became the responsibility of the newly elected provincial government. The new regime

[14] The University of Venda is far smaller than the University of the North. For example, in 1993 only 4,657 students were enrolled at Venda, in comparison to 13,000 at the University of the North (SAIRR 1994: 744).

immediately increased funding, established feeding schemes in all primary schools, and devoted considerable resources to the distribution of textbooks.

Trusting that the liberatory rhetoric of the ANC would transcend the clientelistic imperatives of local politics, Jimmy expected the best from these changes:

When I arrived at the new school, Ben Chiloane warmly welcomed me. I thought that I would easily get a promotion because there was no deputy headmaster and only one head of department – Mrs Modike. But I soon realised that I had gone from the frying pan into the fire.

During the final year (matriculation) exams of 1993, Tlasede had performed worse than any other school in Bushbuckridge. Only three (4 per cent) of the 68 students who wrote these examinations passed.[15] Jimmy realised that Ben Chiloane had dug his own grave by appointing too many 'foreigners' as teachers, and that this strategy would make his regime fall foul of the local Comrade power structures. Only five of the fourteen teachers at the school were from Bushbuckridge: four were from Polokwane, four from elsewhere in the former Lebowa, and one from Venda. Most of these teachers were single and hired rooms in nearby villages:

The teachers from Polokwane and the local Comrades wanted to remove Ben as the school principal. They accused him of embezzling school funds, incompetence, and being a reactionary. The school inspectors then appointed a commission to investigate these claims. Some members of the commission also wanted Ben Chiloane removed and they did whatever they could to find irregularities. After the investigations were complete, the commission held a public meeting. Matsikitsane Mashile and Segopela Mashile [the ANC veterans], the community, the teachers and the kids were all there. The commission announced that they found Ben innocent of the charges of embezzlement and incompetence. But, for security reasons, the committee asked all those present whether they still wanted Ben as the school principal. The kids shouted, 'No! We don't want him!' Ben said that under these conditions he no longer wished to be the principal. The inspectors then transferred Ben to another school.

My problems started when Ben departed. Now the hounds were ready to bite. I was caught up in a web because they recognised me as a supporter of the [now-departed] school principal. My support for the principal was genuine – it was out of love for the school. Everybody hated me. The teachers from Polokwane accused me of many things: amongst others, that I was a member of Inkatha

[15] Only 1,392 (25.3 per cent) of the 5,492 pupils who wrote the matriculation exams in the Bushbuckridge circuit in 1993 passed. Only 197 of the candidates obtained university exemptions, and the highest marks in the circuit were awarded to three students who obtained only C aggregates.

[of Mangosotho Buthelezi's Inkatha Freedom Party, who were bitter political enemies of the ANC, especially in the province of KwaZulu-Natal]. They even accused me of being a witch.

The inspectorate came to our school after the principal had been removed. They recommended D. B. Modike as caretaker principal; and Thabo Mashile and J. B. Mohale [Jimmy himself] as her assistants. But the teachers overruled the recommendations. . . . They confirmed Modike and Mashile, but they replaced me with R. B. Lekwane. I was the only teacher with a senior degree, but the teachers did not want me to be elevated. They preferred Lekwane [from Burghersfort]: someone who had a lesser qualification than me, and who was junior to me, both in years and in experience. He had a diploma and I had a senior degree. . . . The teachers said that I had come to the school later than Mashile and Lekwane. Do you see the misfortune [bati]*?*

Mrs Modike [the caretaker principal] hated me because I could write, and she connived with my enemies. The teachers from Polokwane did not greet me anymore and refused to speak to me. The only way in which I could survive was to do my work thoroughly so that the children would support me. I did my work: I taught, I marked, and I gave feedback. They tried to use the students against me, but very few of the students hated me. The kids liked my teaching and the students did not respond when the other teachers spoke badly about me. This made it difficult for my enemies to win the war.

Jimmy's defence of scholarly and professional excellence was closely interwoven with his repudiation of nepotistic practices, which he linked to the political ascendance of the Comrades. He was deeply frustrated by a situation in which political affiliations and loyalties counted more than professional qualifications.

In 1997 Jimmy escaped from Tlasede and volunteered to work at a 'finishing school', also in Bushbuckridge. The Department of Education had established this school specifically to accommodate only the large number of students who had previously failed their Grade Twelve exams. Jimmy described working at this school as a most fulfilling teaching experience:

They looked for some of the best teachers in Bushbuckridge to go there. I loved it. The coordinator of the finishing school, Mr Shokane, was a nice person and he was very encouraging. He was a friend. Although we taught only the kids who had previously failed – those underachievers – we obtained a 60 per cent pass rate at the end of the year. We attained position four in the whole circuit.

In 1998 the Department sent a circular that all teachers enlisted at the finishing schools should return to these finishing schools. I did as instructed. But, in my absence, the management of Tlasede wrote a petition to the Department of Education, complaining that I had absconded and that I was being paid for nothing. Because I had been absent for fourteen days without notice, they requested that I be dismissed. All the teachers signed, even Thabo Mashile. Thabo used to drink with me, but he did not tell me anything. There is no such thing as a friend!

On the day of the judgement the inspector came to the finishing school and called me out of the class. He told me that the teachers of Tlasede had petitioned for my dismissal, and asked, 'Why are you teaching here?' I replied, 'Because the government had directed me.' Even the inspector did not know about the circular. I then asked him to accompany me to Tlasede. When we arrived, I was very angry and screamed at the principal, saying, 'I'll take you people to court for defaming me!' I then took the circular board and read the contents of this circular to the inspector and to the teachers. The school management and principal had even signed the circular. Then I asked them, 'Did you not understand what you signed?' The inspector realised the mistake and dismissed the meeting. The management committee apologised to me. I reluctantly accepted their apology. As we drove back to the finishing school, the inspector asked me, 'Why do these people hate you?'

National-level reforms, driven by the spirit of the constitution, continued to promise some improvements. In 1998 the South African Schools Act was promulgated, providing a new administrative framework for all schools. In terms of the Act, school governing bodies (SGBs) were to have twelve members, comprising the principal, two teachers (now called 'educators'), seven parents, and two pupils (renamed 'learners'). 'Student representative councils' (SRCs) now became 'learner representative councils' (LRCs). The Act also outlawed corporal punishment. All teachers in Bushbuckridge were forced to sign forms, distributed by the provincial Department of Education, acknowledging that corporal punishment was now a criminal offence, punishable by six months' imprisonment. Henceforth, the Department expected teachers to impose non-corporal punishments, such as warnings, temporary suspensions, and expulsion. School rules also became less draconian. Primary school boys were now allowed to wear long pants; girls were permitted to dye, straighten, or lengthen their hair; and pupils who wrote love letters received counselling and even sex education (Niehaus 2000b: 403–5). But the overly generous recognition of pupil rights promised by these reforms did not meet with Jimmy's approval when he returned to Tlasedi in 1999:

I found it extremely hard to restrain myself and not to fight with the other teachers. One day there was a staff meeting at which these people from Polokwane spoke a lot of shit. They said that we should appoint kids to control the late coming, and that the kids should discipline themselves. They also suggested that we should open a bank account so that the kids could use their own school fees. I became angry, stood up, and shouted at them at the top of my voice, 'This is bullshit! This happens nowhere else! Let's not implement unpractical things!' I had very little support at the meeting. Even my friends – such as Thabo – did not openly want to side with me. Hereafter, many teachers no longer spoke to me. But I did not care. What I said was for the community's benefit.

Jimmy was also shocked to discover that the old pattern – male teachers having sex with schoolgirls – continued. He said that Jerry Moloi, one of his enemies from Polokwane, was the greatest culprit:

I heard that during break Moloi would take girls to his home and screw them. He allegedly threatened the girls that he would fail their English and Biology [exams] unless they slept with him. Once a young man called Mapayile came to our school and reported that Moloi had tried to rape his girlfriend. Mapayile used to be the SRC president at school.... In the past Mapayile and Moloi had been friends and the two of them worked together to depose Ben Chiloane as the school principal. Moloi even lived with the young man's brother.... The ANC [presumably the chair of the local branch] and the Civic [Association] advised Mapayile to report the matter to the police. Mapayile took the girlfriend to the police station, but the results of the examination showed that she had not been raped. This might have been because Moloi had used a condom. The Civic later held a community meeting. Four girls testified that Moloi had shown them pornographic videos before sleeping with them. Unfortunately, the school recess punctuated this process.

In the same year, Jerry Moloi allegedly blackmailed a woman who applied for admission to Tlasede with a fraudulent report card, saying that he would only support her application if she slept with him. Though she complied with Moloi's request, the admissions committee still turned down her application:

When her husband heard about this he went straight to Moloi's quarters threatening to shoot him. The husband also reported Moloi to SADTU [the South African Democratic Teachers' Union] and to the chief. Moloi agreed to compensate the woman's husband by paying him R4,000 in monthly instalments of R700. He also signed a document swearing that he would never again be seen in the village. Hereafter Moloi requested a transfer and was offered a new teaching post in Phalaborwa. Moloi told the Department that his life was in danger and apparently cited me as the culprit who arranged for thugs to kill him. In that way he framed me as a scapegoat. This was one victory that was scored on my part. Moloi was a ringleader and my most powerful foe.

Unfortunately, Jimmy still had other enemies. On one occasion teachers from Polokwane even accused him of trying to bewitch them. This incident shows how Jimmy's persona of a resentful, envious, and excluded colleague, who showed great courage in defying and challenging the power structures at school, had started to resonate with the stereotypical image of the witch.

In those days we used to drink at Five Star Restaurant after school. One day I sat there having beers with my friends. After some time, I went to use the toilet at the railway houses across the road. Some of these teachers from Polokwane lived in those homes and they saw me coming out of the toilet. Ralushai, the teacher from Venda who is my friend, then warned me. He said to me, 'Jimmy! The teachers who live in those railway houses say that you are a witch. They say that you sprinkled potions in the toilet for them to die. Now they are not using the toilets.' I just laughed.

Joining the African National Congress (ANC)

At one stage, Jimmy thought that his unpopularity among teachers at school and his inability to secure promotion were due to his inability to develop appropriate political connections. People with lesser qualifications, but with better reputations within local ANC structures, were progressing faster than him in their occupations.

For this rather opportunist reason, Jimmy joined the Impalahoek branch of the ANC in 1996. But he found it hard to suppress his disquiet at many of the decisions taken by the branch:

At one ANC meeting they chose me to be a political educationist and an additional member. There was a chairperson, deputy chairperson, secretary, deputy secretary, treasurer, and five additional members, including myself. My task was to orientate those who wanted political education about the struggle. I received all the ANC manuals and I enjoyed this work. It was like teaching the Comrades. I had to brief them about ANC policies.

But I made no progress within the organisation. People said that I was too big for my boots. When I got into the office I thought that I was an important man. I thought that everyone looked up to me to effect changes in the way that the organisation was run. One of the tasks of our branch was to see that the municipality addressed the water problem and ran the other social services, such as the clinics, smoothly. The people who chose me told me that government had given the Water Committee [of the municipality] R70,000. But the Committee members could not account for the money. I suspected that the municipal officers 'ate' [misappropriated] it. I chaired one of our branch meetings and when the question of water came up for discussion, I asked about the money. I wanted the Committee members to return the money. But I did not have any support from the other branch members. The ordinary rank and file appreciated what I did, but the branch members were not impressed with me. I wanted to quit because I thought that I was in the wrong place. The politics of the day were the politics of bread and butter [a possible reference to nepotism and feathering one's own nest]. But I wanted real politics. I realised that I would not survive. So, when our terms expired in 1999, I resigned to save my skin. Hereafter I no longer attended any branch meetings.

In 1993, I introduced Jimmy to Edwin Ritchken, a doctoral student in Political Studies at the University of the Witwatersrand, who was also an ANC activist. In 1995, Edwin invited Jimmy and another of my research assistants to serve on the steering committee of the Bushbuckridge Rural Resource Centre, which he had helped to establish in Shatale township. Jimmy eagerly participated in the committee:

Edwin obtained the funding from somewhere to build the centre. There was a good kitchen for cooking chips and cookies, computers, a library, a garden, and also paralegal aid. The Centre offered legal advice to people on a number of issues such as unfair dismissal, UIF [the unemployment insurance fund], pensions, and contracts. This was a very good idea and our committee ran it. When Edwin received his PhD there was a graduation party at the Resource Centre and people slaughtered a beast. Most of the people on the committee were senior ANC guys. We [Jimmy and his friend] were the only small guys and Edwin introduced us to the big guys. We attended several of the meetings. But there was so much in-fighting. Some people did not see eye to eye. At one meeting we had to choose a speaker. Some argued for a speaker from Limpopo Province and others said they wanted Matthews Phosa [the premier of Mpumalanga Province]. To me it did not matter [who spoke], but this showed that the people were in different camps. There was also a rift between the people who supported Limpopo and those who supported Mpumalanga [see page 16 on the border dispute]. We could see that the centre was not well run. In 1997 the steering committee accused someone of stealing R33,000. He was taken to court, but was found not guilty. In 1998 the Centre went insolvent.

As a result of these experiences, Jimmy became disillusioned, not only in the capacity of the ANC to positively transform people's lives, but also in his own ability to participate meaningfully in organisations. Although he had had misgivings about the promises of the liberation movement since the onset, I sensed that Jimmy's frustration about his own marginal status within the organisation made him even more cynical when he subsequently spoke of politics.

Redeployment

In 2002, the post-apartheid government implemented a comprehensive rationalisation strategy that demanded the national redeployment of teachers. Throughout the year teachers were transferred from school to school within the Bushbuckridge circuit:

In my absence the school governing body [SGB] had decided to change Tlasede into a special school for commercial subjects. This was another plan by the teachers to remove me. When Tlasede became a commercial school, I became redundant. Seven of the fourteen teachers at Tlasede had to be transferred and I was one of them. But God is good. The teachers who wanted me to be redeployed were, themselves, redeployed. Some of my enemies left, but I am still at Tlasede.

In 2003, I was told that I had to go to Nxumalo High School. But when I arrived, the principal said, 'No! This is a mismatch! I don't need History and English teachers. I want Business Economics and the Sciences.' He then sent me back, and I had to be reabsorbed [into the teaching staff] at Tlasede. Until today, I am still waiting to be told to which station I should go.

With Jimmy's enemies redeployed, his position at Tlasede improved greatly. He finally sensed a chance of promotion:

At first Mrs Modike [the principal] did not like me, but things had drastically changed. She appointed me to the School Governing Body and asked me to do the school's correspondence. I wrote letters to the Department of Education, asking them to improve the infrastructure, water, and fencing at the school. These days I literally run the school. . . . We recently held a staff meeting and she said that she had earmarked me to become a Head of Department. The meeting lasted from 1:30 pm until 5 pm. Three teachers stood up and said, 'No! We can't allow this man to be promoted!' They were Maatsie and Matsepe from Polokwane, and Mokoena from Ohrigstad. But she replied, 'I don't understand. Why not? He is qualified, competent and experienced.' They argued that I had arrived at the school after Matsepe and that I did many things wrong. But the principal asked them, 'What don't you understand? Matsepe only has a diploma.' Finally, the principal recommended me, and the nine temporary teachers at the school all supported me.

Jimmy's enemies attributed his sudden, newfound, success, as well as the demise of their own power clique at the school, to witchcraft:

After the staff meeting Matsepe became seriously ill. He was first taken to Tintswalo Hospital and was then sent to the Mediclinic at Nelspruit, where they operated on him. The doctors said that he had kidney problems and that his blood now had to be cleansed each week for the rest of his life. Some people claimed that I bewitched Matsepe. Priests at their church told them that I am responsible for Matsepe's illness. Once they gossiped about me in the staff room, but one of the new teachers told them they are mad. These days they are so scared of me.

The staff [of Tlasede] once arranged to visit Matsepe at the Mediclinic. The teachers chose me to arrange the transport, to collect money, and to organise the programme for prayers. Can you give these tasks to a witch? Who consoled the sick guy? Who made the appointment for meeting his family?

Arrested Development?

In the previous chapter we saw how the violence and insecurity Jimmy encountered during the formative years of his life formed a backdrop to understanding the 'aura of factuality' that witchcraft possessed for him. His life trajectory during subsequent years, shaped by his experiences of circumcision, university studies, the liberation struggle, and of working as a teacher in under-resourced schools, were similarly conducive to this conviction. Of greater significance than the violence and conflict he encountered in these settings was his perception of temporality.

As elsewhere in Africa, the political struggles in Bushbuckridge involved a distinctive 'tempo-politics' – that is, attempts 'to manage the flow of time and create alternative futures' (Smith 2008: 234). *Marxist Modern* (1999), Donham's innovative monograph on the Ethiopian revolution of 1974 as experienced in the Maale District, illuminates the local situation. He describes the revolution as a 'modernist project'. Zemaca students, who entered the district from Addis Ababa, advocated a concept of history, premised on the ideas of linear progress, forward and upward movement, and of increased status through time. The students implemented changes to 'jump ahead' towards a new hopeful future. In Maale the young revolutionaries found common ground with Protestants who expressed contempt for pagan ways and also subscribed to utopian visions of universal belonging. However, they confronted and were opposed by elders who saw history as regressive decline from a prosperous past. These 'traditionalists' were orientated towards a time when an authentic ritual king – called *kati* – ruled the land and ensured the fertility of plants and animals by interceding with the ancestors. The visions of linear time were pronounced, but by no means peculiar to Ethiopia. They are also a hallmark of developmental practice (Ferguson 2006; Smith 2008), Pentecostal theology (Meyer 1998), African nationalist politics (Ferguson 1999), and the politics of liberation in South Africa. This conception of linear time is apparent in the violent rejection of 'backward institutions' such as chiefs and Bantustans by the Comrades, and in the proclamation of an 'African Renaissance' by President Thabo Mbeki (Mbeki 2008).

Jimmy was a marginal participant in struggle politics who often despised the manner in which Comrades intimidated others. He was equally dubious about Pentecostal religion, whose demands he saw as excessive. However, he shared a commitment to linear time and he too invested in the future. Indeed an expectation of increased status through time formed a meta-narrative to the telling of events in his personal life. Jimmy invested in personal progress rather than revolutionary social change, and he identified education rather than 'the struggle' as the key in bringing about a hopeful future. Jimmy endured a painful circumcision ritual, delayed gratification, and invested in his studies to attain respectable masculine adulthood.

Modernist projects seldom realise their most important objectives. As a consequence of the Ethiopian revolution, the state sank its roots deeper in Maale society, collecting more tax and conscripting young men to fight in foreign wars (Donham 1999). Development projects frequently fail to reach their goals (Smith 2008), and nationalist politicians found that their expectations of 'modernity' were misplaced, after their countries experienced abjection or expulsion from the global economy (Ferguson 1999). Despite the greater political stability that prevailed in South Africa after 1994, Jimmy did not feel that his investments in the future had given returns in the manner he had anticipated.

Jimmy constantly experienced profound distress about lagging behind, being halted, or even moving backwards (cf. Smith 2008: 15). Jimmy was circumcised only at the age of eighteen, had penetrative sexual intercourse only when he was nineteen, and had to wait until he was 35 for the birth of his one and only son. During 2001, when Jimmy was 37 years old, he and his wife, Lerato, still lived with his parents and had failed to set up their own independent household. Despite marrying an extremely supportive wife, obtaining excellent marks for his Bachelor of Education degree, and being a brilliant teacher at a time when South Africa's new government was creating new opportunities for black people, Jimmy's expectations for occupational advancement failed to materialise:

Today, after teaching for thirteen years, I am still waiting for a promotion. I thought the university could afford me the opportunity to secure a good job. But here I am now. Many of the students whom I taught are earning good salaries. None of them have proper qualifications. They don't even have diplomas. But they become mayors and regional managers at the Bushbuckridge municipality. You can understand my concern. If I knew that they would not recognise talent in teaching, I would never have joined the profession.

Jimmy underlined the importance of promotion:

My salary is R5,600 after tax and an HOD [Head of Department] gets R7,000-something. With a principal it is between R10,000 and R12,000 after tax. . . .

I have applied for countless other jobs, but only twice did they invite me for interviews. During both of these interviews I obtained the first position, but they never hired me. Do you remember? . . . Once we had to write a letter of complaint about the selection procedures followed for one of these jobs. In 1998 I applied for the principal's post at Tlasede. I was short-listed, but never received an invitation for an interview.

After he told me these stories about his working life, I could understand his reasons for being so cynical about the idea that circumcision makes one a man. In Jimmy's experience, not only was adult masculinity not instantly attained, but it could be delayed, or even permanently blocked.

But Jimmy was most concerned about the particularities of misfortune: why should his path be obstructed, rather than the paths of others? In telling this story, Jimmy compared his experiences to my own. During fieldwork I regularly discussed with him the tensions between me, who aspired to be a good scholar, and the petty-minded university bureaucrats who constantly obstructed my work. My personal tensions with politicians of the academy were by no means trivial. In 2000, I resigned from the University of KwaZulu-Natal in protest against the dismissal of my Head of Department, Caroline White. I also found it hard to hide from Jimmy my irritation at the incompetence of some of my seniors. But, at the same time, he observed my progress from junior lecturer in 1990 to full professor in 2002. Jimmy also saw that despite my temperament, which was rather similar to his, I had been fortunate enough to secure new jobs.

Jimmy did not see his own trouble at work as being only structural. He did not blame his lack of progress on the structural violence of apartheid or on the inequities of the post-apartheid situation. Rather, he saw the thwarting of his ambitions as rooted in envy and jealousy in the sphere of interpersonal relations. Jimmy repeatedly told me that he suffered from a condition of misfortune (called *bati* in Northern Sotho). He suspected that the lack of return on his investments in education and in work might have been a result of secret, sinister forces that were somehow blocking his progress.

4 'Then I Did Not Believe'

Jimmy was extremely ambivalent about the student activism that he witnessed at the University of the North. But he was more critical, and at times even condemnatory, of the political campaigns by the Comrades of Bushbuckridge. This was particularly so when local youth intervened in the morally ambiguous field of witchcraft. Although Jimmy accepted the power of witchcraft as real, he did not believe that the Comrades had the capacity to reveal the true identity of witches.

At least a dozen elders lost their lives when the anti-witchcraft movement swept through the villages of Bushbuckridge in 1986. Comrades burnt three suspects to death in the village of Casteel, executed an apostolic minister and three women pensioners in Brooklyn, and stoned to death a drinking-tavern operator in Buffelshoek. Previously, villagers had accused some of the alleged witches of transforming children into zombies.

The only person killed in Impalahoek during these campaigns was Jimmy's paternal aunt, and Luckson's eldest sister, Doris Mosoma. In 1982 a group of boys saw a monkey in a tree outside a café. They threw stones at the monkey and pursued it, until it mysteriously disappeared into Doris's yard. Some children gossiped that the monkey was her witch-familiar. Three years later, in 1985, the six-year-old child of Doris's next-door neighbour, Maatsie, died of measles (*maoko*). The Maatsie family buried the child in a shallow grave behind their home. Merely one month later, Doris unscrupulously drove her cattle through Maatsie's yard, damaging the child's grave. Onlookers claimed that they actually saw Doris sitting on top of the child's grave, scooping soil from the mound with her hands. The Maatsie family was extremely angry and sent men to consult a witch-diviner (*mungoma*). He allegedly confirmed that Doris had bewitched the child. Eventually the Maatsie and Mosoma families met, but they failed to resolve their dispute.

One morning in 1986, about fifteen Comrades arrived at Doris's home. They smashed open the door and found only Doris and her daughter inside. (Two of her sons worked in Johannesburg, and her third son lived in another section of Impalahoek.) The Comrades dragged both women out into the yard by their feet and then proceeded to stone

Doris to death with bricks. As soon as they left, Doris's daughter ran to her brother's home to inform him about what had happened. The two children reported the matter to the police, but they were unable to identify any of the assailants. Because Comrades warned people not to attend the burial of any witch, very few people attended Doris's funeral.

This event provoked much bitterness and anger. Jimmy, vehemently denying that there was even the slightest possibility that his aunt, Doris Mosoma, practised witchcraft, viewed her killing as murder. Like many other neighbours, Jimmy was of the opinion that the Maatsie child was not bewitched, but died because her father had unwittingly polluted her. At the time of the child's illness both her parents worked on the Witwatersrand. Her father was notified, came to visit her, and gave her a sip of his cold drink. (Her mother was pregnant and remained in the city.) Informants said that because her father was 'hot' (*fiša*) from having sexual intercourse with his pregnant wife, he should have avoided all contact with his sick daughter.[1] Convinced by this alternative explanation, Jimmy affirmed:

We were extremely angry that people could do this to my aunt in the broad daylight. To this day the Mosoma and Maatsie families are not on speaking terms.

Rumours of Luckson Mogale's Witchcraft

But Jimmy was even more dismissive when he heard talk, in the aftermath of Doris Mosoma's funeral, that his own father, Luckson Mohale, might have been responsible for her death. A few mourners speculated that Luckson had sent familiars to put a special aura (*seriti*) on Doris. This aura made those who looked at her think that she was a witch. Jimmy rejected these insinuations as ridiculous. 'What made people suspicious,' he told me, 'was that my father buried her [Doris] with his own money.'

According to Jimmy, the source of these malicious rumours was Aaron Mohale, his father's eldest brother. Whilst the 'equivalence of siblings' was one of the most fundamental principles in Northern Sotho and Shangaan kinship systems, and siblings rarely accuse each other of

[1] In local beliefs corpses, bereaved persons, women who had aborted, and pregnant women are in a dangerous state of heat called *fiša*. For example, it is believed that the aura (*seriti*) of a deceased person contaminated everyone who came into contact with him or her. To avert misfortune, bereaved families observed a week-long period of mourning. Pregnant women presented a confusing duality (they were both one and two) and observed the same prohibitions as widows. Sexual intercourse was also a potent source of contamination. Sick persons, children, and those initiated at the circumcision lodge were generally recognised as being most vulnerable to pollution. See Hammond-Tooke (1981: 112–40) and Niehaus (2002a) for different accounts of pollution beliefs in the South African lowveld.

witchcraft today, the relations between siblings were sometimes very tense in the past. It is certainly true that, during the era of subsistence agriculture, an ideology of shared blood propagated solidarity between patrilineal descendants, and that these bonds were essential to the integrity of the hamlet (*motse*) as corporate unit. But the earlier practice of primogeniture, in which the eldest son inherited the bulk of the father's estate and cattle, often generated severe conflict between siblings.

When the Mohale hamlet was dispersed to different village sections during the population removals of 1960, Aaron appropriated all 16 cows. Luckson was extremely dissatisfied about this and also complained that Aaron was the only Mohale sibling to be allocated a fertile field (*dirapa*) next to the Makgwedi River. Aaron, in turn, resented the manner in which his younger brother, Luckson, had usurped the proprieties of age-related rank and had publicly shamed him by paying for the funerals of his two sons, who died during 1973 and 1977, respectively. When his sons died, Aaron was working for the South African Railways in Johannesburg and failed to come home when informed of their deaths by telephone. (This was possibly because of his severe alcoholism.) As their younger uncle (*mangwane*) and executive member of the Mapulaneng Burial Society, Luckson took responsibility for arranging both funerals. Jimmy said that he

was only twelve years old at that time, but at the funeral I heard one of my aunts saying, 'Luckson wants others to think he is generous. He has eaten our child.'[2]

Aaron was subsequently hospitalised for alcohol poisoning, quit drinking, and joined the Zion Christian Church (ZCC). A serious rift, nonetheless, emerged between Aaron's and Luckson's households:

My father advised us never to visit our uncle's home and their children never came to our home. I spent 18 years not visiting this uncle. They don't live too far. They live just down the road, near the Roman Catholic Church, but I still don't go there.

In subsequent years, Aaron made further allegations. He claimed that Luckson had bewitched Doris Mosoma's daughter, who also died in the 1970s (see Figure 4.1). He even claimed that Luckson had caused the death of their own mother, Nana, in 1984. Though Nana was already extremely old, Aaron believed that she had not died from natural causes. Aaron observed that on the day of Nana's death a baboon climbed on top of the roof of her home. He claimed that Luckson had sent the baboon. Four years later Maria Khubayi's child Tebogo, died. Aaron again alleged

[2] In many other parts of Africa 'eating' is a prominent metaphor for witchcraft (Schatzberg 1993: 451–8). This is also true of Bushbuckridge.

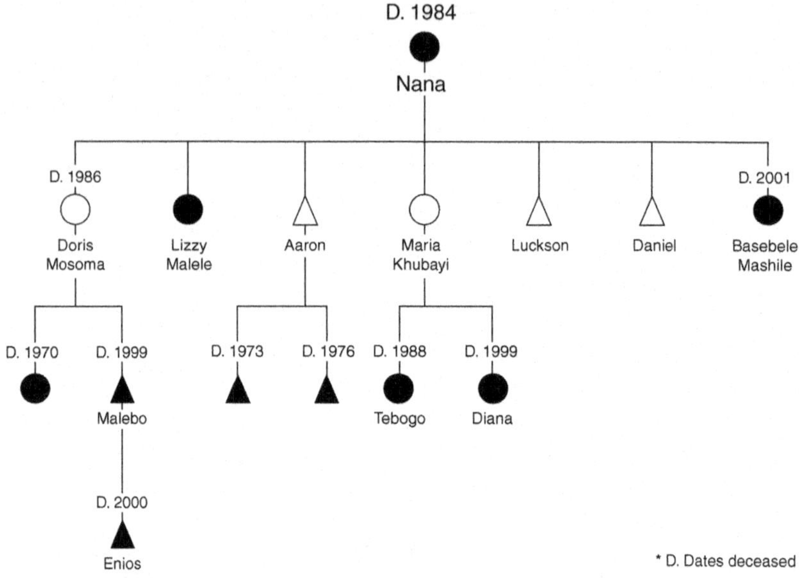

Figure 4.1. Deaths amongst Luckson Mohale's cognates, 1970–2001

that Luckson had poisoned the child. Not many people accepted these allegations. Jimmy, for one, believed they were senseless. On the contrary: in the light of his childhood experiences, he claimed that Nana herself was the witch and that she had been trapped, as she was trying to bewitch others.

One cannot simply explain the witchcraft accusations that were levelled against Luckson Mohale in terms of systemic, repetitive, and persistent structural tensions, such as those between siblings over inheritance. They were also a product of the conjunction of unplanned, unanticipated, and anomalous events that instantly erupt from the ordinary plane to the larger scheme of things (Sahlins 2004: 155–6). Of significance in this regard was the almost simultaneous occurrence of Luckson's retirement and presence at home, four more tragic deaths amongst his cognates, and also of a whole series of uncanny sicknesses and misfortunes within the Mohale household.

In the decade between 1988 and 1999, there seems to have been a lull in misfortune, and not a single one of Luckson's cognates died. In 1996, Luckson's employer, Louw Transport, became insolvent and, after many years' service, Luckson received a retrenchment package of only R10,000. He decided to retire for good. He opened an auto-teller account with First National Bank in Hoedspruit and hid his card from his fellow household members and kin. But Luckson could not consistently ignore the competing claims that his two wives and his thirteen children made upon his money. Within a year the account was exhausted, and since then his only source of income has been a small state pension.

The issue of Luckson's witchcraft resurfaced in October 1999, when, in the space of only two weeks, Malebo Mosoma (Doris's son) and Diana Khubayi (Maria's daughter) both died. Within the next few years Enios Mosoma (Doris's grandson) and Basebele Mashile (Luckson's youngest sibling) also died. During each funeral, Luckson's seemingly contrived or unbecoming behaviour attracted attention.

Malebo Mosoma's Death, October 1999

Doris Mosoma's son Malebo was born in 1945. He secured a job at the South African Railways in Johannesburg, and married *ngwa* Molobela in 1970. Together they had four children. After Doris's brutal murder by the Comrades in 1986, Malebo appropriated the lion's share of her herd of cattle, her smaller animals such as goats, pigs, and chickens, and her other possessions.

Malebo's wife, *Ngwa* Molobela, died in 1994, and he soon remarried. His new wife was a woman from Trichardtsdal, who had two children from her previous marriage. This created great tensions. Enios Mosoma (*ngwa* Molobela's eldest son) accused his father, Malebo, of misusing his mother's estate, going so far as to report him to the police station. To diffuse these tensions, Malebo left Enios his home in Impalahoek, and built a new home for his second wife in the mining town of Phalaborwa. After work on 15 September 1999, Malebo returned to Phalaborwa in his Toyota van after having visited his in-laws, where he drank heavily. At an intersection in town, Malebo saw an oncoming truck, but proceeded, believing that the truck driver would stop. Unfortunately, the driver went ahead and hit Malebo's van on the side. Malebo died instantly.

Luckson, valuing his kinship ties with his sister's son, Malebo, assumed full responsibility for arranging the funeral. When informed of his nephew's death, Luckson rushed to Phalaborwa, and took Malebo's second wife to visit the scene of the accident. Malebo's half-brother wanted the van's engine, but Luckson and the wife refused, and asked the owner of a scrapyard to remove the van:

My father worked very hard. He was even there when they performed the autopsy and told us that Malebo's intestines were placed on the one side, and his heart and liver on the other. Can you bear to look at these things? Can you see! This man is brave!

Luckson was dismayed to discover that Malebo had only R300 in his bank account. Because this was not enough to bury the deceased, Luckson went to see Malebo's former employer, the South African Railways. The personnel office said that they could contribute R7,000 towards the funeral, but that the money could only be released in two weeks' time. Luckson and Malebo's second wife then arranged with the undertakers, TERAS, to bury Malebo on credit. They chose a coffin and a tombstone and arranged for the deceased to be buried at the home of his son, Enios, in Impalahoek. But there were further problems after the funeral. The South African Railways paid the R7,000 into the deceased's bank account, which had already been frozen. The undertakers, TERAS, summoned Luckson to court for failing to pay for the funeral. Luckson therefore had to consult a lawyer to arrange for the money to be transferred into the account of Malebo's second wife. Malebo's second wife quickly returned to her own parents' home, before any firm arrangements could be made for the ritual of removing her widow's mourning clothes (*hlobolo*).

Although some believed that Luckson had behaved in an admirable manner, Luckson's cognates were furious, and condemned his assertive behaviour. He appeared to have overvalued his connections to his sister's son. Aaron argued that Luckson's concern was insincere, and said that, in actual fact, Luckson and Malebo were sworn enemies. At a previous funeral, Malebo had publicly accused Luckson of witchcraft, and a fight had been narrowly avoided. Moreover, Luckson had opposed Malebo's claims when he fought over his mother's estate. Jimmy observed:

My father hated the older nephew [Malebo], and we also hated that man. In 1999 my father tried to organise an invocation for the ancestors [phasa] *at our home and he asked everyone to 'pop out' [contribute] money. All the houses of his family had to be present, but Malebo, the first-born son of the first house, refused to attend. Malebo told others that my father would sprinkle potions* [dihlare] *on the sacrificial goat, and would call out his victim's name as the goat bleated when its throat was slit. Because of Malebo's refusal to attend, the entire event had to be cancelled. We [Jimmy and his siblings] were very disappointed because Malebo was so stubborn. We children were interested in the invocation* [phasa] *and we were looking forward to the blessings from our ancestors.*

Aaron alleged that it was to conceal these tensions that Luckson had bewitched Malebo and buried him. In addition to this, Malebo's siblings, his children from his previous marriage, and even his nephews blamed Luckson for ensuring that Malebo's new wife inherited his entire estate. Luckson, in turn, was angry because he did not receive any cooperation from them during the funeral arrangements.

Diana Khubayi's Death, October 1999

Diana Khubayi, Maria's youngest daughter, died two weeks after Malebo's funeral, at the age of only 27 years. Diana was a brilliant pupil at school and obtained a primary teacher's diploma from the Mapulaneng College of Education. She never married, but had one child. Unable to find a teaching post in Bushbuckridge, she decided to visit her older sister in Johannesburg, hoping to find a job. Diana's efforts were not rewarded. Instead, she became seriously ill. Though she complained of excruciating headaches and her sister took her to a good hospital, the doctors failed to make any conclusive diagnosis.

Diana then returned to her parents' home in Impalahoek:

Those who went to see Diana told me that she suffered from headaches. Dr Kruger at the plaza gave her tablets, but they did not tell me what he had diagnosed. On pension day Diana told her mother, 'Please don't use all your pension money! You'll need the money for my funeral!' She died only minutes after her mother returned from the pension point.

Again Luckson was judged to have behaved inappropriately: this time by undervaluing his ties of kinship with the deceased. Jimmy takes up the story.

I remember that day well. When I returned from school the little ones came running towards me. They asked, 'Where's your father? He is wanted at our grandmother's place.' They said their aunt had died and that my father had to help them take the corpse to the mortuary. My father was at a meeting of the Mapulaneng Burial Society and arrived late. At the home of the deceased he did something unheard of. In our custom we should all sit outside the home and leave the corpse inside. But my father went inside the house and shouted, 'Diana! Diana! Where are you?' He entered her room and spoke to her saying, 'My niece! Wake up! Are you dead?' Many people were offended. It is taboo [diila] *to shout where there is death and to speak to a dead person. What is even more surprising is that my father did not even attend Diana's funeral. He made a shallow excuse, saying that he had to attend another funeral in Violetbank.*

At the ritual for taking off the mourning clothes (*hlobola*), on 3 February 2000, the members of Diana's family assembled to discuss the circumstances surrounding her death. Jimmy remarked that nearly all of the thirty people were of the opinion that witches had captured (*dlo kola*) Diana and changed her into a zombie:

They observed that, before her death, Diana complained saying, 'Why do you want to kill me? You know that I have a little child who needs education.' My aunt blamed her neighbour, who was popular with witchcraft. Others whispered that my aunt, Maria, bewitched her own daughter and used her zombie to sell beer. But at the meeting I also learnt how much they hated my father. My aunt told me, 'Your father is killing our people.'

Enios Mosoma, January 2000

Luckson's paternal relatives experienced further misfortune. Enios Mosoma died only three months after his father, at the age of 37. Though he was known as a 'slow learner' at school, Enios married and obtained a fairly well-paid blue-collar job at ESKOM (the Electricity Supply Commission) in Johannesburg. He always wore extremely flashy clothes and even carried a briefcase. However, his good fortune soon came to an end.

In Johannesburg Enios stole things from the Xhosas and they bewitched him. His favourite pastime was now smoking cannabis [ganja] *and he became mentally ill. Enios returned home and never went back to work. He would hallucinate and speak to himself. His uncles tried to help and Enios improved, but he was still not 100 per cent [healthy]. At one stage Enios's mother bought him a [minibus] taxi, but he had an accident and hereafter he became severely disturbed. His wife left him to go and stay in Arthur's Seat with her son [Enios's only child]. After that, Enios received a disability pension and cleaned people's yards.*

Enios lived alone and was a regular customer of a rather seedy drinking tavern. One evening Enios went to a nearby petrol station, where they also sold liquor, and he was reportedly very drunk. As it was about to rain, a man called Chauke decided to take Enios home. Though Enios resisted, Chauke forcefully loaded him onto the back of the van. The next day, Enios was found dead outside Chauke's gate.

Only the police seemed to accept Chauke's version of what had transpired that evening. Instead, most residents of Impalahoek believed that Chauke had delivered Enios to a sinister syndicate, which had drained his blood, and sold it to a pharmaceutical company for profit.[3] Jimmy too subscribed to this theory:

It was raining and there was some thunder, but Enios's clothes were not drenched. This shows that he was killed inside the house and dumped outside.

But Aaron and Daniel Mohale claimed that it was in fact Luckson's snake (*mamlambo*) that had sucked Enios's blood. Luckson was certainly deemed to have had sufficient reason to bewitch Enios. Jimmy observed that only three months previously, there had been a major confrontation between Enios and Luckson:

[3] It is widely believed that certain local businessmen attain profits by illicit and inauspicious means. They allegedly belong to a syndicate, headed by a white garage owner, which uses machines resembling vacuum cleaners and syringes to extract the blood of vulnerable travellers. The syndicate allegedly sells the blood to pharmacies and to government for profit (Niehaus 2000a). Similar rumours of blood sucking were widespread in East and Central Africa during colonial times and have been interpreted as metaphorical correlates of the extraction of resources from the colonies by colonial powers (Pels 1992; White 2000).

When his father [Malebo] died, Enios accused Luckson of witchcraft. He was a bit insane and came to my father's place, saying, 'You killed my father.' My father then took a whip [sjambok] and beat him severely. The police came to our home with Enios, but my father told the police that he had insulted us.

At Malebo's actual funeral there was another confrontation:

When Enios Mosoma spoke, he directly told my father, 'You bewitch people!' My father was furious, asked Enios whether he knew the Bible, and attacked him with a stick. Enios bled profusely.

Upon hearing of Enios's death, Luckson told others that Enios was troublesome, and deserved to die.

Misfortunes in *Ngwa* Ngobeni's Household

Events happening in the household of Jimmy's mother, *ngwa* Ngobeni, reinforced the perceptions that everything was not as it should be. Jimmy's brothers, Moses and Peter, both suffered unfortunate marital breakdowns. Moses married his first wife in 1979, and though he instantly paid all the agreed upon bridewealth, she stayed at her in-law's home for only a few months.

She did not even quarrel with Moses. Without saying a word she just went back to her own family.

Moses's second marriage was to *ngwa* Siboye, with whom he went to live in Tsakani. In 1985 their first baby was stillborn. *Ngwa* Siboye's parents reportedly consulted a diviner, who said that witches had sent a snake (*mamlambo*) to eat the child from its mother's womb. In 1990, Moses suffered a mysterious infestation of lice, and three years later he had a serious motor vehicle accident in Johannesburg.

Peter Mohale married Violet Monareng in 1989. From the time that she first became part of *ngwa* Ngobeni's household, Violet suffered from persistent headaches and from painful feet, and she failed to conceive. Her infertility placed her under considerable pressure. In 1993, she lied to *ngwa* Ngobeni, saying that she had been pregnant but had suffered a miscarriage. Violet's parents suggested that ancestral spirits might be calling her to be initiated as a diviner.[4] But her mother-in-law, *ngwa* Ngobeni, decided to take Violet to the Zion Christian Church (ZCC) instead, and asked the ministers and prophets to pray for her. Here

[4] Diviners often viewed persistent pain, infertility, disorientation, bouts of aggression, and hot feet as symptoms of spirit possession. In the case of possession, diviners asked the afflicted persons to dance to the beat of cowhide drums until they experienced a trance. Diviners then exhorted the spirits to speak through the mouths of those whom they had afflicted, and to state their demands. Once appeased, the spirits could bestow the powers of divination and healing, and choose the afflicted person to work as their medium. See van Binsbergen (2003: 155–94) for an in-depth description of this process.

Violet fell in love with a middle-aged church member, a relationship that soon became evident to the family.

Violet now started displaying symptoms of insanity:

Each morning Violet told us that she had dreamt uncanny dreams. She said that she dreamt of white people visiting our home,[5] *and of a large clay pot, filled with human blood, standing in the centre of our yard. We thought that Violet was mad. She wanted to show us where the clay pot was, but immediately when Violet came to the spot, she fainted. Other times, Violet would wake up and immediately start running towards the river. Violet collapsed many times at home. Sometimes she would lie totally still, without moving, for about two hours. It was only by feeling her pulse that we knew she was still alive. It seemed as if she was possessed. We sprinkled her with water and called a ZCC prophet to pray for her. Only when she burnt ZCC papers would she be revived. At church they said that she had the power to see the future.*

In 1999 *ngwa* Ngobeni sent Violet back to her natal household, so that the spirits troubling her could be evoked. It was during this time that she told her husband, Peter, that she had been pregnant for three months. Peter realised that he had not been home for the previous six months, but at work, and could not possibly be the child's progenitor. He therefore separated from Violet.

At the same time that Violet struggled with 'possession sickness', Jimmy's brother, Henry Mohale, who was studying Information Science at the University of the North, developed an inflamed appendix:

When we returned from fetching ZCC ministers to revive Violet, we found Henry lying on the veranda. Henry was lean, complained that he was ill from the stomach, and said that he suffered from constipation. He was in agony and he had no appetite. My mother took Henry to Mokgoto [an apostolic healer]. The prophet said that neighbours had bewitched Henry because they were jealous [actually envious] that he was at university. Mokgoto gave Henry holy water to drink and potions [dihlare] *to cleanse him. Henry first had some convulsions, but he later showed some improvement. We told him to go back to Turfloop because he was lagging behind in his studies.*

In 1996, Jimmy's youngest brother, Kagišo, impregnated a neighbour's daughter. At the time he was only eighteen years old. Kagišo told me that, although his father was angry, he never openly expressed his feelings on

[5] White persons are perceived as wealthy outsiders who are neither intimate with, nor envious of, local village residents. Whites are therefore antithetical to the stereotypical image of witches. Residents of Bushbuckridge, nonetheless, believed that witches could use whites as instruments of their craft. In this capacity whites served a similar role as witch-familiars. Dreams of white persons were generally interpreted as omens of great misfortune (Niehaus 2001: 63–82).

this matter. Kagišo, nonetheless, began to feel insecure in his parents' home. Each morning he felt exceptionally tired:

I always felt as if I had slept on bricks all night long or as if a tokolotši *[the ape-like witch-familiar] had abused me. I also had very bad dreams. I once dreamt that a monkey slapped me on my chest. I shouted for help, but my voice did not come out. Even when I woke up, I could feel the monkey on my chest. Whenever I slept I would watch television [a metaphor for very vivid dreams] for the whole night.*

Kagišo soon began to suspect that his father, Luckson, might be the source of all these maladies at their home. He heard from his paternal kin that his father kept a snake that had already killed many of his own relatives. Moreover, he, his sister Jessie, and his half-brother, Andrew, once attended a service of the ZCC. On this occasion a prophet called them aside, and instructed them, 'Tell your father to cease his evil deeds.' Kagišo now recognised that his father often behaved in the most peculiar manner. Luckson always slept in complete darkness and washed three times each day, mainly in the outside toilet. Mindful of these rumours, Kagišo left home in 1998 to stay with his girlfriend's parents. Jimmy was furious when he heard of this and scolded Kagišo, saying that it was his duty as the youngest son to remain at home and to take care of his parents in their old age.

The sounds of voices, saying that Luckson practised witchcraft, became louder and louder, and impossible to ignore. Within a year of Kagišo's departure, Jimmy's daughter, Kgopotšo, complained of something in her ear. Nurses at the local clinic inspected her ear, but found nothing wrong. But an apostolic prophet revealed that witches wanted to transform Kgopotšo into a zombie and had sent an invisible worm to bite her ear. Jimmy's wife, Lerato, and his mother, *ngwa* Ngobeni, also became seriously ill.

During 1998, Lerato developed boils on her legs. Prophets at church diagnosed that witches had placed *xifulane* – a type of potion that enters through the soles of the feet – on her path at home. But once Lerato was cured of her boils, she developed fever and started coughing profusely:

We took Lerato to consult many different doctors, prophets and diviners. Some doctors diagnosed asthma. Others said that she was allergic. Lerato continued sweating and coughing. We would go out early in the morning, look for diviners and prophets, and we would only return at eight [pm]. Then we would report to our parents. But she did not get better. This ate my money. I cannot tell you how much I spent: it might have been more than R8,000. This was close to the time that she had to write her UNISA [University of South Africa, a distance education university] exams. Before Lerato wrote the exams, my mother-in-law advised us to take Lerato to a prophet in White River. He said that there was a problem at my parents' home and he made concoctions for her to drink. The prophet used river water, stones from the big mountain, and spirits, milk, and Vaseline.

Then we made a blunder. Before Lerato had completed the ditaelo *[prescriptions from the Holy Spirit], I brought her home to my parents. She returned to us on the Wednesday afternoon with all her things and my mother was very happy to see her. But at ten o' clock Lerato went to bed, and her problems started again. That evening I went to booze. I told my friends that my wife was better. But after an hour Thabo Mashile [Jimmy's colleague and friend] came to me and said, 'Jimmy! We need you at home! Your wife is seriously ill!' I ran back and found that Lerato had fainted. I took her to hospital. She had convulsions and did not respond to the treatment. . . . At three [am] she became better, and they discharged her two days later. When she came home to my parents, she asked to lie down on the bed. It became so bad. She could not breathe. My cousin had to take her back to her own parents, the Mashiles.*

In the midst of Lerato's sickness, Jimmy's mother, *ngwa* Ngobeni, also began to suffer from a mysterious and untimely disorder:

One afternoon [in May 2000] my mother collapsed on the way home from the market. She told me that she felt dizzy – as if someone had hit her over the head. As she collapsed she felt hands clutching at her and trying to drag her.

Later, in July, my mother attended a funeral in Johannesburg. She returned at ten [pm] and the next day she went to complain at the Wesleyan church that the driver had driven too fast when he took the [mountainous] Pilgrim's Rest road. Then she went to the market and slept early. The next day my mother vomited and had a headache. She found it difficult to stand and to walk. The doctor touched her where the pain was, gave her tablets and told her to return if her condition did not improve. But her condition became worse. Later, her voice was completely hoarse. On 23 February my mother went to sleep, but suddenly awoke. She said that something had grabbed her by the throat, entered her mouth, and wanted to close her voice box. She said that it felt like a frog or a butterfly and she sent her grandson to fetch ZCC tea.

The Mohale siblings embarked upon a protracted quest to find a cure for their mother, but did not meet instant success:

We took her to doctors and to a specialist in Nelspruit. They said it was asthma and a heart problem. They gave us medication for asthma, but it did not help. We thought that our mother would die. A diviner said that witches at home wanted to turn my mother into a zombie. The diviner gave me potions [dihlare] *and instructed us, 'Put this where she sleeps! But this will only help temporarily. If you don't take your mother from the yard you'll lose her!' I came back, spoke to my father, and suggested that we take my mother to my sister Jessie's place in Tsakani. He agreed and we then took her things to Tsakani.*

For the next six months, *ngwa* Ngobeni stayed at her daughter's home. As an active member of the local ZCC, Jessie utilised the churches' considerable therapeutic resources to find a cure for her ailing mother. The ZCC prophets gave *ngwa* Ngobeni water and tea to drink, tied woollen yarn around the thresholds of her body, and burnt papers around her.[6] They also sprinkled substances around the home to ward off witchcraft.

The Mohale *Mpogo*, 16 December 2001

Finally, the prophets pronounced that *ngwa* Ngobeni's health would only improve if she and her husband, Luckson, undertook a pilgrimage to the church's headquarters in Moria, just outside Polokwane. For this purpose, Jimmy and his brothers rented a sedan from AVIS, a car-rental company. *Ngwa* Ngobeni and Luckson Mohale were both baptised in Moria. ZCC prophets told Luckson that bringing about an end to their misfortune would depend upon their asking the local congregation to conduct an all-night prayer (called *mpogo*) at their home, and removing all witchcraft substances from their yard.

Jimmy and his brothers immediately began to make arrangements for the all-night prayer:

We did everything together. The Zionists don't allow meals. But there had to be bread with no butter, tea without sugar, coffee and milk. We also bought jam. There is also an hour for cookies. We collected wood and borrowed electricity cables and lights so that they [the Zionists] could see. We even obtained toilet rolls. In the morning we first attended a get-together for the Mohale people [a clan gathering] in Phalaborwa. We went there by bus. We invited all the Mohale people to attend our mpogo, *but hardly any of my father's brothers and sisters came. Only our uncle Daniel, who is also a ZCC member, and my aunt, Basebele, attended.*

We first served our relatives maize porridge, boiled meat, and drinks. The ZCC congregation arrived later that evening. The minister said that we were all under his control and that we should not sleep. The congregation began by clapping hands, singing hymns, dancing, and praying inside the yard. At midnight the preachers started fortifying our home. They went around the yard and sprinkled holy water everywhere. Then, in the early morning hours [the most potent time of healing], the prophets started making revelations and prescribing remedies from the Holy Spirit [ditaelo]. *There was a family prescription. They instructed the oldest son, Moses, to fetch water from where two rivers converge, and told my father to give it to the entire family to drink. At four [am], Moses fetched the water from Violetbank.*

[6] In Zionist belief, woollen yarn cords of various colours (*dithodi*) and burning red papers could be vessels for the power of the Holy Spirit. In Zionist practice, they are widely used as therapeutic substances. See Comaroff (1985: 221–8) and Kiernan (1990) for a more in-depth analysis of Zionist therapy.

At five [am] the prophets told everyone to confess their sins and to speak the truth. The prophets then spoke privately with my father and with my mother for more than an hour. Hereafter, they asked the family to form a circle and to pray. At the exact moment of the prayer, my father fell from his chair. It seemed as if he had passed into a coma, and it took some time before he regained his senses. Our whole family cried. We thought our father was dying, that he was going to greet God. Some of the congregants said they saw a white man slapping him across the face.

Jimmy's siblings Jessie and Kagišo believed that the holy waters had trapped their father, evidence that he was the one bewitching his own family. Others, such as Jimmy himself, saw Luckson as the victim of witchcraft.

Luckson Mohale's youngest sister, Basebele, also behaved rather oddly at the prayer event. Jimmy said that he had always disliked Basebele and her husband. The couple owned two taxis, maintained a borehole in their yard, and had flush toilets in their home. But despite being wealthy and spoiling their children, the couple were very stingy, and seldom helped their kin and neighbours.

Jimmy also mentioned that there were tensions between Luckson and Basebele. Apparently Luckson complained that, after his mother's death, Basebele took everything she had kept in a trunk and stole the money she had saved. But Luckson never publicly quarrelled with Basebele:

Basebele attended the prayer on the Saturday evening, enjoyed the meal and the tea, and she then returned to her own home. Early on the Sunday morning, Basebele came back to the prayer. She entered the gate without greeting anyone, walked straight to our toilet, and stayed there. When she finally emerged, she walked past our neighbour's home and told him, 'This might be the very last time that you see me alive.' Basebele arrived at her own home and she immediately started vomiting. For the next two days she was seriously ill. Her relatives took her to hospital and her son drove to see a diviner, but things only got worse. She passed away at eight o' clock on Wednesday morning. By then she had been ill for only five days.

Jimmy recalls that at the time of death of his aunt, Basebele, he was visiting his wife, Lerato, at the home of his in-laws:

My brother, Henry, was on holiday with my parents. He phoned me, saying, 'Come back home Jimmy! Our aunt has died!' I walked all the way from Tsakani and when I arrived [at his parent's home] I asked Henry and my father to come with me to my aunt's place. But my father warned us that he was still using prescriptions from the church [ditaelo] *and could not go where there is pollution from death.*

We arrived at 8.30 [pm]. Basebele's son, Ezekiel, was furious and told us that our father had bewitched his mother. He said that our father was still angry because Basebele had stolen our grandmother's old coins, and that our father had sprinkled potions at the prayer to kill his mother. Ezekiel even came to our home with a firearm and threatened to shoot my father.

Luckson was so shaken by these accusations that he phoned his eldest son, Moses, and Moses immediately came down from Johannesburg to protect him. Moses owned a revolver and threatened Ezekiel that he would shoot him, if he ever again threatened his father. Jimmy and Moses believed the explanation for these events was that their aunt had come to the prayer evening to bewitch their father, but was 'trapped' by the yard fortifications put in place by the ZCC ministers and prophets.

Later, two other sons of the deceased also came to Luckson's home:

It was about nine in the evening and we were eating. Two of Basebele's sons, who were about twenty-eight and twenty-nine years old, came and stood by our gate. They greeted us and said that they wanted to speak to our father. 'Your father killed our mother and we want him to give our mother back to us. If he does not, we'll kill him.' My father did not reply. But the boys continued, saying, 'We don't want him at our house. Tell him not to come to our mother's funeral.' Then they left. I could see that one of them had a gun.

Jimmy went to see Basebele's sons (his cousins):

I phoned Ezekiel, but he did not respond to my message. I then went to their house. Everyone looked at me. They asked me, 'Where is your wife?' I replied, 'With my in-laws.' Then they asked, 'Where is your mother?' I said, 'She is staying with my sister.' Then, they said, 'Yes. There is a snake at your home. Why are you staying with the snake?' I could not reply.

Defending His Father

Jimmy realised that something was seriously wrong. People everywhere were accusing his father of witchcraft: not only his patrilineal kin, but also his own siblings, Kagišo and Jessie. In the beginning of 2001, Jimmy told me:

All eyes were looking at my father and I also began to suspect him.

But Jimmy hoped that his father was innocent. For more than six months, he alone lived with his father, seeking to protect him against his accusers.

In the time that I lived with my father, I noticed nothing significant. I saw that my father washed himself in the toilet room [outside pit latrine] as many as three times each day. But by then [at that time] I did not find it strange.

At the back of my mind I could sense that something was not right. Sometimes, I would ask myself, 'What is wrong here?' But I did not know what it was. Then I would leave it as it is.

According to Jimmy the real source of misfortune lay well beyond the gates of his parents' homestead. He suspected that envious women neighbours, who had pestered their household for decades, were still responsible for their misfortune, and had successfully managed to deflect the blame onto his father:

When my mother became ill all the witches [in the neighbourhood] were happy. They thought she would die and they would get meat for their familiars. But my father spoilt their plans by going to the ZCC and also by taking my mother there. This angered the witches. That is why my father's enemies want to overpower him. They have set up my father to try and punish him. This is a sort of bad fortune [bati]. *The witches would come to our home at night, being naked. They would stand in our yard, wash themselves with potions, make their wishes, and say that they want my father to be sniffed as a witch. To make this happen, the witches would take my father's aura* [seriti] *and replace it with the aura of a dead person. This is what causes my father's misfortune.*

In addition, Jimmy suspected that his grandmother, Nana, might have left behind potions and a pot of human blood when she left the homestead. He thought that the polluting influence of these substances still lingered about in their yard.

The anomalous occurrence of misfortune – including multiple deaths among Luckson's close kin and concurrent episodes of illness within his household – constituted sufficient grounds for accusations of witchcraft. Consistent rumours gradually built up a consensus among Luckson's neighbours and members of his kin that he might be perpetrating harm by means of mystical malevolent powers. Luckson became increasingly isolated socially, enjoying only the support of his elder sons. Jimmy seems to have ignored these rumours. He had not personally encountered the sorts of misfortune usually attributed to witchcraft attacks. Although he was deeply distressed by his inability to make any progress in life, he accounted for this in terms of his marginalisation from networks of political power, rather than by seeking an explanation in witchcraft. Moreover, by supporting his father, he sought to preserve the integrity of his patrilineage. But in the light of subsequent personal experiences, his belief in the innocence of his father no longer seemed self-evident; it was not resilient against evidence.

5 'My Second Initiation'

By 2003 Jimmy was no longer defending his father: instead, he had become one of Luckson's most vocal accusers. There was not one single cause for Jimmy's 'conversion', which involved seeing the world around him in a very different light. Rather, he related his change of opinion to mysterious and perplexing incidents of misfortune. Whereas events in the previous chapter afflicted others, Jimmy himself began to have experiences that ran counter to the predicted and even predictable flow of life. These had started with uncanny motor vehicle breakdowns and accidents during the early 1990s. But these incidents became more frequent, and between 1999 and 2003, important social changes took place in the immediate circumstances of his life. In fact, Jimmy's social world fell apart. He encountered marital disharmony, separated from his wife and family, experienced guilt, and faced a situation of financial ruin.

In 2003 Jimmy told me:

These days I am a charity case. I can no longer support myself. I now live on handouts from others. It is really tough, Sakkie [my nickname]. It's like I'm experiencing my second initiation.

Jimmy's use of the term 'second initiation' to describe his predicament in adult life did not refer to the opening up of new vistas, predicated upon the extinction of old social identities. Rather, it denoted a period of intense pain and hardship, which led nowhere.

By now Jimmy no longer merely suspected that something was blocking his progress in life and thwarting his ambitions: he saw himself as being under direct attack by malevolent occult forces. Phenomenologically speaking, witchcraft is invisible and witches cannot be known in themselves or in terms of their internal attributes. Much like the modern labourer described by Marx (1959: 114–16), they are known through their deeds, and through their actions upon the natural and social world. But whereas the labourer's work is productive, that of the witch is purely destructive.

There was so much destructiveness. It had also become clear for Jimmy that its source was closer, more powerful and more sinister, and much less diffuse than something which might emanate from the homes of his neighbours: it lay at the very apex of his own household and family. Jimmy gradually felt compelled to adopt the viewpoint of his patrilineal kin, that his father really was a witch.

Cars

Between 1990 and 1995, Jimmy bought three cars, none of which lasted for more than a few months. In May 1991 Jimmy drove his first car, a Ford XR3, from the road and it literally burst into flames:

I did not even have the car for one year. I took a teacher to his home in Dingleydale and I only remember taking the road back. . . . Thereafter I cannot remember a thing. I had a strange blackout. . . . I felt as if I got out of myself. When I regained my mind I saw myself walking barefooted back towards Dingleydale. I looked around and saw my car in flames. It had gone off the road and was burning to pieces. I only arrived home at about twelve o'clock that evening.

On the Friday morning I felt some pains and I went to the hospital for a check-up. Later, my mother took me to Mokgoto [an apostolic prophet] and he said that witches in our neighbourhood had caused my accident. Mokgoto cleansed me and told me that I had to buy three different types of ancestral cloth – black, red, and white. To remove the misfortune [bati] *he tied a black cloth around my waist and prayed for me. I then had to leave the black cloth in the forest, and I had to place the red and white cloths underneath my pillow and sleep on them. I also had to buy a white chicken to purify myself. I had to slaughter the chicken, pour the chicken blood and eggs into boiling water, and wash myself with the mixture. I also had to say thanks to my ancestors, especially to Ramadimabe [Father of Misfortune, his maternal great-grandfather's mother] for having saved me.*

In 1992 Jimmy and his wife, Lerato, visited me in Johannesburg and purchased a second Ford XR3 from a used-car dealer. They paid him R12,000 in cash. It must have taken them months to save this amount. However, as the couple left Johannesburg in their new sedan, and travelled along the M2 highway towards the East Rand, it blew a top gasket and spurted oil all over the road. Fortunately, Jimmy's brother, Moses, found a relatively skilled and cheap mechanic in Soweto and they made it safely home one week later. But in Impalahoek the sedan soon became sedentary:

The car hardly ever moved. It just stood in my yard for ages. It never capsized, but the people finally told me that its gearbox was broken. I finally sold the car for only R4,000.

Jimmy did not expect witchcraft and accepted that Ford was not really as good a brand of car as he had believed. He heard several mechanics joke that 'Ford' really stands for '*F*irst *O*n *R*ubbish *D*ump'. Therefore, Jimmy purchased a Mazda as a replacement:

In 1995 I bought a Mazda sedan from an Indian guy in Nelspruit for R8,000. But it also ran for only five months. At about six o'clock one evening I fetched my step-brother's wife, who had just delivered a baby, in Casteel. It was raining and I drove the car at about sixty or seventy kilometres per hour. As I passed Tsakani, my fingers started getting numb. Something told me to switch on the headlights. Only twelve metres further on I saw a car parked across the road. There was a sharp descent on the one side and a wall on the other. I tried desperately to negotiate, but I hit the car from its rear. My Mazda's suspension immediately collapsed. I found out that Gift Morema and his newly wedded wife were in the [stationary] car. Gift said that the car would not start and that he alone had to push it. He had his lights off. I asked Gift, 'Do you want to kill me?' We struggled to get the cars going. We did not call the police, but we hired a car to tow it. We had the accident at about six [pm], but I only came home at twelve [midnight]. Gift never paid me. I eventually gave the car to my younger step-brother for only R800.

Later in life, Jimmy purchased and lost two more cars.

Marriage and Love

At more or less the same time as these unfortunate motor vehicle accidents occurred, Jimmy also began to experience marital disharmony. In retrospect, he told me of the love and deep affection that he had always felt for his wife:

I have never loved any woman like I loved Lerato. I have never loved anyone as much as her. Never! She was my childhood lover. She was the one woman who understood me better than anyone else.

But in Bushbuckridge, a man's love for his wife does not preclude him from engaging in extramarital sexual encounters. Kotzé, who conducted fieldwork in another village of Bushbuckridge, felt prompted to write, 'To men multiple sexual relations are a national sport; to women it is a primary source with which to ensure their and their children's survival in the face of male dominance' (Kotzé 1986: 26). Like Kotzé, I was often struck during fieldwork by the openness with which male informants such as Jimmy spoke about their extramarital liaisons.

We can plausibly relate the frequency of extramarital affairs to the system of labour migration, which separated husbands from their wives. But migrant labour itself does not explain multiple relationships (Delius and Glaser 2004). Husbands justified their involvement in these liaisons by arguing that they were naturally inclined, and also traditionally allowed, to be polygamous. To this effect, they would invoke old Northern Sotho proverbs, such as: 'A man is a blanket. We share him' (*Monna ke lepai. Re a apolelana*) and 'A man is an axe. He can be borrowed' (*Monna ke selepe. O lala a adimilwe*). The use of these proverbs concurs with a general tendency by South African men to invoke images of traditional patriarchy to justify extramarital affairs and male dominance (Spiegel 1991). Women, by contrast, committed themselves to 'modernity' or to 'ways of the whites' (*sekgowa*), which they associate with monogamy, and to greater equality in the domestic domain (van der Vliet 1991). Therefore, wives nearly always contested the legitimacy of their husbands' extramarital affairs.[1]

Jimmy first cheated on Lerato with a young woman called Nokhotula Shubane, even before he was married:

I remember well. It was in May 1984. By then I worked as a private [unqualified] teacher at the Impalahoek Primary School. In those days I still played football for Dynamos and after our soccer practice I went to buy some things at the store. There I met a young woman [Nokhotula Shubane] and said to her, 'You! Come to my brother's place tomorrow at six in the evening! You can find me there!' I was not serious and I really did not think that she would show up. The next day I had to organise a trip by the whole school to a sports day in Graskop. After we returned, I drank some beers and I only came home at eight [pm.]. Then my younger brother, Peter, and I still stayed at Moses's place and we had the whole house to ourselves. When I arrived Peter told me, 'Jimmy! Someone came to see you. It is not Lerato. She's in your room!' When I got into my room I found someone sleeping on my bed and I was surprised. Her shoes were small and her dress was different from any of Lerato's dresses. I realised I did not know her and then I woke up this stranger. She said, 'You invited me. So I came.' That evening I was drunk, slept with the woman, and took her home early the next morning. I was scared Lerato might come. I did not love Nokhotula. She was so cheap. She could sleep with any man.

In January 1985, someone came to me and said, 'Hey Jimmy! Your wife is about to deliver!' I did not know anything about this. Later that month, Mr Shubane [Nokhotula's father] came to my home and told me that his daughter expected my child. I denied responsibility saying, 'No! This child can't be mine! Your daughter has many boyfriends. I know some of them.' Nokhotula also told her father that she was not cocksure it was me. We then had to wait for the child to be born. Nokhotula gave birth during February, whilst I was at university. I expected her family to bring the child so that I could be tested for paternity. In the African paternity test we usually check the inside

[1] One notable exception is the Khozi Bay area of KwaZulu, where women invoke an idealised picture of an ancient Thembe Thonga tradition as a charter to assert their own gendered interests (Webster 1991).

of your hands and those of the child [for any resemblances]. But her family never brought the child to me.

During one university vacation I learnt that Nokhotula had been to our home in Impalahoek, but that she did not find me. Her sister told me that the child is a boy who looks like me. Like me, he is dark. But I also learnt that Nokhotula had married another man. Maybe I was the father. I cannot be sure. We did not use a condom.

After we had married, Lerato learnt about my affair with Nokhotula. This happened in the early 1990s. Another woman [Nokhotula's neighbour] asked Lerato why she could not give birth to a baby boy for me, as Nokothula had done. Lerato was very upset and that evening she shat me out. You know how important a boy is in African culture. If any woman gives birth to a boy people are very happy because he promotes the family's surname. Lerato asked me, 'Why do you tell these people that I can't give birth to a boy?'

Later in his marriage, Jimmy had many more extramarital affairs. In Bushbuckridge this pattern is rather uncommon. Elders generally expect young men to have different lovers, but then, as they grow older, to settle upon one particular woman. They either saw men who kept many lovers later in life as immature, or as trying to compensate for the lack of sexual adventure during their youth. However, Jimmy himself described his sexual liaisons as normative. To him, they provided rare sources of pleasure in a world full of frustrations.

In Bushbuckridge the erotic is not separate from interpersonal power, and men saw the sex act as dramatising masculine subjectivity, virility, and even domination. This is evident in the manner in which men described the penis as a weapon and portrayed sexual intercourse as an act of penetration. Men called the penis (usually *polo*) 'knobkerrie' (*molamo*), 'stick' (*thoka*), or 'assegai' (*lerumo*); and having penetrative sex as 'inserting' (*hloma*), 'piercing' (*hlaba*), 'eating' (*ja*), or 'boarding' (*kalama*).

Jimmy engaged in two different kinds of extramarital liaisons. First, he had longer-term relationships called *bonyatši*, with at least four different 'paramours': Carol Zwane, Anatsi Chiloane, Sheila Malatsi, and Patricia Biya. These relations had a definite transactional component: men provided intermittent gifts of money and other commodities to their paramours, although these were not directly exchanged for sex (Spiegel 1991; Hunter 2002):

I met Carol [the first paramour] at a sports competition hosted by the local high schools. She was clad in sunglasses and she was twiggish and short. I proposed to her [requested sex from her] and she invited me to her home. Since then I visited her fairly regularly and she never gave me any problems. Our relationship went on for a long time. She also had other men.

Anatsi was from Mariti and I met her when she was visiting her relatives in Dipping [a section of Impalahoek]. Our relationship only lasted for a short while.

However, it was his relationships with Sheila Malatsi and Patricia Biya that landed him in trouble and placed the greatest strain upon his marriage. In villages where networks of gossip – or the so-called 'pavement radio' (Ellis 1989) – are highly effective purveyors of news, secrets are exceptionally hard to keep. Jimmy's wife, Lerato, learnt of his affairs, and Sheila's other boyfriend, a taxi driver, directly confronted Jimmy at home:

I proposed to Sheila at the shops in about 1995. She was very beautiful and she agreed to my proposal. At the time I did not know that she was also having an affair with a taxi driver from Cottondale.[2] *Sheila began to love me and did not tell me about the other fellow. One day I arranged to take her home to Cottondale, but what I did not know was that her other boyfriend followed us with his taxi. By sheer luck we lost him. I then screwed Sheila in Cottondale.*

Later the taxi driver asked Sheila where she had been and beat her with a whip [sjambok]. *The next morning, he brought Sheila to my parents' home. [Jimmy had been out until late and was still nursing a hangover.] When they arrived I was still asleep, but my parents woke me and said there were people to see me. Lerato was washing clothes outside. I told the taxi driver, 'I understand you are looking for me.' He said, 'This woman will tell you why I'm here.' But Sheila could not say anything because she was still crying. The taxi driver wanted to beat her again, but I told him, 'You're wasting your time. She's not my girlfriend. I only gave her a lift. She even paid me. Is there anything wrong with that? You are getting it from the horse's mouth. She's not my girlfriend.'*

This man then started threatening me and he even said that he'll kill me. I then went inside and fetched a stick to make him angry. I changed the focus. I was now speaking about an insult, not about an affair. He was stupid. He came all the way to my place and could not prove that I was having an affair with Sheila. He was too emotional. I asked her if she paid me and she said, 'Yes.' I then asked her, 'Am I your boyfriend?' and she said, 'No.' Fortunately my gamble worked.

The taxi driver then drove away and took Sheila to hospital. Sheila told the nurses the truth. She told them that she was in love with me. Sheila later sent people to my home to tell me that she desperately wanted to see me. I went to

[2] Some of Jimmy's drinking mates were of the opinion that Sheila was actually married to the taxi driver at the time. However, I find Jimmy's account that he was merely her boyfriend more plausible. This is because Jimmy did not hesitate to tell me that some of his other paramours were married.

the hospital to check her, and the nurses told me that I'm causing problems for her. They said that Sheila had even threatened to kill herself. I realised that I had to stay away from her.

Patricia Biya, in contrast, was described by Ace Ubisi, Jimmy's neighbour, as 'someone who was only after Jimmy's money'. Patricia came from Nelspruit to study at a nearby technical college. Although she was married, her husband worked in Polokwane (about 300 kilometres away). Patricia and her sister, Yvonne, rented a room behind a well-known motel in Bushbuckridge. On a single day in 1994, Jimmy spent R3,000 on Patricia, claimed Ace:

That morning Patricia came to Jimmy and pleaded with him to take her to Komatipoort [near the Mozambique border, about 250 kilometres south], where, she said, her aunt was critically ill. Jimmy asked me to accompany them. He drew R800 from the auto-bank, poured R100 petrol, and drove us to Nelspruit. In Nelspruit he bought us Nandos chicken and took us to the cinema. He then drove to the aunt, who was at a diviner in Komatipoort. When we arrived the old woman looked better. The diviner said that she had regained her health and was free to go home. Jimmy paid the diviner R300, and gave the aunt R100 for food and for transport back to her home. He drew another R400 from the auto-bank in Nelspruit, poured R100 petrol, and gave Patricia's relatives R88 for beers and for food.

When we arrived back in Bushbuckridge, Patricia's sister, Yvonne, was not at home. Her neighbours gave us a note, saying that she was attending a music festival in Phalaborwa, where Brenda Fassi [a very popular artist] was singing. By then we were already drunk, but we also decided to go there. At Hoedspruit we encountered a roadblock and the soldiers saw empty beer bottles lying in the car. But Jimmy bribed the soldiers and gave them R50 not to arrest us. [During the crime wave of the 1990s, soldiers assisted police with crime-fighting operations.] At Phalaborwa there was another roadblock. But luckily I knew the speed-cop. We also gave him R50. Jimmy paid R20 entry fee for each of us. Inside the stadium there were fires where people could roast meat, and he also bought meat for R30 and beer for R70. We danced in the stadium until about two or three in the morning. Then all hell broke loose. The people of Phalaborwa said that they hated Brenda Fassi because she had bewitched their hero, Paul Ndlovu [a famous Shangaan musician]. They were screaming and destroying her instruments. The securities came and called for police reinforcements. We ran like hell, hid behind the bushes, and only came back to fetch our car at four o'clock.

That evening I went to sleep at the home of my uncle [malome] *in Phalaborwa. But Jimmy and Patricia slept in a hotel – for which he paid about R50. We only drove home past eleven [am] on Sunday. Jimmy overtook another car.*

But a traffic officer stopped us and charged us R1,300 for overtaking on the barrier line. He refused our bribe and Jimmy was in a hell of a trouble.

At home Jimmy had no more money. We first sat down and planned what to tell Lerato. We decided to say that we went to Hoedspruit, where we met my cousin from Phalaborwa. He had a television set with him and he could not deliver it because thugs had stolen his money. We took him to Phalaborwa by car and he took us to the festival.

Ace could not understand why Jimmy was so stuck on Patricia, and remarked that he knew very well that she was also having an affair with a student at the college.

In addition to these regular relationships, Jimmy also periodically engaged in 'one-night-stands' with women he met in local drinking taverns (*shebeens*). As elsewhere in South Africa, women who frequent taverns sometimes engage in transactional sex. There is a common understanding amongst the clientele of these institutions that a woman who accepts liquor from a man is willing to have sex with him.[3] Jimmy usually drank at a fairly respectable tavern in Acornhoek called 'Banda'. Owned by a friendly and convivial businessman from Malawi, and frequented largely by local professionals such as teachers, policemen, and hospital employees, Banda has a reputation for being a violence-free zone. The tavern comprises a fairly small building accommodating a liquor outlet and pool table, but is surrounded by shady trees and a well-kept lawn. Without the knowledge of the proprietor, men regularly took young women from the tavern to have sex in nearby motels, or sometimes even used the toilets or bushes behind the tavern. In Jimmy's own words:

I also proposed to these women in the taverns. Sometimes I did not even know their names. Angus Evans [the Coloured owner of a general dealer store in Impalahoek] had a number of spare rooms and he usually allowed me to use these rooms if I gave him a few beers. I never paid these women a lot of money – sometimes only a quart of beer [750 ml] would do the trick.

The money that Jimmy spent on other women drained his salary and this contributed to a series of arguments between him and his wife. But Jimmy professed that he was innocent, and blamed Lerato for misspending her own salary:

One night I asked Lerato for money to take Henry [Jimmy's brother] to university, but she told me that she had withdrawn all the money from our account. I became furious when she refused to tell me what she did with the money. I was so angry that I cut her bank card to pieces with a pair of scissors and I made

[3] See Wojcicki (2002) and Hunter (2002) for fairly detailed discussions of 'transactional' or 'survival' sex in South African taverns.

a lot of noise. My father shouted at us, saying, 'I don't mind if you kill each other.'

Precisely at the time of this conflict, Lerato started to develop persistent health problems. Her symptoms included coughing, asthma, allergies, heavy breathing, fever, and unspecified pains. These might very well have been somatic expressions of underlying anxiety and social problems. Such sickness behaviour enables wives to articulate certain demands, and to renegotiate the content of their marital relationships (Littlewood and Lipsedge 1984). During the course of her sickness, Lerato spent as much time as possible at her parents' home, where she claimed she always felt a great deal better.

Jimmy found the process of managing Lerato's therapy most distressing. He constantly had to take Lerato to doctors, diviners, and prophets; pay excessive amounts for the remedies they prescribed; move back and forth between the homesteads of his parents and his in-laws; and deal with his agnates, who were staunch Zionists. When Lerato's father died in 1998, Jimmy had to assist with the funeral arrangements and contribute R4,000 towards the costs of his coffin. In this manner, Jimmy settled all his outstanding bridewealth debts. Paradoxically, Lerato now lived at her mother's home, almost permanently.

In September 1998, Jimmy and Lerato separated. For the next nine months, he lived alone with his father, and she with her mother:

At the time it seemed to me as if divorce was imminent. I was sick and tired of my wife.

Residing with His Affines, 1999–2002

Henry Mohale worked exceptionally hard as a mediator to save his brother's marriage. His efforts paid dividends in June 1999, when Jimmy and Lerato finally reconciled. To save their marriage, the couple resolved to live together in Lerato's mother's homestead.

Jimmy told me that he recognised that Lerato was pregnant and that he wished to reconcile with her for the sake of his children. Late in 1999, Jimmy and I drove to the maternity ward of the Hoedspruit military hospital to fetch Lerato and her new baby boy, called Katlego. Jimmy was overjoyed that Katlego would perpetuate the Mohale surname.

I found Jimmy's sudden decision to reside with his affines in a strictly patri-virilocal society hard to comprehend. By way of explanation, Luckson Mohale had informed me that it is imperative for sons to leave their parental home in order of seniority. By 1999 Jimmy's younger brothers, Peter and Henry, were already building their own homes. Should Jimmy have continued to reside with his parents, he would have subverted these seniority rules, and he would have unleashed an affliction, called *di feka*

(*eka* literally 'betray'). *Di feka* causes kinswomen to bear crippled children.

Jimmy resided with his affines as a short-term sacrifice. He deferred present-time gratification and began to think about the future. As a newly reconciled couple, he and Lerato had ambitious plans. In 1996 they purchased a residential plot in a comfortable middle-class residential suburb of the town White River. Jimmy initially saw the site as a form of investment. But in 1999 they decided to build a home on the stand:

We started building because I wanted a good education for my kids. I reasoned that Lerato and our three children could go and live in White River, and that I could stay there on weekends and on holidays. I had no prospect of changing jobs. The house would actually be for Katlego. Lerato and I took out a loan of R40,000 from Standard Bank: each of us took out R20,000. To pay back the loan the bank would deduct R900 from our monthly salaries. We also added our savings. I must have poured between R70,000 and R80,000 into the house, and Lerato between R50,000 and R60,000.

We also decided to invest in the future of our children. We sent Kgopotšo and Thandi to WEM [William English Medium, a private school]. It does not matter how intelligent kids are. If they cannot command the queen's language things will be difficult for them. When young people apply for jobs the employers interview them in English. They also need English for tertiary institutions. Our local [state] schools don't see the importance of teaching kids English. Even teachers cannot speak English well. I would have felt very bad if Kgopotšo and Thandi had enrolled at a school like Tlasede [where Jimmy taught].

After Kgopotšo had completed Grade Nine at WEM, Jimmy and Lerato enrolled her at the Combined School in Middelburg (almost 300 kilometres away) for Grades Ten to Twelve.

Kgopotšo is very bright. In most cases she obtained the first position in her class. . . . Thandi was not so good at school and she did not want to go to Middelburg. So she remained at WEM. I took these decisions as the head of the family and afterwards I explained them to Lerato. She understood.

Unfortunately, these ambitious plans did not come to fruition. Jimmy resented living with his affines. He experienced conditions in the home to be cramped (see Figure 5.1) and found the domineering behaviour of his mother-in-law to be intolerable.

It was really not nice to live with my in-laws. My wife, my son, and I stayed in one room, her brothers and their wives in the other two rooms, and Lerato's mother slept with the four kids in her own bedroom. At eating time we all converged in the sitting room. I soon discovered that we were from radically different backgrounds. I drink [liquor] and they are Zionists. I also did not like eating their foods, but I did not want to be fussy. My in-laws tried to control

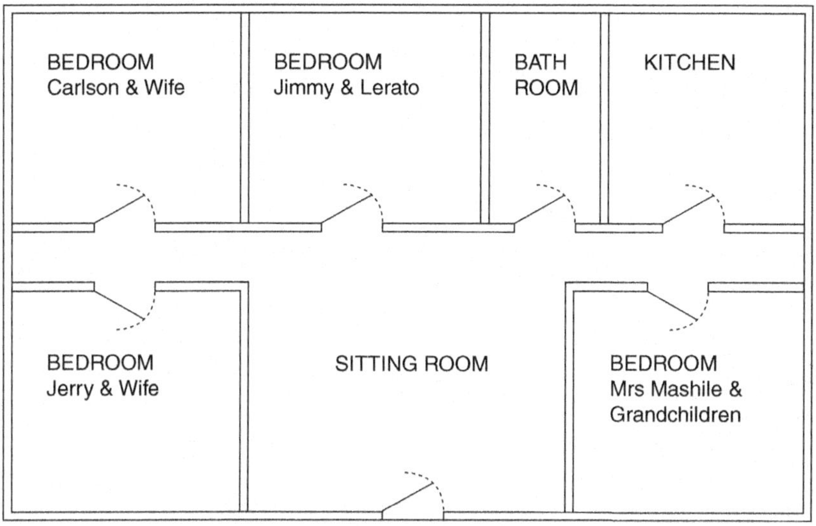

Figure 5.1. Sketch map of the Mashile home

me. I am used to going out at eight [pm] in the evening to meet my friends, but when I lived with my in-laws I could not go out late at night.

By living with his affines, Jimmy transgressed the avoidance rules (*hlompa*) that he ought to have maintained with his mother-in-law:[4]

*In the old way of life you had to wear a jacket whenever you visited your in-laws and they had to bring gifts [*xirwalo *in Tsonga] whenever they visited you. You could only take off the jacket when sleeping. A man could not sit in the same room as his mother-in-law and he was not allowed to share a table with her. You had to speak to her through somebody else [an intermediary].*

But I did not care too much about tradition. I avoided my mother-in-law because I did not like her. She was a rude person and she was pompous, snobbish, and bossy. She was full of bad influences and she wanted to own me. Other people warned me about her. I even heard my father saying, 'That Mashile woman is killing my son.' But her own sons worshipped her. I'm sure that she uses the potions of witchcraft to keep her sons obedient.

That woman is diabolical. She always told Lerato that, as a daughter, Lerato should give her mother money. One Saturday my mother-in-law spoke to another woman at a funeral. She said to her, 'This is my daughter', and she pointed to Lerato, 'and this is my son-in-law. My daughter is a lady teacher and my son-in-law is a teacher. My sons are also teachers. Imagine if

[4] See Kuckertz (1997) for an in-depth discussion of rules of respect (*ukuhlonipha*) in another South African context.

each of them could give me R1,000 each month.' When I heard this I felt like vomiting. How can you pay a person R4,000 for doing nothing? That woman is really twisted.

Jimmy commanded little respect in the home of his affines. He claimed that Lerato obeyed her mother rather than her husband, and she no longer even informed him of any of her decisions:

When I stayed there, Lerato and I again started fighting. I realised that my in-laws were interfering with my marriage, and that my mother-in-law controlled my wife. Lerato no longer wanted to contribute towards any of our projects. Once, she even told me that she no longer wanted to live in the house in White River. My wife never consulted me in anything. Once Lerato was not at home and my neighbours told me that she had gone somewhere to pay for a beast [cow]. Other times I came home and found that Lerato had gone to a stokvel *[rotating credit association] meeting.*[5] *I would not even know that she was a member. Another time I heard that she and her brother had purchased a tombstone and a cow for their [deceased] father, but they did not notify me. She also applied for a job without me knowing.*

Lerato no longer cooperated with me. I paid off the house loan, but she did not. The one day she would be paid her salary, but the next day she had nothing. She could never tell me what happened with the money. It just disappeared. I was worried that she might have been using her money to visit diviners to bewitch me.

I could not confirm the validity of these impressions. On the occasions that I met Lerato's mother, her behaviour towards me was always courteous and kind. In either case, Jimmy absolved Lerato from blame, saying that she was merely an innocent pawn of her mother, who had robbed her of her freedom:

I pretended to be fine, but deep down I nursed anger. I spent lots of time thinking about my future. I saw everything collapsing in front of me. I died inside. Because of this I started drinking too much. I sometimes drank on an empty stomach and came home drunk to throw temper tantrums and shout at Lerato. I wanted to show her that I had done a great deal for her, but that all these efforts were a waste of time. For five months we were not on speaking terms. I also had suicidal tendencies. I wanted to kill my wife and myself. This idea used to come to my mind. It is only my son – Katlego – who kept me going.

[5] In Impalahoek a *stokvel* group usually comprised about ten women wage earners. Each month all members would donate a specified amount, usually of about R100, to the member whose turn it was to receive the money. She would save most of the money, but use a small portion of it to host a party. In the most detailed study of these groups, Bähre (2007) sees *stokvels* as a means of enforced saving and creating networks of trust in a social environment characterised by insecurity and violence.

Jimmy sought to escape from this predicament by seeking pleasure, frequenting Banda's tavern, and engaging in extramarital affairs. He insisted that it was due to his marital problems that he started proposing to other women. But Lerato insisted that the causal arrow pointed in the other direction. She said that Jimmy's drinking and womanising were the cause, not the consequence, of his problems.

In either case, Jimmy's drinking mates told me that they became increasingly concerned about his reckless behaviour at Banda's tavern. Ace Ubisi observed:

Jimmy used to buy beers for us. If there were three girls at the table, he would pick one of them, leave the beers with me, and go to a motel to screw the whore [sefebe]. *After about one or two hours, Jimmy would be back. Then he would grab another whore and take her to another motel or even to the bush. Then, at about three [am], Jimmy would go to Rooïboklaagte to screw his girlfriend, Carol Zwane. He would only come home at eleven [am]. Because he was not on speaking terms with Lerato, she would not even ask where he had been.*

Patrick Monna, an unmarried mine labourer who was also a research participant and mutual friend, told me that he sometimes joined Jimmy in these escapades when he was on vacation in Impalahoek:

Jimmy screwed around like nobody's business. I used to accompany him to Banda and from there we would take two girls to the motel. We usually shared one room. He used the mattress and I used the base bed. We bought each woman four bottles of Smirnoff Twist [a popular brand of flavoured Vodka]. This is strong stuff. It is about 6 per cent alcohol. Other times we used a house next to the chief's office. Nobody stays there. A young man gave us the keys to the house and we bought him beers for the favour. The next morning we also gave the girls R10 transport fees. . . . I always told Jimmy to use condoms. I tried to influence him. But he sometimes took chances.

Lerato twice caught Jimmy cheating on her, but suspected that he had also done so on the numerous occasions he failed to sleep at home. One evening in 2001, Lerato heard that Jimmy and his girlfriend were seated in a parked car, on the outskirts of Impalahoek, waiting for friends. Lerato sneaked up on the vehicle, opened the rear door, and assaulted the other woman. Jimmy, in turn, beat Lerato.

On a rainy evening, early in 2002, Lerato learnt that Jimmy was sleeping in a motel with the wife of a migrant labourer. She arrived at the motel reception, told the security guard that she was Jimmy's sister and desperately wished to speak to him because their mother was seriously ill at home. The security guard knocked at the door and Jimmy opened, wearing only a pair of trousers. Lerato attacked the paramour, who was lying naked in bed, and Jimmy fled from the motel in the rain.

Iris

Jimmy first met Iris Maluleke in 2001. Iris was extremely attractive and was fifteen years younger than Jimmy. She was also from an impoverished family and could obtain only poorly remunerated jobs, such as cleaning at a local supermarket and at the Electricity Supply Commission offices.

Iris's previous boyfriend, Sello Dilebo, had an extremely unsavoury reputation as a petty thief and a womaniser. Though Sello had obtained a teacher's diploma, he worked as a backstreet mechanic in Impalahoek. Sello was extremely violent towards women: he physically abused his girlfriends and was also known as a rapist.

Jimmy told me:

I really could not understand why Iris ever accepted a proposal from such a thug. Sello was once Flerry Mashile's boyfriend and she told me that he used to beat her very badly. Sello met Iris whilst she was doing Grade Twelve at the Tlasede High School. When he got involved with her, Sello called himself 'Try'. He did not use his real name because he did not want Iris to discover that he was really Flerry's old boyfriend, who is a woman basher.

Jimmy's friends and family first learnt of his affair with Iris when his new car, a Mazda 1800 utility van [*bakkie*] was – like the others he had owned – damaged beyond repair. Jimmy had purchased the van for R53,000 from Nelspruit Motors, only six months before the incident. He bought the vehicle on credit, and an amount of R911 was deducted from his monthly salary by stop order:

One Friday I knocked off from work and went to drink with my colleagues. At seven o'clock [pm] I picked up my new girlfriend, Iris, and we took a friend home. As I drove towards the plaza [a shopping centre just outside Impalahoek], I felt as if someone grabbed me by my hands. My eyes closed. Then I made a mistake and stepped on the accelerator. From Chicken Licken [a fried chicken outlet] I drove at a very high speed and I nearly knocked the petrol pumps. The petrol pump attendant even fled to get out of the way. I managed to stop the car. Now I was scared and I was shaking. My passengers got out of the car and said, 'We don't want to die. Go and die alone!'

That is when I asked a youngster to drive the car. I gave him three cans [of beer] and asked him to take my girlfriend and me to a motel in Violetbank. After he dropped us off, I asked him to take the van and to park it somewhere else. I did not want people to know that I was at the motel. He drove the van, but capsized and smashed it beyond repair. The car was a complete write-off.

Jimmy bribed the policeman who investigated the accident with R300, and changed the youngster's statement, saying that he, himself, had in fact driven the van, but had swerved from the road in the morning mist to avoid oncoming cattle. The insurance company accepted his fraudulent statement, and allowed Jimmy to lease a small Corsa sedan from Nelspruit Motors as a replacement.

The Corsa cost R43,000, but with hire purchase the price went up to R66,000. To this they still added insurance.

Whilst Jimmy was shaken by this most recent accident, he was proud that he could win Iris's love. However, Iris's former boyfriend, Sello, did not easily accept defeat, and challenged Jimmy to a fistfight during May 2002:

That evening I drank at a hotel with my friends. We then went to the Spar supermarket to pick up Iris. As I came out of the car to greet Iris, Sello came from nowhere, approached me, and pulled me by the shirt. By then I was already cooked [drunk], but Iris and I started fighting him. She grabbed him and I hit him, but he bit her little finger and she screamed. Only when I beat him on the jaw did he let go of her finger. Many people, even school kids, watched the fight.

From the Spar supermarket we drove to the Plaza [shopping centre]. By then my shirt was torn and Iris's finger was bleeding. We went to buy ice cubes for the pain and also something to clean her finger [presumably a disinfectant]. Whilst we were at the plaza, Sello again appeared and came walking towards me. I asked him, 'Do you want to fight?' Then I said, 'Fuck you! If you beat me, I'll report you to the police station [just across the road] for assault!' But he said to me, 'Jimmy, you're a coward. Let's fight it off.' I only became furious when he swore at me, saying, 'Your mother's arse [Mosona mmago]*!' Sello should not have insulted my mother. I hit him with the fist and he went down. Then I jumped on him and kicked him. By then Sello was already dizzy. But Iris grabbed a [750 ml] beer bottle and hit him on the head. Sello again fell down. I thought he had died, but when I felt his pulse and listened to his breathing, he was fine. We thought of taking him to the police or to the hospital because he was bleeding. But he resurfaced and walked away.*

Jimmy learnt that Sello was actually a distant relative of his wife, Lerato:

After I had beaten him, Sello came to complain at the home of my in-laws. He said that I had taken his girlfriend. I was there when he came. Sello cried after he spoke to Lerato. My mother-in-law must have known about this all along. By then I did not really care anymore. I did not deny any of Sello's charges. I was actually happy when this happened. I did it [engaged in extramarital affairs] with the purpose of causing trouble for my in-laws. I was tired of being at the receiving end. I felt like a tissue paper that could be used to wipe someone else's arse. I did it to remind God that I was still there.

The Small Room in Tsakani, 2002–3

By 2002 it was clear that Jimmy had overstayed his welcome at his mother-in-law's home and he decided to hire a small room in a housing complex elsewhere in Tsakani for Lerato, himself, and their three children. Lerato's cousin leased the room to them for a monthly rental of only R180, including water and electricity.

By moving to the new room, Jimmy and Lerato merely relocated their problems. Lerato and the children still visited her mother each day. Jimmy continued to claim that his mother-in-law was interfering with his marriage. Lerato still publicly complained about her husband's indiscreet extramarital affairs, and the mutual accusations of wasting money continued:

We fought all the time and we stayed in the same house for nine months without having sex. She refused to cook food for me or to wash my clothing. Because of this I would stay with Iris and ask Iris to cook for me. I took my clothes to my sister's daughter, across the road.

During one episode, Lerato answered Jimmy's mobile phone, and upon hearing Iris's voice, she threw the phone down the pit latrine. In another episode during 2003, Lerato learnt that Jimmy had bought Iris's child a birthday cake. Lerato arrived at the birthday party, and whilst those in attendance were dancing to loud music, she attacked Jimmy with a broomstick. In the incident Jimmy fractured bones in his right hand.

Out of desperation, Lerato told Jimmy that she would prefer him to marry Iris as his second wife, rather than to be humiliated constantly by his cheating. Then at least, he would sleep at home. She even offered to pay bridewealth for Iris. But this proposal led to yet another argument:

Lerato told me that I could marry Iris and that she would be happy just as long as she could see the father of her children. But I was angry and I asked her: 'Where will you pay bridewealth for me? Do you know the girl?' Lerato said: 'Yes. She is Iris! You want to make her a second wife.' I replied: 'Who said I want to make her my second wife? She might become my first wife. When you pay bridewealth for her you must also hire bodyguards to look after her. They have to see to it that she does not screw other men. She is a springbok [an antelope known for graceful leaping, also a metaphor for promiscuous women]. I like springboks. They don't bewitch me.

By the time these events were transpiring, I realised how serious the situation had become. I sat down with Jimmy and spoke to him as earnestly as I could. I told Jimmy that whilst his in-laws might well be interfering in his marriage, Lerato had a right to complain about his extramarital affair with Iris. I pleaded with Jimmy to end the affair, to think about his children, and to sleep at home. I said words to this effect:

Your affairs with Iris and with the other women are the roots of your trouble. We live in a new South Africa. Whites cannot go around claiming that racism and apartheid is their culture. Whites have to change. In the same way, black men cannot just claim that affairs are part of their culture. Black men also have to change. In the new South Africa women have rights. You should decide whether you still love your wife. If you do, you must end your relationship with Iris. If you do not, you must think seriously about divorce. People do divorce: Mandela divorced his wife, Winnie, and de Klerk divorced his wife, Marike. Then, even if you do divorce, don't just marry Iris. Be single for a while and find the correct woman. Think of your children. They are suffering. You must also cut down on your drinking. Don't drink when you have problems. Only drink once you have solved them. Also listen to your brother, Henry. He is an educated and responsible person.

Jimmy nodded and looked extremely serious. Unfortunately, my words were not based on adequate knowledge of the facts. I knew that Henry had always tried desperately hard to assist Jimmy in resolving his marital problems. But I did not realise that Henry openly sided with Lerato, and was claiming that Iris had bewitched Jimmy with love potions (*korobela*) to make him forget about his family.

Later, Jimmy told me that he was subsequently taken by Henry and some friends to see a diviner:

Henry came here early in the morning. He told me, 'Put on your clothes! Don't wash! Take your [motor vehicle] licence!' Then I drove with them. We went to a diviner called Nyambi. Henry thought that my paramour [nyatsi] *was bewitching me. We arrived, went inside the divination hut* [ndumba] *and put down R70. The diviner [Nyambi] told me: 'You! Sit here!' Then he took Henry aside and threw the bones [lots].*

At nine [am] he said: 'Let's speak about this man now.' He pointed to Henry and said, 'You are the senior.[6] *You complain about your brother.' Then he pointed to me and said: 'Why are you scared? Your ancestors are strong. If it had not been for them, you would have died a long time ago. Your mother-in-law uses strong potions. She wants you to die so that your wife can inherit your money. If you don't take care of yourself you will be shot.' The diviner then asked me many questions. 'Where is your father-in-law? Is he dead?' Finally he told me, 'Your wife works with papers and you do the same [office work]. She is not a witch, but her mother wants money from her.' Then Henry explicitly asked the diviner, 'Does my brother's paramour* [nyatsi] *use potions?' The diviner replied, 'No!'*

[6] Although Henry is the sixth-born Mohale child, he was named after his mother's father, Hendrik Ngobeni. Since birth, Henry has been closely associated with his maternal grandfather. He speaks loudly like him and is also very intelligent. Because he bears the ancestral name, Henry is deemed to be the senior child.

From the consultation, the two brothers and their friends learnt that it was Jimmy's mother-in-law rather than his paramour who was threatening his life. Henry reportedly pledged every cent that he owned to save Jimmy's life.

Leaving Lerato, 2003–5

In 2003, Jimmy permanently left the room that he had shared with his wife and three children, and moved in with his girlfriend, Iris.

I thought that my wife wanted to poison me, so I went away. I left everything there – my ID [identity document], my [motor vehicle] licence, my blankets and my clothes. I left with only one shirt and one pair of shoes, pants, underpants, and socks.

In retrospect, Jimmy remarked that this was not a decision that he had taken lightly:

When I separated from my wife I did not do so haphazardly. It was a well-thought-out decision. Only if you are in a predicament of my calibre can you understand what it felt like. I knew that I would be disadvantaged, but there was no other option. My other option was death. I viewed the pros and the cons and this was the better devil. I left my children because I did not want them mingled up with my problems. I want them to grow up and to be independent thinkers. I don't want to confuse them. I was in no position to explain my problems to them. I would have been abusing my children by telling them about my difficult relationships.

At the time Iris was living in a small three-roomed RDP (Reconstruction and Development Programme) house elsewhere in Impalahoek[7] with her mother, sister, child from a previous relationship, and her sister's two children. Iris's mother worked as a fruit and vegetable vendor in the nearby town of Hoedspruit, and was seldom at home. Said Jimmy:

I did not really care if her relatives were welcoming. I did not expect anybody to welcome me. I lived the life of a cowboy. I stayed there for about four or five months. It was not nice [at Iris's mother's home]. The children always made a noise during the day and it was hard to sleep at night because of all the noise from the juke-box at Marashea's tavern. I wanted peace and my nerves were jumping all the time. The only thing that I liked was that we paid no rent. I was like a refugee seeking asylum.

[7] During the late 1990s the South African national government made an earnest attempt to improve 'service delivery' in Bushbuckridge. In 1998 government constructed about two thousand three-roomed homes – fitted with electricity, sanitation, and on-site taps – for households earning less than R500 per month (Niehaus 2006b: 532–3).

Later, Jimmy and Iris hired a single room in a housing complex in Acornhoek, paying only R250 per month for rent and electricity:

We lived there for almost a year. This was freedom and freedom was very nice.

But, after experiencing problems with water and with their neighbours, Jimmy and Iris moved to a two-roomed home across the street from Iris's mother and sister. The owner, Judith Shai, worked in Phalaborwa and allowed Jimmy and Iris to stay there free of charge:

Judith wanted to sell me this place, but she still has not had time to negotiate with us. She keeps on promising that she'll come, but she doesn't. I don't even know what she looks like. Only Iris speaks to her on the phone. It is very strange. We have also been receiving free electricity. This guy [their next-door neighbour] connected electricity cables to our place and he pays for it. He says he is grateful because we look after his children when he is not here.

Jimmy's decision to leave Lerato, nonetheless, cost him dearly. Soon after Jimmy left, Lerato instituted a claim for R2,400 per month against him at the Bushbuckridge magistrate's court, to maintain their three children. I saw Jimmy during December 2003, on the evening before he was due to appear in court. He was notably anxious and showed me the potions that he obtained from a diviner to ensure a favourable outcome. But the potions were only partially effective: the magistrate ordered that R1,500 be deducted from Jimmy's salary each month, by stop order.

Under these circumstances there was no way in which Jimmy could complete building the house in White River. Nor could he sell the house to recoup his losses. The house still needed plastering, tresses, and tiles that would cost at least R30,000. By 2005 Jimmy owed the White River municipality R16,000 in unpaid rates. There was every possibility that the municipality could take possession of the home to meet his growing arrears.

These were crippling financial commitments. After deductions from his salary for maintenance, a car he no longer drove, a home in which he would never stay, life insurance, and rent, only R650 remained (see Figure 5.2). This left Jimmy without medical insurance and with virtually no money for food:

See, Sakkie. That's how my wife destroyed me. I will be left with absolutely nothing. I think that the problem started when my mother-in-law took Lerato to the diviners. In court I realised that there was some kind of force on her. She won't listen at all. . . . I am a charity case now. I live on handouts. My younger brother [Henry] knows my situation and he bought me a shirt. I also had to borrow pants, underpants, and socks from the people at school.

Monthly income after tax		R5,100
Deductions	Maintenance Car Home loan Living quarters Liberty Life (Insurance)	R1,500 R1,500 R900 R250 R300
Remaining money		R650

Figure 5.2. Jimmy Mohale's monthly earnings and deductions, 2004

Iris occasionally gave Jimmy some of the money she earned from hairdressing, and I occasionally helped him out by paying him a research assistant's stipend. Perhaps it was his financial desperation that forced Jimmy to swallow his pride, and again seek out my company.

Since leaving Lerato in 2003, Jimmy had only seen her on a few occasions. Lerato once told Jimmy that she wished to speak to him about their home in White River. Jimmy also learnt that Lerato had built a three-roomed home for her and their children elsewhere in Impalahoek. To demonstrate how spiteful his wife had become, Jimmy told me that she had stolen three of his identity documents:

At the time that Lerato and I were fighting I applied for an ID [identity document] at the Home Affairs Office in Phalaborwa. When I went to Phalaborwa to collect the ID, they [the officials] told me that because it lay in their office for such a long time, they decided to send it to me by post. I went to the post office, but discovered that Lerato had opened the box and taken it. At the maintenance court, the magistrate instructed me to bring along my ID. But I told him that I did not have one. Lerato told him that I lied. 'He does have an ID, but his ID is with me.' I asked her to give me the ID, but she said, 'No! You must come and fetch it!' When we went to the court for the second time, she again changed her statement and told the magistrate that she did not have my ID.

I realised that Lerato would not give me my ID so I applied for another document in Phalaborwa. The Home Affairs office in Phalaborwa sent my new ID to Thulamahashe. When I went there, they told me that it was now at the Bushbuckridge municipality. But at the municipality they told me that the new ID was at the chief's office. I went there [to the office] but the clerk said that one of my cousins had taken the new ID and given it to Lerato. I said, 'Eeiisshh. You killed me! We are separated!' I desperately needed the ID and I sent my lady cousin to Lerato's school. . . . But Lerato said, 'No! I can't give you his ID.' My cousin even spoke to the school principal, but Lerato still refused. I even reported the matter to the police, but they could not resolve the problem. The police told me that I had given Lerato the ID and that she had not stolen it. Lerato now had three of my IDs. I have now applied for a fourth one.

Lerato wants me to come to her home, but in our culture this is not allowed. If your wife builds a home, you as her husband should be the first one to sleep in it with her. If she sleeps in the home with another man before you, and you then visit the home, you'll be polluted and you'll die.

Jimmy did not invent this taboo out of thin air. But it is also true that he refused to meet Lerato at any other location in and around Impalahoek.

Jimmy's Political Comeback

During April 2004, Jimmy decided to make a 'political comeback' and to work for the ANC during South Africa's third democratic elections.

Initially, Jimmy was extremely coy, preferring not to tell me about his involvement in the election campaign. I had invited Jimmy for supper one evening, but did not find him at home. Instead, I located him in the company of Bushbuckridge's mayor and a few other ANC officials. I greeted the mayor, joined them for a drink, and Jimmy and I then left for my place. We first stopped at his room, where he quickly rid himself of his ANC T-shirt. I could not understand his embarrassment. After all, Jimmy had told me that he was again attending ANC meetings, and he freely criticised all other South African political parties.

At home, Jimmy told me that he did not really wish to associate himself with many of the local ANC leaders. He said that he was working on the campaign only to make himself visible in the hope that he could attain a position in the newly constituted Bushbuckridge municipality:

Sakkie, I have been applying for jobs with the [Bushbuckridge] municipality for a long time. I have applied to be a 'community liaison officer', 'manager of transport', 'administrative officer', 'and monitoring and implementation officer' and also 'assessment and evaluation' officer. Some of these jobs pay R35,000 per month and others R18,000. I thought that it would be easy to get one of those administrative positions. I have a good CV and some very good references. But I was not even short-listed for a single one of those posts. I applied for the lowest position in Public Works, but I did not even get an interview. For this position you only need a Grade Twelve certificate and the salary is R131,000 per annum. As a teacher with an honours degree I only get R90,000. I was not asking for a higher job. I was only asking to be one of them. The most obvious thing is misfortune [bati].

Most of the guys in those jobs do not have qualifications or expertise. Mohlala – my former student – was appointed as the 'community liaison officer'. He had only Grade Twelve. Why him? This is the million-dollar question. I don't know if it is my lack of political contacts or ANC connections or what? I thought that working on the campaign might help me. I thought that if the 'big guys' saw me campaigning they might recommend me for one of those jobs.

Jimmy was part of a team of about seventy election workers from five different wards, conducting a door-to-door campaign. The team's composition effectively blurred the boundaries between party and state. The election workers were predominantly teachers (on holiday), policemen (on leave), and other government employees. But they had exchanged their suits and uniforms for ANC T-shirts and ANC caps. The team travelled in a convoy of 15 flashy vehicles – BMWs, Audi A4s, Nissan Sentras, and utility vans – all decorated with ANC posters. As the team arrived in a particular village, they asked the headman for his consent, and announced their presence on microphone. They then visited each home in pairs.

We spent about ten minutes in each home. I would tell them, 'We represent the ANC. We have been sent to find out if you had any problems with voting, and what you need the government to do for you in your village.' We then gave a small speech. We would say, 'Vote ANC! It liberated you! It has brought houses, pensions, child maintenance grants, and food parcels!'

The election workers then recorded, on a form, the number of voters in each home and how many intended to vote for the ANC, abstain, or vote for other parties. They also wrote down people's complaints and requests. These procedures effectively constructed voting as an exchange of ballots for resources and social services.

The campaign was a brilliant success. During the elections the ANC received 136,717 of the 147,963 votes cast in Bushbuckridge (92.4 per cent). After the results became known, celebrations were held at three different venues.

But Jimmy told me that he was extremely disappointed.

I am more than bitter. On the campaign I saw many things that offended me. There was money from the ANC for catering, but we election workers were categorised into junior and senior members. Each day the members of the executive branch would go to grab Chicken Licken and drink beer. But the rest of us had to eat bread and drink cold drinks. There were many ANC T-shirts, but they [the senior members] distributed the T-shirts, not us. We were also not allowed to participate in the planning meetings. They treated us like kids and only told us what had to happen at a particular meeting. We could realise that our inputs were not required. But I just kept quiet.

Despite campaigning for the ANC, Jimmy was ineligible to vote in the elections because his wife had taken his identity document.

For me it was more a matter of showing a face than really campaigning. Throughout the day of the election I stayed in my room. I did not vote. . . . I did nothing. I only longed for beer. I only missed my Windhoek [a popular Namibian Lager].

Jimmy had not entirely lost hope. Soon after the election, the government announced that the administration of Bushbuckridge would finally be transferred from Limpopo Province to Mpumalanga. Jimmy thought that with the new provincial leadership in place, he stood a better chance of gaining a position in government.

Problems with Iris

By 2005, Jimmy had lived with Iris for almost three years. Their relationship, too, began to show signs of strain. There were rumours amongst Jimmy's friends that Iris was having an affair with Donald Shabangu, the deputy principal of another high school. Donald was wealthier than Jimmy: his wife owned a bottle store and he drove a BMW sedan. One of Jimmy's friends reportedly saw Donald and Iris buying clothes at a boutique in Sandton City – an exclusive shopping centre in Johannesburg's northern suburbs. Henry (Jimmy's younger brother) also saw Donald and Iris at a soccer match between Kaiser Chiefs and Black Leopards at the sports stadium in Thohoyandou, Venda. When Jimmy's friend and brother informed him, he replied that he had treated Iris with *likubalo* potions that would prevent her from having sex with other men.[8]

In the first week of February 2005, Jimmy went out to drink with friends at Banda's tavern. When he returned home, close to midnight, he found that Iris was not in. Jimmy was extremely hungry and went to see his friend, Patrick Monna, who lived just across the road. Here Jimmy asked Patrick's sister for food, and they sat together, eating and chatting. Iris arrived home after midnight. She called Jimmy from across the road, and when she eventually located him, accused him of having an affair with Patrick's sister. Iris was extremely angry and did not want to listen to Jimmy's explanations. In a fit of anger, she produced a knife and tried to stab Jimmy. He tried to evade the knife, but it cut the fingers of

[8] Men were widely suspected of doctoring their wives or lovers with potions that they obtained from diviners, to ensure that their lovers or wives remained faithful in their absence. *Likubalo* was associated with witchcraft and allegedly worked like a mystical chastity belt. One type of *likubalo* was allegedly manufactured by cutting a small piece of flesh from a dog's penis, drying it and grinding it into a fine powder. Once it had been administered to a wife, her husband closed a pen-knife. This would cause her and any other man who had sex with her to become stuck together like mating dogs. Other types of *likubalo* could cause the lover to start bleeding through the nose and mouth, to be struck by snakes, to be caught by others, his penis to curl up like a millipede, or the wife to have diarrhoea whilst copulating (Niehaus 2002b: 86–8).

his right hand. Iris then threw out all of Jimmy's clothes from their two-roomed home. That evening Jimmy slept at the home of his half-brother, Andrew.

The next morning, nurses at the local hospital cleansed Jimmy's wounds and bandaged his hand. Jimmy later reconciled with Iris. His mother, *ngwa* Ngobeni, heard what had happened, summoned the couple to her home, and instructed Jimmy to separate from Iris. But Jimmy pleaded with her, saying that Iris had not stabbed him. He claimed that he had merely fallen on glass and cut his hand. After the conversation, Jimmy consulted a diviner, who told him that someone had bewitched Iris to cause her to kill him.

Towards the end of March 2005, there was another altercation between Jimmy and Iris. Jimmy went out drinking at Banda's tavern, where one of his friends told him that he had seen Iris with another man in Impalahoek. At midnight, Jimmy located Iris at Marashea's tavern. He asked Iris why she was drunk, and beat her with his fist. But friends rushed to Iris's assistance and they pushed Jimmy so that he fell to the ground. The argument continued for two more hours, and at their home Iris beat Jimmy over the head with a large glass water container.

The next day Iris's relatives organised a meeting. Iris openly said that she no longer loved Jimmy and that she would prefer to find another man who did not have to pay maintenance for his children and would be able to support her. Jimmy, in turn, said that he had seen Iris drinking with other men. Iris's mother remarked that the couple were always fighting, and she advised them to separate.

For the next two evenings Jimmy slept at Patrick's house, and he told me that he seriously contemplated leaving Iris. However, Jimmy recognised the hopelessness of his situation. He eventually apologised to Iris and to her kin for having beaten her, and moved back into their two-roomed home. He simply had nowhere else to go.

In telling me about the period of hardship – which he called his 'second initiation' – Jimmy again emphasised how his expected life course had been thwarted. As a man who had worked for thirteen years, he had no place to call home. He felt that given his intelligence, qualifications, and dedicated hard work at school, he should have been better off. Jimmy was frustrated by the venality of the South African system that did not allow professional qualifications and achievements to triumph. Jimmy accounted for his dilemma in terms of structural factors and anomalous incidents of misfortune – such as motor vehicle accidents, an interfering mother-in-law, and an insubordinate wife. He did not see his extramarital liaisons as being responsible for his distress. Jimmy argued that he simply engaged in sexual practices that were normative to men of his generation. But others, such as his wife and neighbours, contested this view and argued that his sexual affairs were his undoing. In terms of this view Jimmy was culpable, at least in part, of his own downfall. Jimmy never explicitly told me that he experienced guilt and shame. Yet these factors might well have been apparent at an unspoken, perhaps unconscious, level. The politics of culpability and attempts to deflect blame illuminate crucial aspects of the accusation that he made against his father.

6 'I See Things Differently Now'

At precisely the same time that others were accusing Luckson Mohale of witchcraft, Jimmy's social world was falling apart. However, Jimmy did not instantly make this connection and his faith in his father did not evaporate overnight.

A well-known Northern Sotho proverb states, 'A witch does not have a horn' (*Moloi ga a na lenaka*). This proverb basically means that a witch's identity is never obvious, and we cannot observe a witch with the naked eye. It also warns against accusing someone of witchcraft with whom one experiences conflict. Whilst it is true that in Bushbuckridge people relate envy to witchcraft rather like they relate a motive to a crime, the presence of envy is neither necessary nor sufficient. Not all envious people are perceived as having the ability to perpetrate harm. Moreover, witchcraft can be a motiveless crime. Any convincing accusation demands further evidence. Therefore, the anthropological argument that social tensions are the prime determinant of witchcraft oversimplifies matters.[1] It detracts from the polysemy of witchcraft beliefs and underestimates the faculty of mystical beliefs to alter people's life worlds as well as the capacity of these beliefs to alter people's concepts of their own experiences (Niehaus 2001: 113–16).

Tension and conflict between Jimmy and Luckson Mohale were marginal to Jimmy's eventual conviction that his father practised witchcraft. These largely seem to have followed, rather than preceded, the labelling of his father. More crucial were circumstantial evidence, such as observations of his father's uncooperative behaviour during his mother's sickness, the experience of further incidents of misfortune and deaths, and the importance that Jimmy attached to the pronouncements of several diviners and Christian prophets. For him these revelations, described by Peek (1991) as non-normal modes of cognition, constituted authoritative proof of his father's hidden identity.

[1] It is a well-known dictum in anthropological and in historical literature that the distribution of witchcraft attributions and accusations reveals tensions between persons standing in various relationships (MacFarlane 1970; Marwick 1970). But there is a world of difference between general statistical trends and particular cases.

In retrospect, Jimmy said that his father's rather odd behaviour at the time of his mother's sickness sowed in him the first seeds of doubt about his father's innocence. Luckson seems to have been completely unconcerned and to have acted in the most blasé manner:

On the first evening that my mother became sick, we as her sons desperately sought to help. But our father continued to sleep. He did not wake up and did not take action. All that he did was to complain that his wife opened the door. When my mother was so sick I took her to a diviner called Mkhabela next to White River. Mkhabela has a speaking calabash[2] *and I asked him whether my mother will survive. Mkhabela threw his divination bones and said that the horn pointed towards the east. This means life. I asked him three times and each time he nodded in agreement. He then gave me potions to place at home. But these did not work.*

A few days later they phoned me at twelve [midnight]. I was at my wife's parents and I rushed home. At home I could see that my mother was very sick. She cried, 'Take me away from this place! If you don't take me away I'll die! Your father's things will kill me.' That is when we decided to take my mother to the home of my sister, Jessie.

Whilst my mother lived at Jessie's place I could see that this guy [Luckson] never took any interest in her sickness. My father spent a long time without visiting my mother. I eventually became very angry. I had to run around with my mother, but he did not care about her welfare. One day I looked at my mother and started to cry. I had no money [with which to take her to a healer]. I borrowed R600 from the moneylender [mashonisa] *and I had to repay R720 [by month end]. I still owe him R270. It was my father's wife, but he was not interested [in her condition]. I once asked him, 'Why don't you care?' and he replied, 'I don't believe in diviners* [tinyanga] *and in prophets.' But at the same time my father attends church, where they give him prescriptions* [ditaelo]. *He became furious and asked me, 'Are you accusing me of being a witch?' I said, 'I won't recant.' That was the first time that I started to think that my father might perhaps be a witch.*

Not long after, Jimmy had another serious quarrel with his father. Only weeks after Jimmy had purchased his fifth motor vehicle, a brand new Corsa sedan, he took his daughter Kgopotšo to school in Middelburg (about 300 kilometres away):

I went to Middelburg with Suko, a ZCC minister, and with Marumo's wife. We drove at 120 kilometres per hour. Close to the Middelburg turn-off we followed

[2] Hammond-Tooke describes ventriloquism as an authoritative method of divination. Instead of the statements coming from the mouth of the diviner, they are heard as emanating from the calabash or from all around the hut, and are believed to be the voices of the spirits. He writes: 'The rarity of the gift gives this type of diviner great prestige' (Hammond-Tooke 1989: 113).

a truck, pulling a trailer. I wanted to overtake the truck on the ascent. Just then the back door of the trailer opened and bricks fell all over the road. I reduced speed and swerved to avoid the bricks. But my two left wheels went over some bricks and burst. I clung onto the steering wheel and stopped the car.

The truck driver also stopped and came to us. I only had one spare wheel in the trunk, so the truck driver took me to Middelburg to fix one wheel and to buy a new rim. I later got the car going and only drove at eighty kilometres per hour on the way back home. I arrived back at twelve thirty [past midnight]. I woke Lerato and told her the story. Then I still had to take the ZCC minister to Welverdient. Lerato accompanied me and sat in the back seat. I was still scared from the accident. On the way back from Welverdient, I hit a leopard.[3] *It came from nowhere and I heard the knock. That was two accidents in one day.*

I went home and slept. The next day I went to my father and explained to him what had happened. I told him that I hit a leopard when I returned from Welverdient. But my father shouted to me, at the top of his voice, 'No! You were imagining things. You were drunk!' As I drove away I was shaking with anger.

After the incident Jimmy learnt that his wife Lerato had regularly been visiting his father, to complain about his extramarital love affairs. Lerato told Luckson that Jimmy wished to divorce her, and that he was spending all his money building a house for his girlfriend, Iris.

Ngwa Ngobeni's Illness and Duduzile's Death, 2002

Ngwa Ngobeni's decision to stay at Jessie's home in Tsakani soon became a major bone of contention. Jessie had previously worked at Tintswalo Hospital, but at the time that her mother came to reside with her, she was a fruit and vegetable vendor. Her husband Fundani Thobela worked for the South African Defence Force in Phalaborwa. Jessie and Fundani had eight children, of whom five still lived with them.

Only about two months after *ngwa* Ngobeni moved in, Jessie's youngest daughter, Duduzile, who was only 12 years old, began to display signs of illness. Her condition rapidly worsened and she died within two weeks. Duduzile's relatives had always regarded her as extremely intelligent, and noted that she always attained the top marks in her class at school. She was also a choir leader, a drum majorette, and a most reliable child to send on errands.

Duduzile's death was very mysterious. My father once invited the little one to his house and told her, 'I want to send you to the plaza shopping centre to buy

[3] The leopard is the animal associated with royalty and the shoulders of chiefs are draped in leopard hide. However, with the denuding of game in the lowveld, one hardly ever encounters this animal outside game parks (Carruthers 1995). Jimmy believed that the leopard that he struck was an exceptionally powerful witch-familiar.

things.' When Duduzile returned, he gave her money, and said, 'Please don't tell the others – not even your mother – that I gave you money. If you do, they will all come to me to demand money.'

Duduzile's sickness started as flu. She used to complain to her mother, saying that she was not feeling well. Her parents are staunch ZCC members and they gave her [ZCC] tea and coffee. Jessie also took Duduzile to two doctors. The first said the child had fever and gave her some tablets. The second said that she will be alright – nothing else. We believed that he was a reputable doctor. I was not really too interested in what the doctors said. All that I heard is that they gave her some tablets. I knew it was witchcraft and if people are bewitched Western doctors find it hard to diagnose them. The doctors will just use the nearest Western term. They will say she has flu and will give her Panado [a headache tablet]. What else could the doctors do?

Duduzile looked fine when she returned from the doctor. I visited Jessie and she sat next to her. But on the Tuesday Jessie told me that Duduzile was sick and on the Saturday at 7.30 [pm] someone phoned me and asked me to come over to Jessie's place. When I arrived everyone sat outside. They told me that Duduzile had just died. I was shocked and asked them, 'Is this true?' They said, 'Yes. We're waiting for the vehicle from the funeral parlour. We have already phoned.' I was shocked. They told me that Duduzile was fine. They gave her food and she ate it. But by five [pm] things changed. She could no longer speak and froth came from her mouth. It looked as if she had been poisoned. Duduzile died in her mother's hands. Her mother held her and felt that her body suddenly became heavier. Then she knew that Duduzile was dead.

The AVBOB [funeral company] van arrived and took Duduzile's corpse to Tzaneen [a town about 120 kilometres north]. The next day five of us went with my brother-in-law [Fundani] to Tzaneen to make the funeral arrangements. Because he [Fundani] had taken out AVBOB insurance for 12 years, he was under the impression that AVBOB would pay for the entire funeral when one of his family members died. He also thought that AVBOB would bury her. But we discovered that AVBOB would only pay out R2,500. AVBOB wanted to bury the child for a profit. They wanted to ask us R900 for the vehicle which took the corpse to Tzaneen, R2,000 for a beast [cow] and R2,200 for the coffin. AVBOB even said that they did not have a small coffin and wanted us to buy a large one. They calculated and said that we had to pay them [an additional] R7,640. We did not have that money. . . . The parents then decided to let the ZCC burial society bury Duduzile. We asked AVBOB for the R2,500 and told them that they could deduct R900 for transport. But AVBOB did not want to understand. Only after a long argument did AVBOB yield and allow the ZCC to take over. The ZCC fetched the corpse, took the little one to a local funeral parlour, paid R2,000 for the coffin and gave the parents R3,000. It was a very big funeral. We had to buy a beast and eighty loaves of bread for the night vigil.

People came to the funeral by bus and by truck. Marumo [the primary school headmaster] brought three-quarters of his teachers and many school kids.

When we prepared for the funeral, I drove around everywhere with my Corsa. But do you think that he [Luckson] visited the bereaved family? His daughter's daughter was late [dead]. But he never went there. Many people were saying this man is a crook. They were saying that this man has magic.

Before the funeral a fierce argument erupted amongst Duduzile's relatives over who – rather than what – had been responsible for her death. Jimmy was not perturbed when he heard his sister, Jessie, blaming their father. He had heard her express these opinions before. But he was shocked to learn that Jessie's husband, Fundani, and her affines believed that his mother, *ngwa* Ngobeni, might have bewitched Duduzile:

Jessie's in-laws were angry. They told Jessie that they had been to a diviner [inyanga] *and that this diviner revealed how our mother had killed the little one. The diviner said our mother killed Duduzile because she, herself, wanted to be cured. They asked Jessie, 'Why is it that the old woman gets better when the child dies?'*[4] *They called us to discuss this with them, but we defended our mother. We insisted that she is not a witch.*

These accusations placed the Mohale siblings in a conundrum. They now faced an unenviable choice, being forced to decide which of their parents practised witchcraft. When faced with such a choice few children would not side with their mother. But the Mohale siblings remained divided: Jessie and Kagišo had already made a firm decision. But Moses, Jimmy, and Henry still harboured some hope that their father might also be innocent.

Visiting Dr Sugar

On 13 August 2002 (after Duduzile's death, but before her funeral) Moses and Kagišo (the eldest and youngest Mohale siblings) decided to consult Dr Sugar, one of the most renowned diviners of Bushbuckridge, to ascertain what had really happened at Jessie's home.

Diviners such as Dr Sugar derived their power of vision and ability to cure by virtue of being possessed by foreign spirits.[5] According to regional legend the first spirit mediums of the South African lowveld were Nkomo we Lwandle ('Cow of the Ocean') and Dunga Manzi ('Stirring Water'),

[4] This description resembles Foster's (1965) classical description of the 'image of limited good'. Foster maintains that, in the peasant societies of Mexico, all desired things in life, such as wealth and health, are seen to exist in finite qualities. The acquisition of wealth and health necessarily occurs at the expense of someone else.

[5] Harries (1994: 156–63) writes that this form of spirit possession originates in Mozambique in the 1860s. He sees spirit possession as a means of coping with an oppressive situation and its symptoms as similar to those of hysteria. See Honwana (2003) and West (2006) for a more detailed description of spirit possession in contemporary Mozambique.

a Shangaan woman and a Mozambican man. They were said to have been trained by Nzonzo, a powerful water serpent. Nzonzo reportedly captured them and submerged them in deep rivers. Yet they did not drown, but lived underwater for months, breathing like fish. Only after their kin had slaughtered a cow for Nzonzo would the water serpent release its captives. They crawled from the water on their knees, but were now powerful diviners with a wide assortment of potent herbs.[6]

Nkomo we Lwandle, Dunga Manzi and their trainees interpreted persistent pains, infertility, and bouts of aggression as signs that foreign spirits had entered the bodies of their clients. They identified three different kinds of spirits by the languages they spoke: the Malopo, who were Northern Sotho; the Ngoni (derived from the word Nguni) who were Shangaan, Zulu, or Swazi; and the Ndau who came from Musapa in Mozambique. Spirit possession nearly always involved a degree of culpability. The Ngoni spirits of the Swazi warriors possessed the descendants of the Northern Sotho who had killed them at the battle of Moholoholo in 1864. The Ndau, in turn, possessed the descendants of the Shangaan soldiers who had slain them and taken their wives in Gaza, Mozambique. In a ritual, which included drumming, the client danced until she or he experienced a trance. The healers then exhorted the spirits to speak through the mouth of the afflicted person and to state their demands. The healer also appeased the spirits and persuaded them to assist the afflicted person. Once converted from a hostile to a benevolent force, the spirit bestowed his or her medium with the power to divine, diagnose, and to heal various disorders and diseases. The Malopo specialised in treating venereal diseases and sick children; the Ngoni assisted with paralysis of the limbs and red spots; and the Ndau bestowed the ability to detect witchcraft.

Whereas most diviners were adult women, Dr Sugar was a young man in his late twenties. He was always immaculately dressed and was a certified member of the Traditional Healers' Organisation (THO), a nation-wide association of diviners. Members of the organisation pride themselves in dispensing natural herbal remedies, devoid of the harmful side-effects of the toxic tablets produced by pharmaceutical industries. Dr Sugar specialised in sniffing out witches through the use of divination lots, and relied upon powerful Ndau spirits for assistance. He did not quite have the prestige of the famous witch-diviners (*mungoma*) of Phunda Maria (bordering the Kruger National Park), or Mbuzini (near the borders between South Africa, Swaziland, and Mozambique).[7]

[6] Hirst (1993) observes that this myth resonates with the experience of birth. The foetus too lives in fluids inside the womb.

[7] West and Luedke (2006) argue that the idea of borders and of borderlands features prominently in the conceptions of folk healing in south-east Africa. The power to heal is frequently associated with the ability to cross borders, whether literal or metaphorical.

These witch-diviners usually command suspects to sit with their feet outstretched, and identify witches by beating them behind the neck with a wildebeest tail.

Dr Sugar charged R800 – sixteen times more than the usual fee of R50 – for a divinatory session in Bushbuckridge. This exorbitant amount attested to his special skills and gave his revelations about the unseen dimensions of the events greater authority than those of any of the diviners that Jessie's husband and in-laws might have consulted.

Kagišo (Jimmy's youngest sibling) gave the following account of their interactions with Dr Sugar:

After casting his divination bones, he told us [Moses and Kagišo] that someone within our own family is bewitching our mother. We compelled him to tell us the truth. He said, 'There are very dangerous things at your home.' So we asked, 'What things?' He again threw the bones. Then he looked at me and said, 'Why do you ask questions when you are so young?' Dr Sugar was straight. He said, 'Your father has a snake [mamlambo]. *' I was shocked to hear that word. 'Your father bought this snake because he wanted to be a foreman in the company where he worked. Your father has friends. He recruits them to kill others. They work like a society.*[8] *You should put medicine at your home.' Dr Sugar then told us that someone had already died at our home. We immediately remembered Kevin's death in 1984. He said, 'Your father killed this person. On the day that he died you sat at the table and your mother said his death was amazing.'*

As we walked away, Moses remarked, 'Maybe our father does have this thing?' Moses knew all along. At home I told my friend about the witch-diviner's revelations. But my friends warned me, 'Don't show your father that you know. He will kill you.'

On the day after Duduzile's funeral Moses and Kagišo asked their brothers, Jimmy and Henry, to accompany them to Dr Sugar so that they, too, could hear the truth. By now Jimmy had already suspected that his father might have practised witchcraft, but his encounter with Dr Sugar convinced him of his father's hidden identity. Jimmy described the consultation in the following words:

Just after we returned from the graveyard Moses asked Henry and me, 'Let's go and find out what harms our mother and what killed our sister's daughter.' We each popped out [contributed] R200 to pour petrol into my Corsa and to pay for the diviner. Whilst the other mourners were still with the bereaved family,

[8] In popular belief witchcraft is sometimes modelled on rotating credit societies, such as *stokvels*. Witches reportedly take turns to kill members of their families and contribute their flesh to the entire group for consumption in cannibalistic feasts. This practice is believed to have been more common in the past. Nowadays witches allegedly turn nearly all of their victims into zombies.

we climbed into the car. Moses and I sat in front and Henry and Kagišo sat behind [in the rear seat]. My father could see that people were not satisfied and he approached our car. But in his presence we said, 'Let's go!' Then we drove away, leaving him behind. We could see that my father was very angry.

When the four of us arrived, Dr Sugar said to us, 'Don't ask! I will tell you why you came here!' He instructed Moses and Kagišo to leave because he wanted to speak to Henry and to me alone. Dr Sugar told me about my childhood, and also about the deaths of Kevin, Enios [Mosoma, see pp. 86–87] and Jessie's daughter. Then he said, 'You've lost four cars. You nearly died when your cars overturned. Now you have this one. You are lucky. Your ancestors saved you.'

Dr Sugar's pronouncements made a deep impression on Jimmy: he felt that the diviner's narrative corresponded very closely to the events in his life. Jimmy believed that the pronouncement that the ancestors had saved him referred to his near-fatal car accident outside Middelburg and to his collision with a leopard on the dirt road outside Welverdient. By generating a shift to a non-normal mode of cognition, the divinatory revelations forced Jimmy to review known facts in a different perspective, and also to reorganise old elements in new arrangements (Peek 1991: 202).

I wanted to know what caused these accidents. Then Dr Sugar answered, 'There is something at your home. You can't see it. It breaks cars. It is your father. He is the one! He is a witch! Your father inherited a snake from his mother and he ordered potions from Durban to strengthen his witchcraft. He is very dangerous. Your father has killed many people and now he is trying to kill his wife. He has also sent a tokolotši *[the ape-like witch-familiar] to screw his sons and daughters-in-law. The* tokolotši *comes out at night, gets between the wife and her husband and then has sex with the wife. But in the morning she thinks that she had sex with the husband. You should praise Kagišo. He is younger than you, but he saw this before you did.' Dr Sugar also said that he could see what our mother's problems were and that he could come and fortify her and her home.*

These revelations provide apt testimony for Geertz's (1973a) assertion that religious formulations do not always provide comfort and confidence, but also have the capacity to disturb and to shake people out of their complacency. But Jimmy downplayed the dramatic impact of the encounter. In his account, Dr Sugar's divinatory revelations merely articulated a widely shared consensus, confirming what he had already suspected:[9]

I knew all along my father was a witch.

[9] Turner (1967b) and Peters (1972) argue that amongst the Ndembu and the Azande, respectively, divination provides a means of formulation and expressing a social consensus. They accord diviners a far less prominent role in shaping people's worldview than Peek (1991) does.

But Kagišo insisted that Dr Sugar's revelations were a crucial turning point for Jimmy and had a powerful cathartic effect.

Jimmy was shaken. He had always trusted our father with all his heart. When Jimmy came out of the divination hut [ndumba], *you could see that he was upset. He told us that Dr Sugar spoke the truth and that he believed everything Dr Sugar said. Then he started to cry. Jimmy said, 'I never ever want to see our father anymore! My dad is a witch!' He even asked Moses to drive back home. All the way back home, Jimmy sat on the back seat, crying. That evening Jimmy did not drink any beers at home.*

Luckson immediately confronted his sons when they returned from Dr Sugar. Jimmy recalled that he scolded them in the following words:

'I know you are from a diviner. Why do you go to diviners now that the child is dead? Why did you not go to the diviners when the child was still alive?' I just looked at him. Where the hell did he get that information from?

Jimmy observed that in the week after Duduzile's death, several uncanny events happened at her mother's home. In his opinion these events confirmed Dr Sugar's revelations that witches had captured Duduzile, and tried to change her into a zombie:

After everyone had left I was worried that my sister, Jessie, would be unable to cope. . . . One morning the next-door neighbour came to Jessie's home and said, 'I dreamt about your daughter. In my dream I saw your child running. Some people were trying to grab her. She then developed wings and flew away, like an angel.'[10] *My sister responded and said, 'A dream is a dream! My daughter is late [dead] and she can't come back. No person can bring her back!'*

But later Jessie came to me and said, 'My brother. I have a problem. When my husband is gone at work, people come to my home each evening, stand at the corner, and blow a rheebuck horn.' She pointed to the corner where they usually stood and said, 'I don't know who they are, but they call the name of my deceased daughter when they blow the horn.' My sister later invited the men's dance group [mkhukhu] *from her church [the ZCC] to sleep at her home. That evening she switched the lights off early and sent out the boys to investigate [who was blowing the horn]. When the boys came back they said that the culprits were my father and his friend, Pheko. The ZCC prophets also told Jessie that our father and his accomplice had killed Duduzile and wanted to turn her into a zombie. But my father and Pheko found it very difficult [to do so] because Duduzile was no ordinary child. She had an aura* [seriti] *of seniority and she was a child of the ancestors. My father and Pheko searched for her, but they could not find her.*

[10] Residents of Bushbuckridge do not dismiss dreams as being irrelevant to their everyday lives. Like divination, they provide cryptic images of transcendent realities that are translated and discussed, leading people to evaluate known observations in the light of a new paradigm (Jedrej and Shaw 1992).

Although Jimmy and his siblings informed their mother, *ngwa* Ngobeni, about the diviner's revelations, she could no longer remain at Jessie's home. By now the tensions between her and her son-in-law, who still suspected her of practising witchcraft, had become unbearable. *Ngwa* Ngobeni therefore decided to return to her husband, Luckson. She would rather risk living with a potential witch, than with those who suspected her of witchcraft.

This episode suggests the over-determined and at times circular character of witchcraft. In certain respects, the roles of accused and accuser constitute each other. This is apparent in Ashforth's (1993) description of Madumo, who is accused by kin of bewitching his own mother, but sees the experience of being labelled as a witch as a sign that he himself is a victim of witchcraft. Likewise, *ngwa* Ngobeni and Jimmy himself were both accused and accusers. Accusing others was one of the few ways out of being accused, of shifting culpability, and of claiming protection and support.

Before she returned, *ngwa* Ngobeni's sons asked Dr Sugar to fortify her and her home against her husband's witchcraft. Jimmy recalled:

I fetched my mother and took her to Dr Sugar. He cut small incisions on her body and rubbed potions into them. Then, when my father was attending a night vigil [for another funeral], Dr Sugar came to fortify the home. He sprinkled potions so that my mother could return. This was done so that my father's tokolotši *and* mamlambo *would not kill her when she entered the home. Later, we collected my mother from Tsakani. When my father returned, he was surprised to find his wife at home. He asked my mother, 'Where were you? Even your sons won't tell me where you were. This is not normal.' She was cheeky and replied, 'Ask those who bewitched me where I was.' My father then asked her, directly, 'Do you think I bewitched you?' But my mother did not answer [him]. Finally, my father asked her, 'Do you also wish to kill me?' My mother replied, 'No! I don't necessarily want to kill you. But I'm prepared to kill anyone who disturbs my children and wrecks their futures. I am prepared to kill anyone who is involved with witchcraft and wants to kill me.'*

On another occasion Jimmy also asked minister (*moruti*) Mkhari from the St Engenas church [another ZCC congregation] to fortify his mother's yard:

Mkhari also told us that there was a pot full of human blood in the centre of the yard. He said that there was a snake inside the pot. He also said that there were powerful familiars – a tokolotši, *and a zombie – inside the home. Mkhari told us that witches used the zombie to torment our family. I think the minister spoke about Kevin who died in 1984. Mkhari wanted to cleanse and strengthen himself at Moria [the ZCC headquarters] before he could fortify the home. Because Mkhari had lost his job at the Air Force base in Hoedspruit, he asked me for R100 [for transport] to go to Moria. When the minister returned from Moria, he used a concoction of many things [to fortify the home]: spirits, salt, coffee and chillies. He sprinkled these around the whole yard and also put river stones in the garden.*[11] *My mother told us that after he left, she could sleep nicely and no longer awoke with bodily pains.*

Jimmy heard through the grapevine that Jessie's affines – the Manzini family – were still extremely angry about Duduzile's death and had consulted a diviner, asking him to use vengeance magic [*letswa*] to strike down the responsible witch. However, the diviner demanded R2,500 – an amount they could not afford.

'I See Things Differently Now'

For Jimmy the weeks after Dr Sugar's revelations were ones of deep reflection and contemplation. The revelations compelled him to reorganise knowledge he had previously taken for granted and to see the unfortunate events that had plagued his father's agnates, the members of his own household, and also his own life in a completely different light. He no longer saw these incidents of misfortune as random events of chance. He now saw them as patterned, and recognised a very powerful, sinister, and malevolent hand behind their occurrence.

Jimmy now believed that his father, Luckson, had inherited his witch-familiars from his grandmother, Nana. For Jimmy there was now little doubt that his father had been responsible for the death of his agnates Doris Mosoma, her son Malebo, and her grandson, Enios:

My father sent his familiars to put the aura [seriti] *of a witch on Doris. This made people believe that she is a witch whenever they looked at her. My father caused this misfortune for her. His familiars made people brand her a witch. This is because she knew that he was a witch.*

Moreover, Jimmy argued that his father had cast a bad spell [*bati*] on Enios. Like a dark cloud hanging over a person, this spell had made Enios vulnerable to attack by the ritual murderers.

At home, Jimmy said, his father secretly collaborated with the other witches in their neighbourhood. Together with them, he bewitched his own son, Kevin, and caused the spouses of his children to desert them.

My father disliked Violet because the white person that she dreamt of was really the tokolotši *of his homestead. My father hated her. He bewitched her so that she did not conceive. In all the time that she spent with us, she never had a*

[11] There is a popular saying, 'a witch cannot cross a river' (*moloi ga a tshele noka*). River stones are therefore believed to obstruct the progress of witches, and to block their paths.

baby. All the shit business was the work of my father. My father will make you quarrel for no reason at all.

He also used potions to let me separate from my wife. He must have used setenya *or* patanya *[well-known potions] to make us get bored with each other. If your father is a witch he will cast a spell on your family. Then strange things will happen, but you will not take them into consideration. It is only later that you might ask yourself. 'This was strange. Why did I not see this before?' We did not believe we should question our father because he was senior to us.*

He also held his father responsible for his mother's illness, Duduzile's death, and for destroying his sedans and Mazda 1800 utility van in order to prevent him from driving his mother to consult diviners.

Dr Sugar's revelations did not merely make Jimmy see older events in a new light, but also made him more receptive to gossip about his father. Stories that he previously dismissed now seemed plausible to him. He heard that a Malawian man called Mataitai ('miracles'), with whom Luckson worked in Phalaborwa, might have given Luckson a snake:

Mataitai worked together with my father at Louw transport in Nelspruit. He drove a Ford Anglia and he always demonstrated his magic. The other workers said that Mataitai's potions made you powerful and caused white people to like you. When you used his potions you could tell the white manager, 'Fire this man.' Then the manager will immediately do so. My father worked as a foreman and the whites always liked him. He called the shots at work and the employers always took his word.

Jimmy also heard from a childhood friend called Boyboy that his father had been accused of witchcraft when he worked for Potgieter (the owner of another transport business) in Nelspruit.

Boyboy attended school with my brother, Moses. Boyboy knew my parents very well. He sometimes slept over at our home. One evening Boyboy found me at Banda [the tavern in Acornhoek]. He asked me, 'How are you my brother? Where is your father? Do you still visit him?' I said, 'No. I don't visit my father any longer.'

Boyboy then told me, 'Your father is a witch. I used to work with your father at Potgieter transport in Nelspruit and he used to screw us at night with his tokolotši. *Everyone complained about him. Do you know the scar on your father's forehead? Let me tell you where it comes from. Where we stayed in Nelspruit we did not have enough accommodation. Some of us used to sleep in the trucks. One evening your father went naked to bewitch one of our colleagues called Mbembe. Your father slept in the truck and Mbembe slept in the house because he was senior. We saw your father's silhouette pass by Mbembe's window. When Mbembe saw that it was your father he asked: "Luckson! What are you doing here?" Your father replied, "I'm only passing."*

But before long your father came back. Mbembe stood up, took a stick and hit your father all over his body. Your father screamed, "Mbembe don't kill me!" But Mbembe said, "You are bewitching me! The diviners told me about you!" The other truck drivers then came to your father's rescue. He was bleeding.'

'I hated Mbembe when he beat your father, but later on things also started going wrong for me. I went to see a diviner and he told me that your father screws us with his tokolotši. *The* tokolotši *screwed us all night long so that we would be weak in the morning. The* tokolotši *also screwed our wives.'*

Boyboy told me that this happened in 1995 and in 1996. He also said that many truck drivers, who worked with my father, capsized. Some even died. My father killed these people.

Jimmy only once confronted his father. One evening when he was extremely drunk, he went to his father's home, and screamed at him. Jimmy reportedly accused his father of practising witchcraft and of attempting to kill his mother and himself. But since then Jimmy had not spoken to him. For three years he avoided his father at all costs. Jimmy even refused to accompany me in my car whenever I drove past his father's home.

Being Fortified in Phalaborwa

These revelations of witchcraft reinforced the oedipal tensions of anxiety and repressed anger that Jimmy harboured towards his father. Jimmy told me that he now had frequent nightmares of being bewitched:

I have dreamt of my father several times. In one of my dreams he wore a black blazer and he held a community meeting of some sort. I was seated and he spoke about me. He said of me, 'I don't like this youngster! He is troublesome! He blocks my witchcraft!' Whilst he spoke I ran away. My father saw me running past ngwa *Nokeri's home and he started to chase me. I ran and he came following me. At Chiloane's place he caught up with me. He overpowered me and tried to kill me.*

But my brothers arrived and asked him, 'What are you doing to Jimmy?' My brothers then grabbed my father and assaulted him. I saw Henry holding a hammer and I snatched the hammer from Henry and started beating my father. I beat him on the knees. I wanted to kill him. He yelled from the pain. Then I said, 'We can only sort this out one way! If the diviners and the prophets won't kill you we'll contribute money and hire men [retainers] to do the job.' My father asked, 'Are you really going to kill me?' Then I replied, 'Yes.'

The dream clearly expressed Jimmy's fear of death. It is significant that in the dream Jimmy confounded the images of the Mapulaneng Burial Society, of which his father is a spokesperson, and of a gathering of witches. It is also significant that he describes his siblings as rescuing him. This alludes to the enduring cooperative nature of the bond between Jimmy and his brothers.

Whilst disturbing, the revelations, nonetheless, enabled Jimmy to pinpoint the source of the multiple misfortunes that he and his relatives encountered. Jimmy now focused on cleaning the misfortune from his body and on fortifying himself against witchcraft. For this purpose, he accompanied his siblings, Jessie and Kagišo, to consult a renowned Apostolic prophet in Phalaborwa.

The practice of Zionist and Apostolic healers, who treated clients at home, resonated with those of diviners. As in the case of diviners their calling was preceded by a bout of illness. But in this case, Christian healers exorcised rather than accommodated the possessing spirits. During the process of recovery the afflicted person entered into a close relationship with the Holy Spirit, who bestowed the powers of divination and healing, showing the causes of sickness, the prognosis, and appropriate remedies. As a method of divination Christian healers used a multicoloured cord called 'chain' (*moketane*). The healers cast the cord to the ground and observed its position to gain insight into aspects of the client's condition. Moreover, Christian healers used inorganic medicines, providing a stark contrast with the organic potions used by diviners and witches (Hammond-Tooke 1989: 140, Niehaus 2001: 31–6).

Jimmy described the therapeutic encounter as follows:

We arrived in Phalaborwa by taxi at 6.30 [am] and the prophet immediately recognised my sister. He said that he had seen Jessie in his dreams. The prophet operates at the taxi rank rather than at his home and he made us sit on stones. The prophet told me that the problem with my body is that witches had sent a tokolotši *to beat me up at night. But my maternal ancestor [identified as Ramadimabe] protects me. He said our family is disintegrating and that I complain of money. This is because the witch-familiars take my money. I go to sleep with R200, but when I awake there is only R150 in my pocket. He also said that there are ghosts* [sepoko] *on my body. These ghosts cause people to hate me. People look at me and they quarrel with me for no reason. This was also correct. The prophet also said that my wife had been bewitched, so that we should fight all the time. Every time we speak about money we quarrel. This is why we don't progress. The prophet warned me not to drive my car because witches had placed a* tokolotši *in my car. This will cause an accident. If I do not fortify my car I would die.*

The prophet told Jessie that our mother had been bewitched. Whilst we slept at night the witches used her as a familiar. He also told her about the death of a child. Someone gave the child R3. But the money was bewitched. The child used it to buy biscuits and when she ate the biscuits, it turned into snakes inside her stomach. The snakes bit the child to death. The prophet also mentioned to

Jessie that zombies visited her home and tried to open the doors and windows. . . . I was not interested in all those things [revelations]. They are not new. I already knew.

Jimmy found these revelations to be truthful. Experiences at school also made him think that he might well have a ghost [*sepoko*] on his body:

I am always friendly at work, but the other teachers quarrel with me for no reason. I will go to school in the morning. Then someone will insult me for no reason. I asked Mokoena for periods for my students to write a test. But Mokoena became long-faced and went hysterical. He shouted at me. 'You are just here to offend me. I can give anyone periods, but not you.' I replied, 'Fuck you! Don't belittle me in front of the kids!' He then told the principal that I just go into the classrooms to harass people where they were teaching. She [the principal] also did not want to listen to me.

Previously Jimmy attributed his problems at school to his marginality, lack of political connections, and nepotistic practices in the new Department of Education. Now these explanations receded into the background, and witchcraft became a powerful, all-encompassing, single-stranded explanation for his lack of progress. This change constituted an important shift in explanatory paradigm.

A new diagnosis paved the way for new therapies, which he saw as creating the possibility of eventual healing and recovery. Jimmy returned to Phalaborwa the next day to fetch prescriptions from the Holy Spirit (*ditaelo*) that he used to fortify his body against witchcraft:

The prophet said we should come back the next morning for the prescriptions. We paid nothing for the consultation, but we gave him R70 so that he could take a taxi to fetch water for us from the big mountains and scary rivers at Lulekani. He said that the R70 was too much. His powers are from God and if he became greedy they won't work. That evening I went into a drinking house, drank, got drunk and slept.

The next morning at 6.45 [am], I was back in Phalaborwa. At 6.55 the prophet appeared. He gave me fortified wool and told me to put it in my house. He also gave me prescriptions for washing my car and for washing my body for seven days. For this he demanded no fees. But he said that I would have to pay him R400 if he came to Impalahoek to fortify my car. This is because he might come across a mamlambo *[the snake-like witch-familiar] and risk his life.*

Jimmy did not request the prophet to accompany him to Impalahoek, because he did not have enough money.

The same day I started feeling better. After I had washed myself I could feel the changes. That evening I came home and slept. I slept with my wife and with my boy. At five [am], I awoke. At that exact moment a huge thing fell from the tree in front of our house. I heard no footsteps. I looked outside and saw nothing. But I was not scared. Something just told me to sleep. The next morning early I visited my sister [Jessie]. She just laughed. She said that the familiars could not get me because of the woollen cord. 'You surprised and trapped the witch whilst you were sleeping.'

After he had been fortified, Jimmy gained newfound confidence, and this is indicated by the changing nature of his nightmares, in which he was able to thwart witchcraft attacks. It is interesting that in the dream it is now he who rescues his siblings rather than vice versa.

In my last dream I saw my neighbour. She stood at our fence and pushed against the gate. She asked me, 'I want to speak to Henry.' But I said, 'No. You can't.' I could see that she meant Henry harm. Then I wrestled with her. She pushed me and tried to overpower me. But I showed her that I was fortified. She was disillusioned. She became angry and turned back. . . . I won't say that my life is back on track, but I am surviving.

7 Seeking Revenge

After the unbanning of the ANC important changes took place in the nature of witchcraft accusations and the political management thereof. During the uprisings of the 1980s local political activists such as the Comrades took an unambiguous stance against witchcraft. The Comrades attacked witches in an attempt to root out evil, and thereby stake a claim to being legitimate and influential political actors. But, since 1990, the national executive of the ANC has strictly forbidden its members from engaging in witch-hunts. In line with this policy, police officers received instructions to 'stamp out these barbaric killings' by arresting all witch-hunters (*Weekend Argus*, 18/19 March 1995).

Because villagers still expected political leaders to assist them in their struggles against witchcraft, the ANC's policy placed local politicians in a Catch-22 situation. By suppressing witch-hunting they could earn a reputation of siding with witches and risk losing support among villagers. But if they acceded to the popular demand to act against witches, they risked being condemned by the ANC national executive to whom they are accountable. Therefore, witch-hunting now involved considerable political contestation (Niehaus 2001: 156–82).

At first, the local ANC leaders took a cautious approach and sought to strike a balance between these conflicting demands. For example, ANC leaders did not stop the witch-hunt of December 1990 (see Chapter 1), but rather sought to minimise its violence by forcing the accused to burn witchcraft potions in public. But over the years local ANC leaders have became more inclined to comply with the directives of their political superiors, and have refrained from involving themselves in witch-hunting. On a number of occasions during the 1990s, villagers took suspected witches to the police station. The police eventually earmarked a small section of land, behind the station, where the accused witches could live. In November 1994 the police went so far as to arrest four witch-hunters from the village of Rooiboklaagte and to lock them in the cells. More than four hundred protesters gathered outside the station, sang freedom songs, and demanded that the witch-hunters be released. Such episodes left the villagers with the impression that the new government would not be sympathetic to the plight of the bewitched.

Only isolated instances of witch-killing occurred in this context. One morning in 1999, residents of a section of Impalahoek found the badly mutilated corpse of Elias Pheko lying in the street outside his home. Elias was an elderly man whom many suspected of practising witchcraft. Although it was commonly assumed that some of the old man's accusers had attacked him with bricks during the night, no arrests were made. Elias simply had too many enemies: it proved impossible to determine which ones had been responsible for his death.

There has also been a re-invention of vengeance magic – an older strategy for dealing with witchcraft. Until the 1960s villagers frequently consulted 'doctor witches' (*dingaka baloi*) to take revenge for the deaths of their close relatives. These ritual specialists treated the corpse with a potion called *letšwa*, which allegedly caused the killer to die in a similar manner to that of his or her victim. But following the conversion of many villagers to Zionist and Apostolic churches the practice of vengeance magic came to be seen as illegitimate. The dualistic cosmology of these churches drew a Manichean opposition between the forces of good (*botse*) and evil (*bobe*), and between the activities of healers and witches. During the 1990s, however, the criminalisation of other modes of punishing witches left many villagers with little alternative other than to deploy vengeance magic. Villagers deemed vengeance magic to be eminently appropriate because it operates in the same mystical domain as witchcraft: a domain located outside South Africa's formal legal system. Thus the practice of vengeance magic has again blurred the boundaries between good and evil.

Events that occurred in a neighbouring village were pivotal in the resurgence of vengeance magic. During 1997 there were many uncanny deaths in the village, and the local Civic Association collected donations of R10 from each household to hire the services of a diviner to fortify their village against witchcraft. The diviner first announced that all witches should leave, and he then set about laying potions at all roads and footpaths leading into the village. Last, the diviner asked everyone to remove their shoes whenever they entered the graveyard, so that they would not bring soil from the domain of the dead into the realm of the living. He also warned people not to drink, nor to smoke in the graveyard. Only days thereafter an elderly woman collapsed and died near the bus stop. Villagers had long suspected her of being a witch, and believed that the diviner's potions had struck her down. In the next three weeks there were no more deaths in the village.

Thus, when Jimmy and his siblings met in 2003 to discuss what they should do about their father's witchcraft, they decided upon using vengeance magic. They feared that if they hired retainers to kill him, they could be arrested and forced to serve lengthy prison sentences. Jimmy had listened carefully to some of our interviewees describe the dreadful conditions they had experienced in South Africa's overcrowded prisons. In particular, he feared being raped by the notorious '28' prison gang (see Niehaus 2002c; Gear 2005). The Mohale siblings eventually decided to hire a diviner to make their father's witchcraft rebound, and thus to avenge Duduzile's death.

Contesting the Truth, 2004

From being his father's fiercest defender, Jimmy had become his most vociferous and vocal accuser. But he soon learnt that not everyone shared his newfound conviction. His wife, Lerato, and even his younger brother, Henry, still firmly believed in Luckson's innocence. Lerato regularly visited Luckson to complain about Jimmy's extramarital affairs. She also informed him that his children were holding secret meetings at the home of Andrew (Jimmy's oldest half-brother), where they were accusing him of witchcraft. Luckson told Lerato that he was completely amazed and that he had been totally unaware that his sons were so resentful of him. Lerato said that she knew he was innocent and vowed to support him: she even offered to pay for the family to consult a witch-diviner (*mungoma*) to prove once and for all that he was not a witch.

Lerato also complained to Henry about Jimmy's extramarital affairs and his mistaken belief that their father practised witchcraft. This upset Jimmy enormously, because he had always greatly admired his younger brother. By then Henry had already obtained an MA degree in Information Science and was working as a subject librarian at the University of Limpopo – formerly known as the University of the North. Unlike Jimmy, Henry refused to accept Dr Sugar's revelations. Jimmy told me that his father had bewitched Henry to cause him not to believe in witchcraft:

We four brothers [Moses, Peter, Kagišo, and Jimmy] all agreed that my father is a witch, but not Henry. Henry seemed to believe Dr Sugar when he was there, but my father buried potions underneath the gate. As soon as Henry visited my father and got into the home, our father would ask him, 'Do you really think I am a witch as the others say?' Then Henry would answer our father, 'No!' It is the potions that changed his mind. Henry did not like me to say that our father is a witch. Can you see what potions can do to a person?

For about ten months, Jimmy and Henry refused to speak to each other. Jimmy was angry because Henry refused to accept the revelations about their father, and also because Henry was interfering with his marriage and siding with his wife against him. Once, Henry even invited Lerato and her children to visit him and his wife at the University of the Limpopo for almost three weeks. Neither Lerato nor Henry had informed Jimmy about the visit.

Henry stayed with their father, Luckson, whenever he visited Bushbuckridge. In 2003, much to Jimmy's dismay, Henry decided to build his parents a new seven-roomed home at a cost of more than R85,000. Jimmy expressed himself as follows:

We all tried to discourage Henry from building this large home for one man and his wife. Why did he build the home? So that my father's snake and tokolotši *[ape-like familiar] could each have their own rooms? So my father can acquire more familiars?*

However, Jimmy observed that Henry never completed the home because the builders he employed absconded from work as soon as they heard of Luckson's witchcraft.

First, Mashile laid the foundation of the house, but he left for no reason. Mnisi then built the house, but he complained of his legs and his feet. Then he also left. Hereafter, Skukuza worked on the house. But when Skukuza heard that my father is a witch, he also left, saying, 'I hear your father does what my father does.' [At that time Skukuza accused his own father of witchcraft.] Henry hired two new bricklayers, but they also left. Lastly, he paid Rocco R4,000 to roof the house, but to this day the roof is incomplete. All those people complained about my father.[1]

Rebecca Mohale's Sickness

Only after the sickness and death of Moses's daughter, Rebecca Mohale, did Jimmy and Henry again speak to one another. Rebecca studied catering at a college in Phalaborwa and then found work as a chef at a luxurious holiday resort, about thirty kilometres north of Bushbuckridge. Rebecca was twenty-seven years old and single when she became seriously ill. During September 2004, Rebecca fainted at work, and her colleagues brought her back to Moses's home in Tsakani.

In conversation with Jimmy, I often insisted that Rebecca should be taken to medical doctors (in addition to consulting diviners), and that the Mohale family should obtain a medical diagnosis of her condition. But Jimmy was evasive. He seemed to suggest that it was a complete waste

[1] Most houses in Bushbuckridge are not built through a single contract with a single building company. Given financial constraints and the irregular availability of cash, houses are usually built in different stages, and frequently involve several contracts with many different builders. Moreover, companies seldom build houses. Instead, they are constructed by networks of otherwise unemployed young men, who are recruited on a personal basis. The nucleus of these networks is often former prisoners, who learn building skills as part of their rehabilitation from crime in jail. These factors might well explain the frequent changes in building personnel that Jimmy observed.

of time even to talk about clinical medicine when it was so blatantly apparent that Rebecca had been bewitched:

When Rebecca's illness was still in the initial stage, her mother and her aunt, who is a nurse, took her to Tintswalo Hospital. But they waited for hours. They went there at seven [am] and only returned at five [pm]. The more doctors they consulted, the more her illness worsened. They went to a private doctor and came back with tablets. He could not tell them what was wrong. The second time they went to Tintswalo was in mid-October. Again, the doctors could not see anything wrong and did not hospitalise her. They also consulted the clinic, where my aunt works. We tried everything, but there was no improvement. Dr Gumede was the only one who gave us a diagnosis. He looked at her and said that she had tuberculosis.

In South Africa tuberculosis is the primary AIDS-related sickness. At least one third of South Africans are exposed to it as children. Tuberculosis remains dormant, but is reactivated by the suppressed immunity associated with HIV (see Walker, Reid, and Cornell 2004: 73; Iliffe 2006: 45). Many of Rebecca's neighbours gossiped that she had begun to develop opportunistic infections. They said that she suffered from hallucinations, resembling the sort of dementia that occurs in the latter stages of AIDS. But Jimmy vehemently denied this:

Rebecca had an HIV test the second time they took her to hospital and she tested negative. After the result we realised that she does not have AIDS and that she could be bewitched. That is when we went to the prophets.

Rebecca's mother, too, believed that Luckson had bewitched her daughter:

One day my father visited Rebecca, and my sister-in-law argued with him. She asked my father, 'Why is it that Rebecca gets better, but as soon as you enter the house she becomes worse? Why is it that she calls your name whenever she hallucinates?' Since that day my father no longer visited Rebecca.

As Rebecca's condition became critical, Jimmy and his siblings consulted an array of Christian healers and diviners.

One day my brother [Moses] phoned me from Johannesburg. He said, 'Jimmy please, help me. My daughter is very sick!' I saw Rebecca, and took her to a prophet in Violetbank. I parted with R800. He gave Rebecca many things. She became better, but only for a little while. Her hallucinations became so bad. She had to be bedridden.

Early one morning at five [am] Moses's son woke me and said, 'My mother sent me to fetch you now.' I ran to her home and when I arrived I saw everyone standing outside. They told me that the young woman was ill. Rebecca never slept, but she hallucinated and showed signs of madness. We used Moses's car and took her to a diviner called Rola – her name means to lift something which is heavy. I asked for the bones [divination lots]. Rola said that witches were trying to capture [dlo kola] *a young woman in our family and change her into a zombie. But Rola would not tell us who was responsible. We had to pay R50 for the bones and another R150 for* femba.

During the *femba* rituals I witnessed in Bushbuckridge the patient usually sat on the ground with her feet outstretched, as described in the previous chapter, and the diviner used a switch manufactured from wildebeest hair to sniff witch-familiars from the patient's body. The familiars allegedly entered the diviner's body through the nose and she instantly assumed the familiar's behaviour. The diviner could, for example, slither like a snake or shriek like a cat. Finally, the diviner sneezed out the familiars, thereby ridding the client's body from the heavy, oppressive feelings of misfortune.

Jimmy recalled that, on this particular occasion, Rola's daughter beat the ancestral drums. Rola herself danced until she experienced a frenzied trance. She first assumed the identity of an ape-like witch-familiar, then that of a grunting baboon, and finally that of an elderly male person, said to be the witch himself:

I was very scared when Rola did the femba *with the wildebeest tail. First, a* tokolotši *came out from Rebecca's body and then howling baboons. My father also came out. I clearly heard my father's voice. He was arguing with me, saying 'Why do you try to help your brother's family? Why do you pretend that you are intelligent? I don't have time to argue with boys. I have already taken the meat [presumably of the victim], but this Shangaan does not allow me to eat.' He was referring to my maternal ancestor – Ramadimabe. After my father shouted at me, he became angry and went for the child [Rebecca]. Her legs were stretched forward, but he hit her very hard on the back. My father then left the divination hut. As he left, he said to me, 'I will see you* [ke tlo go bona – *the most potent curse*]. *You are a youngster, but you interfere with my business.'*

On occasions such as during the *femba* ritual, diviners typically speak in a low-pitched, guttural, tone. Their cryptic speech is usually barely audible. Yet Jimmy claimed that he clearly heard his father's words. These seemed to confirm to him an ongoing battle between his father, as immoral wreaker of death and destruction, and both himself – acting in a positive social way to save his kin by consulting diviners – and his ancestress Ramadimabe, who has been his mystical protector since he was named after her in babyhood. By assuming that Ramadimabe, despite her Northern Sotho name, was Shangaan, Jimmy associates her with his maternal rather than paternal kin.

Rola, the diviner, convinced Jimmy that she had successfully removed Luckson's aura [*seriti*] from Rebecca's body. Rola explained to Jimmy that witches had already captured the child's breath (*moya*) and that they were now waiting for her to die. But both the diviner and Jimmy were convinced that Rebecca's ancestors fiercely protected her and had successfully thwarted the witches' intentions. Rola stretched Rebecca's limbs (*go olola*) to let the heat escape from her body. She then asked Jimmy to let Rebecca undergo an apprenticeship to become a diviner.

But these measures did not cure Rebecca. Jimmy simply commented:

I took her home, but she did not get any better.

Convincing Henry Mohale

After Jimmy heard Rola's revelations and personally encountered his father's spirit, he became confident that any diviner who was worth her or his salt could convince his brother, Henry, of their father's culpability. Hence in November 2004, Jimmy asked Henry to accompany him to another local diviner, called Staal ('Steel' in Afrikaans) Mashego. However, Staal told the two brothers that their problems were far too severe for him to handle. Instead, he advised them to consult the more powerful diviners of Phunda Maria. Staal's assistance went beyond mere advice: he even offered to drive Jimmy and Henry to Phunda Maria in his own Toyota Conquest:

We first drove to Polokwane: Staal and I slept at the home of my brother-in-law in town and Henry slept at his own home in Turfloop. The next morning we woke up early and by four [am] we were ready to fetch Henry. Henry took R300 and the three of us drove to Phunda Maria.

At 8.30 [am] we arrived at our contact person and we told him, 'Let's go! Take us to the most powerful diviner you know!' He took us to Chaoke. We paid R55 and he threw the lots. Chaoke then said, 'You guys have a problem. You guys are from far. I can see. It is a big problem. People are no longer staying in the house. You want them to stay together and to resolve the problems.' Henry then punctuated [interrupted] the diviner and asked him directly, 'I want to know if my father is a witch.' But the diviner was evasive. He ended up saying, 'I can't tell you exactly. We diviners may not say whether people are witches or not. If we tell people they might end up killing others.' We did not want Chaoke to continue and thanked him.

Our contact person then took us to Rambane. We went into his divination hut [ndumba] *and we asked him directly to tell us what is wrong. Rambane said, 'There is a problem in your house. I can see a* tokolotši *and snakes. They are troubling people. The* tokolotši *screws your wives at night and the snake steals your money. The snake also eats your children. It will also eat you if it is not stopped.' We asked Rambane, 'Who owns the snake? Is it our father or our mother? Who owns the snake?' He replied, 'Are you resilient? Will you be able to handle what I tell you?' Then he said, 'Your father is a big witch. He obtained a snake from Malawians and Zimbabweans.' I then turned to Henry and asked him, 'Henry! What do you say about this?' The diviner continued, 'Your father knows right now that you are here. That man is so powerful! He can kill you.' I again asked Henry, 'See! What can you say?' At last Henry replied and told me, 'Yes. Now I am satisfied* [convinced]. *'*

Henry then asked Rambane, 'Can you help our father to throw away the snake?' Rambane said, 'No. I can't. The snake is in him . . . There is no way of getting rid of it. The only way that you can help this man is to have him killed with vengeance magic [letšwa]. *' I asked Rambane, 'Have you got potions that can kill our father?' He replied, 'No. My potions are too weak. It won't do anything to him.' I then asked, 'Do you know someone else?' He said, 'Yes. There was an old man here who could do it. But he is now late [deceased]. I will recommend another Shangaan – Zingiri.'*

We approached Zingiri's house. There was a very large tree inside his yard and many NW [Northwest Province] cars parked in the street outside. These cars had come from about seven hundred kilometres away, so you can see how popular he was. Zingiri asked us to enter, but instructed Staal, 'You stay outside.' He told us, 'I knew that you were coming. You are from far away and you are anxious. Give me two minutes. Then I'll be with you.' Then he said, 'My consultation fee is R55.' I punctuated [interrupted] him and said, 'We don't want divining lots.' He said, 'Wait! You are from two divination huts [ndumba]. *The first diviner told you stories and because of this you were angry. The second diviner was good, but he does not have potions.' I said, 'Yes! It is the second diviner who referred us to you.' Zingiri then asked, 'What do you want me to do?' I said, 'I want you to kill our father!'*

Zingiri continued, saying, 'Since you are here I feel obliged to tell you something. When you still stood outside my home I threw my lots. This is what I can tell you. Your father is a real witch and he has a big snake. This man is like a university. He provides all the other witches with potions to kill their victims. He can provide potions for everything: even if you want people's cars to capsize or if you want them to divorce. He has killed many people and he will still kill many more. Your father is a ruthless witch. . . . I can kill him, but I do not have the correct potions with me right now. Please give me a week. Then I'll go and get them in Mozambique. You must return, fetch me, and take me to your place. I will do my things there and when I'm done the owner and his snake will both die.' We asked Zingiri, 'How much will this cost?' He replied, 'The price is not negotiable. This man is dangerous. He can kill me. I ask R3,000! Take it or leave it.'

Hereafter we drove back to Polokwane. Now Henry was convinced. Now he knew for certain that his father was a witch. Henry said that for as long as our father is alive he will not complete the house that he is building for our parents.

Once back home in Impalahoek, the Mohale brothers – Jimmy, Moses, Peter, and Henry – agreed to contribute R1,500 each to pay Zingiri and his assistants to kill their father. They agreed to fetch Zingiri during the Christmas vacation.

The Horrible Journey to Bochum

The Mohale siblings had set a firm date to travel to Phundu Maria. But they were compelled to change their arrangements. Peter Mohale unexpectedly asked his family members to accompany him to visit his in-laws in Bochum – a village outside Polokwane – on 25 November. Peter had to make his final bridewealth payments and to attend the ceremonial unveiling of a tombstone.

Before the journey, Jimmy had a premonition that their father would attempt to bewitch them on the way to Bochum. He had a nightmare in which he dreamt of a burning car. For this reason he and his brothers first consulted a local diviner to ascertain whether it was safe to travel:

I said to Peter, 'Peter, my brother, our father is a witch. We can't just go to Bochum.' My brothers said, 'Alright.' They agreed that we should see a woman who is a diviner in Casteel. After we paid R50 for the divination lots, she told us that it would be safe to travel. 'You'll go to Bochum and you'll return.'

Jimmy also made an invocation to his maternal ancestor, Ramadimabe, to ensure her protection. Yet, despite these precautions, their journey to and from Bochum turned out to be a horrible experience:

We were supposed to leave for Bochum on 25th November, but we only left on the 26th. There was a problem. Peter had not made the arrangements for transport on time. He also did not have enough money. Peter told us that he had R2,000 in his bank account, but on the 25th the auto-teller indicated that he had no money left in his account. We had to go and borrow money from a moneylender and from our cousin in Casteel. Mahero, the taxi owner, asked R1,400 to transport our party of 15 people to Bochum. The transport was so expensive because that place is so far – more than three hundred and something kilometres.

We were satisfied with the taxi and early in the morning we fetched the people. There was Moses, Jessie, Peter, Kagišo and his wife, Henry, myself, four of our children, and Philipos, our cousin. We also had to fetch three other people from Polokwane. Peter's in-laws phoned us and said that they wanted to unveil the tombstone at eight [am]. We agreed to leave at four [am], but we could only manage to get away at five [am]. First, we discovered that our driver was too drunk to drive and we had to look for someone else.

We drove from here to Scotchia [only about ten kilometres]. But then the engine gushed oil and then spilled water. We had to phone Mahero and ask him to bring another taxi. Mahero came at ten past six, told us that the bearings and the engine were fucked up, and then asked us to transfer to a new taxi. But we had only driven a few kilometres further when we discovered that the new taxi was also a wreck [sekorokoro]. *We therefore asked the driver to drive very slowly. Because the accelerator did not function properly we could not drive through Polokwane and we had to use a route on the outskirts of town. We only arrived at Bochum between ten and eleven. By then the taxi could not hoot and had no brake lights.*

Peter's in-laws fined us R80 for being late and asked for R80 to buy a coat for the old man [Peter's father-in-law]. They also told us that if we wished to take the bride we should be manly enough to do stick fights with the other men. But we were not prepared to fight. So we had to pay another R70.

In Bochum we called a mechanic to fix the taxi. After he worked on it the taxi's indicators could function and we were happy. But whilst we ate meat with our in-laws a terrible argument erupted. The mechanic demanded R180, but Henry said that he only had R120. The mechanic then drove away in his red BMW, fetched a revolver, and threatened to shoot Henry and the driver. To save Henry we had to give him R60. At six [pm] we bade our in-laws farewell and they gave us a complete goat [a slaughtered carcass] to take home.

Even before we reached Polokwane the temperature was in the red and the car overheated. We stopped to pour water, but it did not help. We then went to the home of Ronald Mokoena[2] *in town [Polokwane] and he gave us a five-litre water canister. But we drove for only ten kilometres and then our lights went off. The car had now become an animal – it kept on overheating and its lights did not work. At Stephen's Lumbers the car was completely stationary, but Moses insisted that we should continue driving home. He did not want to spoil the goat's meat. We called two mechanics to fix the lights. They arrived and worked on the taxi, but as soon as we tried to drive the lights again switched off. Then, when the lights worked, the car would not start. We pushed the car for two kilometres. Then it started, but the lights went off. A ten [pm] we arrived at Moria. Now the car started and the lights worked, but it overheated. We poured water, but the water boiled out of the radiator and burnt my brother. By twelve [pm] we realised that it was a futile exercise. While the taxi stood in the*

[2] Ronald was raised in Impalahoek and attended school with Henry Mohale. After completing a BSc degree in Engineering, he became an inspector of mining equipment in Polokwane. Ronald and Henry have continued to be good friends. As elsewhere in South African urban areas, 'homeboy' networks are an important form of sociality.

road, a bus came and missed us by inches. The mechanics could not understand and decided to tow the taxi to Lenz.

That evening we hired another sixteen-seat taxi to take the women to sleep at Henry's home at Turfloop. We men slept in the vehicle and it was very uncomfortable. We woke at five [am] and by then we had not washed. The mechanic said that the top gasket had blown and that the oil had mixed with the water. They went to Polokwane to buy a new top gasket, oil and oil filters. They said that the car would be ready by nine [am], but we only left at 2.30 [pm]. The mechanics demanded R500 for their work. We did not have the money. But we promised to pay them later.

At Magoebaskloof [a mountain pass] our brakes failed and the wheels seemed to be burning. Actually, the brake drums were smoking. We drove through Tzaneen, but before we arrived in Gravelotte the car again overheated. We had to stop and pour water every two kilometres. Once we even poured twenty litres of water. At Gravelotte we stopped the taxi and bought cold drinks to refresh ourselves. But when we climbed into the taxi the lights again did not work. Between six and seven [pm] we drove through Mica. Ronald Mokoena came to help us and drove in front of us with his car – a Toyota Conquest. We also put on the taxi's hazard lights. At Mica we poured fresh water, but the car again failed to start. We then phoned Mahero [the taxi owner] and told him that we were stuck. The men at the garage helped us push the taxi and after a hundred metres it started. But then water came out of the exhaust system. My mother phoned us and said, 'Leave the car and come home.'

At Mica we decided to hire another taxi – from Mahero – and we transferred all the people into it. Ronald, Henry, and I drove in the Toyota Conquest and only the driver and Kagišo were left in Mahero's taxi. We thought that it would be easier to travel with a lighter load. But the taxi still did not start, still overheated, still smoked seriously, and its lights still did not work.

Eventually we used Mahero's one taxi to tow his other taxi, using jumper-cables from Ronald's car. The Conquest followed behind. We told the driver to flash the hazards, but then the battery went out. As we got to the Klaserie turn off, the jumpers broke and the taxi went across the road. Fortunately there was no oncoming traffic and we could push the taxi back into the road. We again tried the jumpers, but at the descent, they again broke. We finally left the taxi with the driver and with another man and drove to Bushbuckridge in the Conquest. Here we found Mahero towing another taxi. We decided to buy booze. By then we had spent two nights without sleeping.

When the Mohale siblings eventually arrived at the home of their father, Luckson, the old man was furious. He scolded Moses, saying that Moses should have listened to him, and that he himself, as head of the family, should have led the journey to Bochum. For Jimmy, Luckson's expression of anger confirmed that he had in fact, used his malevolent powers to disrupt their journey:

When Moses arrived at our parents' home, our father insulted him. Our father told him, 'This is not your home! You are not the head of the family! When I say you should phasa *the bridewealth money [invoke the ancestors to bless the money], you should do so!' My father also asked Moses for the goat's meat. He was adamant. Moses left the meat with him and everyone dispersed. My father was too angry to listen to how we suffered along the way. He was only interested in the meat. The journey was a nightmare. That is how people can cause shit for you.*

Siegel (2006) has commented that witchcraft provides a means of naming the occurrence of anomalous, unexpected events that would otherwise be unnameable and extremely difficult to conceptualise. Jimmy's perception that their father was responsible for their horrible journey to Bochum bore out well-established fears. But other explanations for these events were indeed possible. Whilst listening to this story, Ace Ubisi, one of Luckson's neighbours and a mutual friend, shook his head in disbelief. Ace said that that he did not suspect witchcraft, and remarked that Mahero was renowned for hiring out dysfunctional taxis.

Taking Revenge

Once the Mohale siblings had recovered from their journey, they resumed planning to take revenge against their father. Their plots were somewhat reminiscent of the scenes described in Dostoyevsky's famous novel in which the three Karamazov brothers plot patricide (Dostoyevsky 1990). But rather than face their father directly, the Mohale siblings relied upon the assistance of diviners. Jimmy remembered that before they had left for Bochum, he and Peter asked the diviner of Casteel what they should do about the 'horrible man' who constantly bewitched them:

She replied, 'He is a bad man. I warn you. Don't ever try and use guns or your bare hands to kill him. Get a diviner. I know of someone who uses a mirror. When you see the culprit in the mirror he will give you a needle and ask you to pierce the image. Then the witch will die. I don't know precisely where he is at this moment, but I will find out for you.' We then asked her, 'Do you know someone else?' She kept quiet for a long time and then she said, 'Yes! I do! But I'm scared to tell you about him. He too, is a witch. . . . If there is anyone who can kill the man who bothers you, it is him.'

Jimmy and his siblings decided not to honour their agreement to revisit Zingiri in Phalaborwa. Instead, they decided to use the services of a seventy-year-old local diviner called Maluleke. He resided closer to them and was half as expensive. Moreover, Maluleke's reputation as a witch confirmed that he could operate in the same mystical realm as their father. This again points to the circular character of witchcraft (cf. Geschiere 1997). In their quest for revenge, during a desperate time, the Mohale siblings chose to discard earlier Manichean oppositions between 'moral' and 'immoral', and to deal directly with the powers of witchcraft.

We found the old man. There was nothing inside his divination hut [ndumba] *except a spear and a few pieces of ancestral cloth. Maluleke asked us, 'My sons, what do you want from me?' We said that we wanted a potion* [letšwa] *to kill our father. He replied, 'Hey! Can't you see there are no potions inside this hut? Why don't you go to a powerful diviner? Why do you come to me?' Only much later did he say, 'Let's talk business, boys. I'm very expensive. For the complete job I want R1,500.' We wanted to give him the money, but he refused. He said, 'Boys, I'm not a crook. I only accept money once I've done my job.'*

Jimmy constantly emphasised the cheap rates and flexible terms of payment that the diviners and Christian healers that he consulted asked for their services. This is perhaps to disguise how much money he spent on their services. In the ideology of diviners and Christian healers expensiveness is often inversely related to effectiveness. A diviner is supposed to be motivated by a genuine concern for helping impoverished villagers rather than financial gain.[3]

At five [am] the next day [29 December 2004] we went to fetch Maluleke and his wife. He asked us to take him to the Inyaka dam [close to Graskop]. Maluleke was dressed in scary regalia. He wore black headgear with feathers and a tail hung down his back. He was also clad in sandals and in red Swazi ancestral cloth. Maluleke took along coins, a chicken, white and black ancestral cloth, maize porridge, boiled meat, and some other concoctions, that I did not know. He said that he would use these things to trap our father's snake.

At the dam we got underneath the bridge. Here Maluleke and his wife knelt on the river bank and submerged their upper torsos into the water. They then poured the meat, porridge, coins, and potions into the water. The things that they did were meant to lure the snake into a trap. They also took the chicken, smeared potions into its mouth, and left it there.

Jimmy explained the symbolic properties of these items as follows:

There are chickens at all homesteads and the chicken will make the snake believe that it is in someone's yard, where it is welcome. The chicken was only meant to deceive. The snake loves money and it also loves the white colour. The boiled beef and the maize porridge will be the snake's provisions, but they have

[3] See Lan's (1993) discussion of money in the popular ideology of Zimbabwean diviners.

potions in them. After realising that it has been deceived, the snake will go back to its owner and kill him for having abandoned it.

After Maluleke and his wife had set the trap for Luckson's snake at the dam, Maluleke asked everyone to return to Moses's home, where he fortified all the Mohale siblings and their children. He made incisions on their ankles, elbows, and foreheads, into which he rubbed a potion.

After this Jimmy took Rebecca to a minister of the Zion Christian Church (ZCC) and two further diviners. The ministers gave her tea, washed her with water from a well, and splashed her with water from a waterfall. The diviners claimed that witches were trying to turn Rebecca into a zombie and commanded Jimmy to burn an herb called *lebuhlu* in Tsonga. They instructed Jimmy to invoke his ancestors and rub some of the herb's ashes onto the young woman's chest and back. Jimmy also gave Rebecca some of the herb to eat.

On Friday 5 January 2005, Jimmy was very optimistic that Rebecca would recover:

I went there yesterday morning. Rebecca's brother told me that she had asked for a cold drink and for chips [potato crisps], drank, and ate. She then relieved herself. Now Rebecca can also talk to people. The brother told me that he saw a large, thick snake disappearing at the toilet. The diviner [Maluleke] told us, 'Don't do anything to any snake that comes into the yard. The snake has to go back to its owner and kill him.' Rebecca is becoming better: she eats, she goes to the toilet, and she knows who she is. Our neighbours were spreading false information. They said that she had AIDS, but it was proven otherwise.

Jimmy's hopes and expectations were misplaced. Rebecca passed away only ten days later:

At five [pm, on 15 January 2005], I met Henry and Ronald at Banda's tavern. Henry told me that our relatives had phoned him and asked us to go to Moses's place. Ronald took us there by car. When I arrived my mother was outside on the veranda. I sat down next to her and said, 'Yes.' Moses's wife told me that things had changed. She said that Rebecca woke early in the morning, washed, dressed, and chatted to the other women. Rebecca then became drowsy and went to sleep. She woke at eleven [am], sent a child to buy a Coke, and drank two glasses of it. Hereafter, she ate soft porridge and again went to sleep. At four [pm], Rebecca started having convulsions and hallucinations. She would say, 'People are taking me away! Stop dragging me!' Rebecca could no longer recognise her own mother. At six [pm] the convulsions stopped and her feet started going cold. It was as if she had stepped on ice. They checked and realised that she had no pulse and that she was not breathing.

When I got into the house Rebecca was already dead. We laid her body on a reed mat and went outside to get rid of [disperse] the children. We then phoned the Elite funeral parlour. They came past twelve [midnight] when the kids were already asleep. We gave them Rebecca's ID [identity document] and waited for Moses's in-laws. We soon informed my father that Rebecca was late [dead]. He should have removed the corpse, but he did not come. Therefore I had to take the corpse to the mortuary. My father only came on the Sunday and was very angry. He asked: 'Who took the corpse to the morgue?' They answered, 'Jimmy.' He then said that we should not have done that in his absence. He even went to the extent of crying.

I asked Jimmy why Rebecca's condition had deteriorated so suddenly:

We were surprised and could not understand why it happened. We went to another diviner – called Ubisi. He threw the bones [lots] and said, 'I can see you are here because of a woman. This person was sickly and I see darkness.' We said, 'Yes! It is true. Our daughter died.' Ubisi continued, 'Yes! I can see from my bones that the man you consulted is powerful. This man fortified you, but he did not fortify the child. That is why she died.'

On the basis of these revelations, Jimmy argued that Rebecca's death was not due to any mistake by Maluleke. Rather, it was Rebecca's own relatives who had committed a fatal error:

Moses's wife made an error because she did not allow Maluleke to fortify her ailing daughter. The snake was lured to the dam, but did not come back to strike its owner [Luckson]. Because Rebecca was not fortified, the snake killed her.

This alleged error served as a 'secondary elaboration', excusing the failure of the anti-witchcraft rite. Incidents such as these confirm how the open-endedness and lack of verifiability of witchcraft give it the capacity to absorb contradictions of various kinds.

During the emotionally laden week before Rebecca's funeral, the relationship between the Mohale siblings and their father became increasingly tense. Although Moses was extremely angry, he wanted to see that his daughter, Rebecca, was buried in a dignified manner. Therefore, Moses asked all his younger siblings to refrain from speaking ill about their father in public, and to allow him to attend the funeral. Privately, Moses believed that Luckson had bewitched his daughter. But he did not wish outsiders to witness the strife within his family. Jimmy recalled:

Moses came to me before the funeral and lectured me. He instructed me, 'Behave yourself when your father is here! Speak to the old man! Refrain from making negative comments! Pretend as if nothing has happened between us! Acknowledge that he is the head of our family!' Moses was adamant that our father should be given that respect. He allowed our father to lead the proceedings and to sit in front. Moses acted as if my father was the one who had to be comforted.

Jimmy promised Moses that he would comply and worked exceptionally hard to assist with the funeral arrangements. But he could not find the courage to face his father, either during Rebecca's night vigil or on the day of her funeral:

Before the funeral I was tired and stressed. I decided to get drunk because I did not wish to see my father and I did not want to say anything in the programme. I can't stand the man who makes my life a misery. It would have been too tough for me to pretend. I bought a case of Castle Lights and I drank till all the beer was finished. I was so drunk that I slept inside a van that was parked in the street outside Moses's home. My father was there in the tent. That evening they killed five snakes in the yard.

On the morning of the funeral my father met Andrew [the eldest sibling of Luckson's second house] at the gate. [By then Andrew was severely ill.] I heard that my father was very rude to Andrew and told him, 'Don't come to this funeral. This place is polluted [fiša] *and you are sick.'*[4] *But Andrew replied, 'This is not your house. This place belongs to my brother. Do you think I am happy when my brother's daughter dies? I must come and bury her.' Andrew then entered the yard.*

After the mourners had returned from the graveyard and eaten the funeral meal at Moses's home, a quarrel erupted between some of Luckson's paternal relatives and his sons.

Our relatives asked my father, 'Where is Jimmy?' My father then told them, 'I don't know. We're not on speaking terms.' The relatives then wanted to call a family council after the funeral. Many people around here complained that my father is a witch. But people from afar did not know. They believed that our family problems were minor and could easily be resolved.

When I woke up in the van I was hungry. I took food and ate some of it. Then I heard people quarrelling inside Moses's garage. When I entered I saw Peter grabbing Daniel [Luckson's younger brother] by the throat. Henry ran behind the two of them and quarrelled with our cousin. Moses screamed, 'Go to your houses! You come here to tell me shit when I lost my daughter.' Moses then went into the house to fetch his gun and everyone fled. But when Moses returned, our cousin Leonard came with a calendar to discuss a date for taking off the mourning clothes [the hlobolo *ritual]. Moses told him: 'Bugger off! You don't know how this person died, but you want to discuss the mourning clothes.'*

During this commotion Moses protected the man [Luckson] who killed his daughter. We African people are strange. We are resilient. We can endure and

[4] In local cosmology the aura of the deceased continues to pollute places of death. This aura is dangerous, particularly to persons in vulnerable positions, such as those who are sick. See Niehaus (2002a) for a more in-depth discussion of local concepts of the body, pollution, and taboos.

even protect our enemy. If the people know that their father is bewitching people they won't publicise it. They will only say it in private – inside the family.

Whilst everyone was fighting my father remained exactly where he was, glued to his chair. Eventually, his nephew [sister's son] came to his rescue and took him home in his van. This was the last time that my father visited Moses's family. He was not there when we cleansed the home or when we decided upon a date for taking off the mourning clothes.

After the funeral we again called Maluleke [the diviner] to Moses's home and asked him to make vengeance magic [letšwa] *for my father. Maluleke went into the cemetery on the Sunday and pierced a green reed into the soil of Rebecca's grave. He told us that it had to be a hollow reed that one could blow like a flute, and that he had put potions inside. When the wind blows, the reed will whistle, and the potions will call the witch to follow the deceased.*

Andrew Mohale: Luckson's Next Victim?

On 31 March 2005, only two months after Rebecca's funeral, Andrew Mohale, the oldest child of Luckson's second wife, *ngwa* Usinga, also died. Andrew was once employed and had been married. However, in 1995 he lost his job, and his wife and child deserted him. Since then he had been unemployed and single. He became sick at more or less the same time Rebecca displayed her first symptoms of illness. Many neighbours gossiped that Andrew suffered from an AIDS-related sickness. But Jimmy again disagreed:

Andrew was not promiscuous and his [former] wife is not sick. The doctors checked Andrew for AIDS and those things and they gave him medication. He is thin, very thin. It is scary how much weight he has lost. But he has no lesions or sores. There is also no coughing. Andrew's condition fluctuates. Sometimes he is bedridden, loses his voice, and hallucinates. If you see him it is like seeing a dead person. Occasionally he has hiccups and finds it difficult to speak. His mother tells me that when he hallucinates he responds to unknown, invisible people. He would say things like, 'Here I am! Hey! Why do you call me?'

It seemed logical to Jimmy that Andrew was yet another victim of Luckson's witchcraft:

Andrew was the first person to accuse our father of witchcraft. Long ago he used to tell us that our dad is a witch and that we should be careful of him. But we never believed Andrew because he smoked cannabis [dagga] *and drank a lot.*

After the onset of Andrew's illness, he lived with his mother, and she and his brothers took care of him. One Sunday Andrew's condition worsened and his brothers took him to a diviner in the village of Casteel. The diviner stretched all his limbs and extremities to make the heat escape from his body and predicted that Andrew would recover. At the time of Rebecca's funeral, Andrew could still walk unaided and he was able to assist his brothers in erecting the funeral tent and in collecting firewood. After the funeral he walked all the way from the bereaved family to his mother's home – about two kilometres away. But two days later he was completely bedridden.

As Andrew's condition deteriorated further, his brothers took him to another diviner, who revealed that witches were trying to transform him into a zombie. The witches had already taken his body and hidden it inside a cave, and they were now trying to capture his remaining aura (*seriti*). The diviner cut small incisions in different parts of Andrew's body with a razor blade and rubbed medicines into them. He explained to Andrew's kin that the constant hiccups and belching were signs of a monstrous animal inside his stomach, making a noise. The diviner then cooked potions in a pot, of which he gave Andrew half a cup to drink. In addition to this, he smeared Andrew's body with an ointment that would allegedly make him invisible to witches at night. Andrew's brothers confirmed this diagnosis when they examined his faeces and observed what appeared to be snake scales and a large tooth.

At five o' clock the next morning, Jimmy, Moses, and *ngwa* Usinga took Andrew back to the diviner. The diviner said that Andrew's amnesia was a sign that witches were taking hold of his mind. The diviner then tried to retrieve Andrew's body and to unite it with his aura (*seriti*). He took Andrew to a dry river bed, where he washed Andrew's face with river reeds and with charcoal, and told his kin to dress him in ancestral cloth. Diviners use charcoal – a substance that defeats the heat of the fire – and river reeds as cooling substances to counter the polluting heat of death. (Widows use black charcoal to immunise themselves against the lingering effects of their husband's death. Elderly women tie river reeds around the neck of an aborted foetus and then bury it in cool river sand.) The diviner also poured a libation for his own ancestors and sprinkled concoctions on the ground to protect Andrew from malevolent forces.

To retrieve Andrew's body from the witches, the diviner started shouting, blew a rheebuck horn, and beat small drums. He said: 'If you hear my voice, shout, Yes!' All the time Andrew stood right next to the diviner, but he could not hear him. Finally, the diviner gave Andrew medication to sniff. The diviner said that Andrew would be cured, if only he could sneeze. Sneezing is a sign of life.[5] *We were very happy when Andrew sneezed. When he came to he told us that he had heard children and adults crying. But he said that he could not see them.*

[5] Jimmy said that in Bushbuckridge sneezing is often associated with the erection of a man's penis. 'When a man is very ill, but he can still be sexually aroused and get an erection, we believe he will survive.' This conception is remarkably similar to the symbolic resonance between smoking, sneezing induced by the taking of snuff, and sexual intercourse in Lesotho (Murray 1975).

The diviner helped Andrew back from the dried-up river bed into the car, and instructed him not to look back.[6] *We paid the diviner R350. We were eight people and he convinced all of us that Andrew would live.*

Jimmy neglected to tell me, however, that his belief that his father had bewitched Andrew was not subscribed to by all the diviners consulted. Patrick Monna, Jimmy's friend and drinking mate, recalled that he once accompanied Jimmy to a diviner who provided very different revelations.

One evening when Andrew was sick, Jimmy stayed at my place. That evening he could not sleep. He said that he had some dreams, in which he saw that Andrew was lifeless. Between four and five in the morning Jimmy woke me and I accompanied him to see an old woman. She told us that Andrew won't live, but will pass on. She also said that Jimmy's father is not a witch. He only used potions at work, like many other men did in the older days. This was not to kill people, but to fortify themselves so that they could be loved by their bosses, and can drive trucks without needing to rest. Jimmy was very angry when he heard this. He said that the old lady spoke shit. He suspected that she was a friend of his father.

On Monday, 1 April 2005, I recorded details of Jimmy's life history in the home he shared with Iris. Just after three that afternoon, *ngwa* Usinga knocked at the door and told Jimmy that Andrew had died.

Andrew's Funeral

Jimmy did not participate in arranging Andrew's funeral. He feared that he might have to encounter his father, and resented the fact that his cousins, who still defended Luckson, were playing such a prominent part in the funeral arrangements. Jimmy even suspected that they might be his father's accomplices in witchcraft.

Jimmy excused himself from participating by saying that he had already contributed enough by taking Andrew to several diviners:

*On Monday my younger mother [*ngwa *Usinga] sent a woman to call me and ask me to help them take the deceased to the morgue. But I said, 'No. I don't want to participate. Let my father do everything. I have taken Andrew to prophets and to diviners. I have lost! The witches have won! Now they must take over. Let them take Andrew to the morgue.'*

The funeral, on Saturday, 7 April, was well organised and well attended, thanks in part to the role played by the Zion Christian Church

[6] To turn back is to revisit the illness. This conception might also be influenced by Biblical mythology about Lot's wife who turned into a salt pillar when she stared back to witness the destruction of Sodom. Frequent overlap occurs between divination and Christian healing.

(ZCC), of which Andrew had become a member in the latter stages of his life. Many dignitaries came, including the Bushbuckridge mayor and municipal manager. Luckson wore a brand new suit and occupied a prominent position throughout the proceedings. But Jimmy refused to attend.

His siblings were furious that he had showed Andrew so little respect:

My brothers were very angry because I was not there. They came to my house at about eleven in the morning and fetched me to attend a meeting. I told them that I had not washed, but they did not want to hear any excuses. They dragged me into the car and drove off. We stopped at the café next to Fundani, where there was a gathering of about twenty-five people. My brothers and sisters were there, waiting for me. They put me on trial and asked me to respond to their questions. Moses, Pretty, and Henry asked me the following questions. One: Why did I not attend the funeral? Two: Where do I stay? Three: What did I want them to do when I got ill? Four: When did I plan to get married? Five: What will I do to defend myself against my father's wrath?

I told them that it was very unfortunate that we should discuss these issues after our younger brother, Andrew, whom I loved so much, had died. 'Why did you not ask me these questions when I took Andrew to the diviners during the night?' I told them directly that I did not go to the funeral because my father is a witch and because I was scared that he might bewitch me. I also told them that I did not have a permanent place to stay, and that I was hiring a two-roomed home. Only once the dust had settled between my wife [Lerato] and me, would I look for a permanent place. I said that there was nobody, beside them, who would look after me when I'm ill. Finally, I told them that I did not intend to marry again. I had been deeply disappointed in my marriage, but did not want to start another family. This is because I am already forty years old, and because I already have children. 'If I had the legal resources, I would fight for the custody of my children. But I don't yearn for any more children because I don't want them to struggle.' I said that I alone had tried to defend myself against the witch, without their assistance.

In African culture we believe that if we stay with a woman without notifying your family, you stand alone. That is why I did not dare to mention Iris's name. I was scared that my brothers and sisters would demand that I pay bridewealth for her. At the meeting my female cousin even said, 'You are staying with another bitch! We don't know her and we don't want to know her!' I was not upset. I was more in a sorrowful mode. Because it was a burial I had to be disturbed.

They told me that they were collecting money to go to a diviner in Casteel and asked me to pop out [contribute] R40 to help them. Moses, Kagišo, and Rodney went, and the rest dispersed. I also did not go to the diviner. He uses wool – not divining lots. I later heard that the diviner said that our father killed the young boy. He said that our father's snake will be full of blood for a while. But after only three months, this man would be forced to kill again. The diviner also said that he could help us kill our father. We did not have to pay him upfront: actions first, payments later.

This encounter signalled a change in Jimmy's status. Not only did he, previously a defender of his father, now become Luckson's fiercest critic, but he also came to be seen as an outcast by his own siblings and cousins. They were concerned about his behaviour and by his homelessness. Men of his family did not desert their own children like he did. Nor did they live without a definite address. Moreover, they saw Jimmy's refusal to attend his half-brother's funeral as a renunciation of sociality and of kinship, and as a betrayal of them. Jimmy was in danger of complete isolation.

In the following month, Jimmy's fear of his father's occult powers became even more intense. He also refused to attend the ritual that signalled the end of the mourning period for Rebecca's death, held on 4 June 2005.

Moses informed me, but I did not want to go because I knew that my father would be there. The ceremony started at one o'clock [pm]. I went to see what was happening there and I took the tarred road. As I got near the woman's bakery, two men appeared in front of me. The one man was my father and the other his cousin. My father was clad in a navy blue suit and his cousin in a charcoal suit. They were clean-shaven and neatly dressed. They never saw me because they did not expect me there. I wore a baseball cap, a T-shirt and running shoes, and I followed behind them. As they turned to my brother's place, I continued with the journey. When I reached a telephone next to the Nazarene church, I phoned Moses. I told him that I was on my way to his house, but that I saw the crook on his way there. This time Henry also did not want to see our father. Many people were surprised to discover that Luckson's sons did not attend the ritual.

The Dissipation of Revenge

All attempts by the Mohale siblings to avenge the deaths of their kin proved unsuccessful. After Maluleke had failed to make Luckson's witchcraft rebound, the Mohale siblings could not assemble enough cash to finance a second attempt on his life. Jimmy and Henry were both extremely hard pressed for money, and Moses, who had always been extremely generous, lost his job. In May 2004 the transport company for which he worked in Johannesburg was liquidated. After that time, Moses was able to secure only temporary positions. In December 2004 he returned home, living only on monthly stipends from the UIF [Unemployment Insurance Fund]:

There could be no vengeance magic because vengeance magic involves money and we no longer had it. I tried to get money, but I could not get any money for us to go to Venda. Neither could Henry. My father also has a way of disorganising people. Whenever we tried, people had excuses. This man [Luckson] has a way of doing it. He caused the others to get uninterested in the whole thing.

Many other diviners said that they were afraid to challenge Luckson, and that their feeble powers were no match for his.

In describing how his father practised witchcraft, Jimmy exaggerated many Oedipal themes in the father–son relationship. He clearly expressed intense hatred and enormous fear of Luckson, but there was also some ambivalence, and perhaps even disguised admiration. Jimmy commented that there were no witches quite as intelligent and competent in their malevolent craft as his father. This was very apparent in Jimmy's description of the rivalry between Luckson and Jimmy's aunt, Basebele (pp. 92–3).

Basebele was a witch who thought that she was superior to my father. She undermined him, disrespected him, and insulted him. But she made a serious mistake when she challenged the strength of my father. By then he had had enough of her insults. He needed only four days to squash her. I tell people that my father is not a witch. He is a super witch.

8 AIDS and Oedipus

The HIV/AIDS pandemic appeared rather late in Bushbuckridge, but then escalated very rapidly. A comprehensive verbal autopsy survey, conducted by epidemiological researchers on common signs and symptoms of deaths in the Agincourt[1] area of Bushbuckridge, shows AIDS to be responsible for a dramatic reversal in mortality rates. Until 1995 infectious diseases and malnutrition were the predominant causes of deaths among children; accidents and violence among adolescents and young adults; and cardiovascular diseases among adults of middle age and over. But thereafter AIDS became the most common cause of death in all age categories (Saloojee and Kahn 2005). Between 1999 and 2007 life expectancy decreased by 14 years for women and 12 years for men (Kahn, Garenne, Collinson, and Tollman 2007: 29–34). A different survey confirms this bleak picture. It shows sero-prevalence among women receiving antenatal care at Tintswalo Hospital increasing from 2 per cent in 1992 to 21 per cent in 2006 (MacPherson, Moshabela, Martinson, and Pronyk 2008: 2).

Perceptions about the spread of HIV and AIDS in Impalahoek dovetail with these statistics. Only in 1997 did I record some sort of recognition by my informants that AIDS-related deaths had started to occur. Three were acknowledged in total for that year, but these deaths soon became too numerous for them to keep an informal account. AIDS-related death soon affected nearly all families in the village.

Reasons for the rapid escalation of the pandemic in Southern Africa might well include the presence of more infectious and virulent strains of HIV (Iliffe 2006: 10–11). On the social side, it was facilitated by a unique constellation of factors – the legacy of a migrant labour system that compelled spouses to remain apart for extended periods of time, traditions of polygamy, and the wide prevalence of 'transactional sex' in situations of economic privation and 'structured gender inequality' (Lurie 2000; Philips 2001; Wojcicki 2002; Campbell 2003; Hunter 2002; 2010). In South Africa extremely diffuse sexual networks

[1] Agincourt is located only twenty kilometres south of Impalahoek. During 2000 the Agincourt study population comprised 68,631 persons residing in 11,212 households in twenty-one village sections.

(Thornton 2008) comprising different concurrent partners (Epstein 2008: 49–65) create a super-highway for the transmission of HIV.

These factors were very apparent in Bushbuckridge. Not all are attributable to the fact that there has been continuous oscillating migration from this region to South Africa's urban and industrial centres, although this certainly plays a part. A multiplicity of partners is evident in diverse relationships, ranging from romantic affairs in school, long-term extramarital liaisons, male-to-male sex in prisons, and brief sexual encounters arranged in drinking taverns. Multiple sexual partners are the norm for those involved in both monogamous and polygamous marriages. Transfers of bridewealth, gifts, and money are a dominant theme in these relations, often distributing resources to the desperately poor. This is clearly borne out by the demographics of 42 AIDS victims which I documented. The 15 deceased men were amongst the 'wealthier of the poor' and had the capacity to sustain different sexual relationships. Some worked as migrant labourers while others were locally employed as teachers, soldiers, and policemen. By contrast, the 27 deceased women were unemployed and/or single, with a primary source of income being their husbands or lovers (Niehaus 2005b: 181). Many female AIDS victims were married and infected by their husbands. Others were described as young and beautiful women, constantly on the lookout for wealthier men to satisfy their desires for money and fashions (Stadler 2003a).

Villagers saw drinking taverns, scattered along the national road from Nelspruit which curved through Bushbuckidge towards Phalaborwa, as prime sites for the transmission of HIV. Here women sold sexual services to taxi and truck drivers for as little as R20 plus a few beers or ciders. There was also a well-known beer hall in Hoedspruit, where soldiers from the local military base drank. The soldiers, many of whom had served on peacekeeping missions in countries as far afield as Rwanda, often assisted the police with crime prevention operations. While congregating in local drinking houses, they frequently purchased sexual services. Women sex workers could charge R100 for a single encounter, plus an extra R50 for sex without a condom.

Interventions by non-government organisations – which conducted concerted AIDS awareness campaigns throughout the 1990s – shaped local understandings of the virus. For example, the Health Systems Development Unit (HSDU) launched a prominent sexual health project in 1992. Staff members gave talks on sexual hygiene to various constituencies, including police, clergy, teachers, headmen, diviners, and youth at schools. The organisation also trained teachers as sex educators. In 2000 the 'LoveLife' campaign built a youth centre five kilometres from Impalahoek. The centre hosted motivational workshops, dancing, studio broadcasting, computer training, drama, basketball, and volleyball.

Groundbreakers of the campaign promoted a lifestyle of positive sexuality based on romantic love, being faithful, abstaining, or using condoms. LoveLife youth with their distinctive hats and T-shirts were literally seen as 'billboards' of the campaign (Wahlström 2002).

AIDS has also become an important topic in the curriculum of 'life orientation' classes in local schools. Teachers at the Impalahoek Primary School warned younger learners not to play with scissors, razors, and pins; not to touch bleeding friends; and also not to inflate any balloons (condoms) they found lying around in the village. They also demonstrated safe sex to pupils older than twelve, using stage props such as artificial penises and different kinds of condoms. AIDS activists targeted high schools for even more excessive propaganda and addressed learners each week. Far from being untouched, pupils were over-saturated with these messages (cf. McNeill 2011).

Despite great publicity about unsafe sex, medical treatment for people with AIDS has remained woefully inadequate. By singling out HIV/AIDS for excessive health propaganda and by focusing on prevention rather than care, these campaigns created the impression that AIDS was a deadly, incurable, and untreatable disease. Since the 1990s a network of 3 hospitals, 7 health centres, and 57 clinics in Bushbuckridge provided voluntary counselling and testing, and treated the symptoms of opportunistic infections. In 1999 the Rixile ('rising sun' in Tsonga) Wellness Clinic was founded at Tintswalo Hospital. The clinic provided further education, hosted support groups, monitored CD4 counts,[2] assisted people in applying for disability grants, and also helped them obtain nutritional support. People also tended to seek help in the later stages of sickness. However, patients complained of intolerably long queues, in which waiting commenced at 6.45 am and many patients were not seen by a doctor until late in the afternoon. Conditions were spartan.

After a notoriously lengthy delay in government provision of antiretroviral drugs (ARVs),[3] it eventually became possible for patients to obtain Nevirapine from Masana Hospital (30 km away), and by 2005 the Rixile Clinic began to supply HAART (Highly Active Antiretroviral Therapy) to patients who registered a CD4 count of below 200 (MacPherson, Moshabela, Martinson, and Pronyk 2008; Mfecane 2010).

[2] CD4 cells – also called T-helper cells – are a type of white blood cells that fight infections. A CD4 count is therefore a measure of the strength of the immune system.

[3] Under the presidency of Thabo Mbeki, government opposed calls by physicians to provide AZT (Azidothymidine) and Nevirapine to women in the last stages of pregnancy to reduce the chances of mother–child transmission of HIV. South Africa's health minister argued that these drugs produced dangerous side-effects, did not combine well with tuberculosis medication, and offered no protection against infant vulnerability to the transmission of HIV by means of breast-feeding. However, in 2003 the constitutional court compelled government to make Nevirapine available in all sectors of the health-care system to satisfy citizens' 'right to life'. See Mbali (2004), LeClerc-Madlala (2005), Posel (2005), and Fassin (2007) for informative accounts of the politics of AIDS and ARVs in South Africa.

Despite such developments, residents of Bushbuckridge encountered AIDS with stubborn silence and fatalism. People are extremely reluctant to undertake tests for HIV antibodies or to report for voluntary counselling at the health-care facilities. They tend to seek help only in the latter stages of sickness. Moreover, those living with HIV seldom disclose their condition, and often refuse antiretroviral treatment. Even in the case of tuberculosis, which is frequently related to AIDS, Pronyk (2003) calculates a mean delay of ten weeks from the onset of symptoms until the commencement of treatment among 298 patients at Tintswalo Hospital. This is frequently a response to the terrible stigma of AIDS, and also to perceptions of how kin and neighbours have shunned, ostracised, and abandoned those infected with the virus.[4] Jimmy's life story casts light upon these extremely complex processes.

Real or Fictitious AIDS? The Deaths at Marashea's Tavern

When I researched the impact of AIDS in Impalahoek, Jimmy eagerly told me how several of his acquaintances and neighbours had contracted the 'dreaded disease'. Jimmy was well aware of biomedical perspectives on AIDS. We frequently criticised the South African government for having underestimated the seriousness of the pandemic in rural areas, and for having failed to provide antiretroviral therapy to those infected with HIV. Jimmy knew that there was no cure for AIDS, but seemed to be receptive to my stories about Judge Edwin Cameron who had effectively managed to control the symptoms of HIV for almost 15 years,[5] and to my claim that HIV-positive persons taking correct medication could enjoy a near-normal life expectancy.

But I detected a change in the tone of Jimmy's talk when he told me of a series of deaths that occurred in the neighbourhood next to Marashea's tavern, where he lived with Iris's family during 2003.

Jimmy counted 16 deaths and 6 cases of serious illness within fifteen households in the neighbourhood.

(1) *Morema.* The female household head died from unknown causes when she was only 49 years old, and worked in Johannesburg.

[4] In a random survey, 2,500 residents in the mining town of Carltonville were offered a free and anonymous test for HIV antibodies, but not a single person accepted (Ashforth 2002: 1). Another study of 726 HIV-positive patients found that 92 per cent had not told anyone of their status (Pawninski and Lalloo 2001: 448). By 2006, 80 per cent of South Africans needing antiretroviral drugs were not receiving them (Thom 2006).

[5] Edwin Cameron is a judge on the South African Supreme Court of Appeal and also chair of Council of the University of the Witwatersrand. He was diagnosed HIV-positive in 1994 and described his experiences of living with HIV in the monograph *Witness to AIDS* (Cameron 2005).

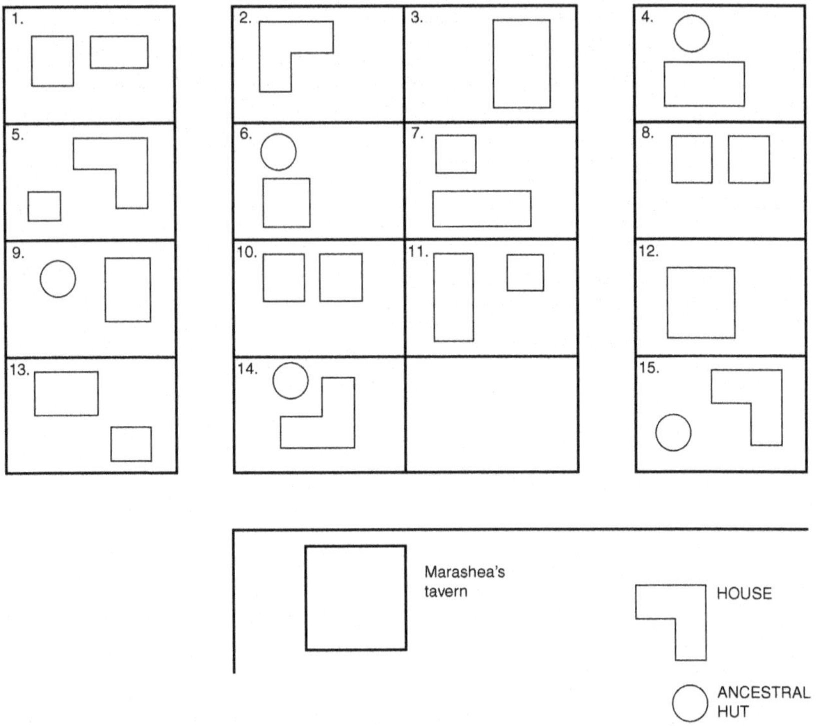

Figure 8.1. The houses opposite Marashea's tavern

(2) *Mathibela.* After 1999, six close relatives of Jonas Mathibela and his wife Roniah passed away. They included two of their daughters, a daughter-in-law, and three grandchildren. Another Mathibela daughter married a security guard in Thulamahashe, but returned to her parents after she became critically ill. The Mathibela couple themselves and their neighbours attributed these deaths to AIDS.

(3) *Dlamini.* The woman household head was a senior teacher and occasionally suffered from serious bouts of sickness.

(4) *Monna.* A young woman member of the household died during 2005. She was single and known to have frequented various drinking taverns. Neighbours speculated that she had died either from AIDS or from complications arising from a backstreet abortion.

(5) *Maplanka.* Nana Maplanka's daughter died in 2005, and she lived with a seriously ill husband, another daughter, and with three healthy grandchildren.

(6) *Dlamini.* Afisi Dlamini's youngest daughter passed away after a long bout of illness in 2004. She was about thirty-eight years old and had previously lived with a bus driver, who was a renowned womaniser.

Joan left two children, of whom the youngest had recently passed into a coma.

(7) *Nxumalo*. One member of the household was said to have died of AIDS.

(11) *Maluleke*. This is the household of Iris's mother, where she and Jimmy resided for six months in 2003. Iris's sister died in 2004, when she was only thirty years old. She worked at a citrus farm and then at a local tavern. Before her death, Iris's sister was exceptionally lean, had dark lesions on her arms and legs, and sores on her mouth.

(12) *Khaulemu*. In 2003 one household member died from unknown causes.

(13) *Mohale*. This is the household of Jimmy's younger mother, *ngwa* Usinga. We discussed the death of her eldest son, Andrew, in the previous chapter, and noted that neighbours attributed this death to AIDS.

(14) *Morema*. During the course of 2005 Mahlamula Morema died of old age, and his forty-seven year old son, Daniel, from AIDS-related diseases. Daniel had worked as a miner, but was declared unfit to work and received a disability pension. Despite being very sick and terribly thin, Daniel occasionally worked as an instructor at a local driving school. Daniel's brother was disabled and his sister suffered from tuberculosis.

In houses (8), (9), (10), and (15) no sickness or death was reported.

Jimmy told me that he sincerely believed that not all these deaths were due to AIDS, and he suggested that some of the deceased might well have been the victims of witchcraft. This belief is in line with many studies elsewhere in Africa, documenting a resurgence of witch-finding and witch-cleansing movements in response to the pandemic (Anderson 2002; Ashforth 2002; Probst 1999; Schoepf 1988, 2001; and Yamba 1997). Ashforth (2002) observes that residents of South Africa's largest black city, Soweto, often interpreted the symptoms of AIDS as a type of slow poison (called *isidliso* in Zulu) inflicted by witches. Sowetans alleged that witches insert the poison into the gullet of their victims in the form of a small creature that slowly consumed them from the inside. *Isidliso* covered many symptoms – literally anything that affected the lungs, stomach, and digestive tract – that all lead to a slow, wasting illness.

The situation in Bushbuckridge was a little more complex. Villagers were of the opinion that a person either died of witchcraft or of AIDS, and they did not believe that witches could actually send AIDS. But there were often fierce disagreements over whether AIDS or witchcraft was the cause of particular deaths. Outsiders and neighbours were more inclined to mention AIDS, especially when gossiping in private spaces. Unrelated elders had few scruples in attributing the deaths of younger people to wild, irresponsible sexual conduct (Stadler 2003b). But insiders and kin often attributed the very same deaths to witchcraft. For example,

Jimmy accepted that more distant acquaintances had died from AIDS, but insisted that his niece, Rebecca, and his half-brother, Andrew, had been the victims of his father's witchcraft.

He argued that whilst witches could not send HIV, they were perfectly capable of creating 'artificial AIDS': that is, witchcraft-induced sickness that mimics the symptoms of AIDS. In this manner, he said, witches took advantage of the pandemic and used it as a shield to mask their nefarious activities. He suggested that Khaulemu, who was a herbalist from Malawi, together with Jonas and Roniah Mathibela, might have bewitched the residents of their neighbourhood:

If anybody gets ill, people will say that he or she has AIDS. Sakkie, I know that AIDS is there. But when you die of AIDS, your partner will also show symptoms of the disease. I don't think it is AIDS when a person dies, but the partner shows no symptoms and lives for another ten years. These cases are questionable.

Jimmy speculated that Jonas and Roniah Mathibela might have bewitched their own children and grandchildren. The couple contradicted usual expectations of behaviour towards sick relatives. They spoke indiscreetly about the dreaded disease when their descendants became ill, and completely disregarded the revelations and prescriptions of prophets and diviners. This created the impression that they might be hiding something (McNeill 2011).

When their daughter became ill, she went to a diviner. All the time her parents only visited her twice. Her mother [Roniah Mathibela] just said, 'I won't waste any time by visiting my sick daughter. My daughter has AIDS and she'll die.' The diviner used divination lots and warned the daughter that she would die if she returned to her parents' place. But the parents took her to their home against her will. The daughter told her father that she did not wish to feed his snake [become a victim of his witchcraft]. At their home she became so seriously ill: she became very lean, even though she did not have diarrhoea. She still felt well when they took her to hospital, but her leg suddenly went cold and the cold moved up her body. That's when she died.

It seemed to us that Roniah was proud that her daughter had AIDS. She did not just speak about AIDS inside the home. She even spoke about it outside, when she chatted with others. The daughter's boyfriend, Lucky, visited the bereaved family to deliver a bag of maize and some groceries. He also promised to support their child with R300 per month. Lucky is well. His health is still good. How can Roniah claim that her daughter died of AIDS, when the boyfriend is still alive? Many neighbours did not visit Mathibela's place. They asked why they should comfort parents who continue to kill their own children. Jonas is a Mozambican who has a snake [mamlambo] *to feed. Roniah loves money. They bewitch their own children so that they can get child support grants from their grandchildren.*[6] *They only use AIDS as an excuse so that the deaths look credible. . . . They get potions from the Malawian diviner [Khaulemu] and kill their victims in such a manner that the deaths look like AIDS. These parents are fly-by-nights! They are witches!*

The allocation of blame for deaths in the neighbourhood was an intensely political act, involving fierce contestation between different generations and also between insiders and outsiders, and invoking contrasting scenarios of fatalism and hope.

Disease, Stigma, and Silence

Residents of Bushbuckridge responded to AIDS with measured silence and discretion. They almost always confined talk about specific cases of AIDS to the backstage regions of social interaction (Goffman 1971). But even then villagers avoided mentioning the words 'HIV' and 'AIDS' directly. As an alternative they deployed various euphemisms. These include the saying that the infected person has the 'three letters' (*maina a mararo*), 'germs' (*twatši*), 'the painful sickness' (*kukuana hloko*), 'the disease of right now' (*bolwetši gona bjalo*), or had purchased 'a single ticket' (in English). Another expression was that a person was 'on diet' (*dayeta*). People also displayed excessive avoidance behaviour towards the sick person, and kin secluded him or her from fellow villagers. Only a select few carers were allowed to enter the room, and those polluted by birth, sex, or by death were strictly prohibited.

Whilst villagers recognised the sexual mode of transmission of HIV, they were not puritanical about sexual matters. At times adults condemned the sexual irresponsibility of the youth. But they had fairly permissive attitudes towards heterosexual promiscuity, condoning sexual exploration by boys, accepting illegitimate children without undue fuss, and not allowing adultery to cause too much disruption. Such attitudes derive from the very positive perception of sex as a means of pleasure, procreation, and of ensuring a balanced supply of blood in the body. Getting married and bearing children were ideal attributes of adult personhood, and men took pride in having multiple lovers. Celibacy and singleness were generally deemed to be more dishonourable than promiscuity.

The sexual route of transmission does not, then, explain people's reluctance to speak about AIDS. Talk about sex was proscribed in certain ways. Elders, particularly parents, were prohibited from speaking directly to the younger generation about sex and vice versa. But the mother's brother

[6] In 2002 the South African Department of Health and Welfare introduced maintenance grants of R170 per child for unemployed mothers. Although the African National Congress presented child maintenance grants as one of its major achievements in the provision of social welfare, men often see these grants as evidence that government favours women (Niehaus 2006b: 537).

and father's younger siblings were obliged to speak to their nephews and nieces about sex in a pedagogical manner. Grandparents too could joke to grandchildren about sex. In these forms of talk elders referred to sex indirectly: by means of euphemisms. But it was considered acceptable for villagers to talk freely about sex to spouses, lovers, coevals, friends, and to outsiders such as anthropologists. Matrilateral cousins had a reciprocal joking relationship, in which they frequently shared lewd sexual jokes. During fieldwork men spoke freely to me about their experiences of contracting gonorrhoea, syphilis, and *lešiši* (literally, 'shudder' – a disease men contract when having sex with a woman who has recently aborted).

A more plausible reason for stigma, silence, and denial is the association of AIDS with death, and the construction of persons living with HIV as 'living corpses' (*setopo sa gopela*) who are 'dead before dying' (Niehaus 2007). This conception seems to be an outcome, perhaps unintentional, of the manner in which public health discourses have framed AIDS as a terminal condition. By singling out AIDS for excessive propaganda, non-governmental organisations have created the impression that the syndrome is somehow deadlier than other diseases, and by focusing on prevention rather than care, they have created the impression that nothing can be done to assist any person who is HIV-positive. These messages came too late. They came at a time when many villagers had already been infected, or at least considered themselves to be infected, with HIV. Experiences of inadequate medical treatment, of being turned away from hospitals, and of being forced to rely upon outpatient care have often reinforced these perceptions.

The concept of HIV-positive persons as 'dead before dying' explains the seclusion of the sick people, excessive avoidance behaviour, and also the discreetness when talking about AIDS. Villagers saw death as extremely contaminating. They believed that upon death the breath (*moya*) and aura (*seriti*, literally shadow) of a deceased person separated from his or her corporeal body (*mmele*) and assumed a dark, sorrowful form (called *thefifi*) that could pollute any object or person on contact. This association of AIDS with death possibly informs the local belief that HIV could be contracted not only through sexual intercourse, but also through sharing a toilet or cutlery, nursing a sick person without using latex gloves, coming into contact with his or her germs, or even breathing the same air.

Primary caregivers were expected to comfort and strengthen (*pharola*) the sick person verbally. They had to avoid upsetting the sick person, naming his or her disease, or referring to the imminence of death. Rather than referring directly to death, people signified it by non-verbal means, or through the use of euphemisms. When a young man died during initiation, the master of the lodge would break a clay pot in front of his mother.[7] Symbolic inversions such as turning around the logs in a fire and placing their thick ends in the centre also showed that there had been a death in the home. The most common sayings were that a person had been 'taken by hyenas' (*tšerwe ke phiri*); 'gone to the place of the ancestors' (*o ile badimong*), or that the 'house had fallen' (*o wetše ke ntlo*) or the 'water had dried up' (*meetse a pshele*). In similar vein, villagers avoided direct reference to AIDS, instead using indirect expressions.

The anomalous symbolic location of persons with AIDS, betwixt and between life and death, contradicted usual schemes of classification and signified danger (Douglas 1970). Villagers often felt less disturbed by a corpse than by a 'living corpse'. They regarded persons who were near death as burdensome and pitiful. Elders recalled that euthanasia was fairly common in the past. To relieve a terminally ill person from pain, they said, relatives wrapped him or her in blankets, placed them at the gate of their cattle kraal, and drove the herd of cattle over him or her.

The symptoms of AIDS signified an anomalous mixture of living and dead tissue and blood. A body afflicted with the syndrome was thought of as literally decomposing whilst it was still alive. Black spotted marks (skin lesions) as well as the loss of body functions and of reason were the clearest indications of this death-in-life. Persistent diarrhoea, constant vomiting, and coughing from tuberculosis indicated a loss of breath, aura, or life; whilst swollen glands, mouth sores, soft fluffy hair, and the person's dark colour showed rotting blood. Emaciation and boniness, too, were reminiscent of a corpse.[8]

Informants explicitly told me that they avoided tests for HIV antibodies because a positive result would cause them to die of stress: forcing them to think and to dream of death, dying, and of graves. They also feared that others might discriminate against them.

But there is another less obvious, unspoken, reason to avoid, contest, and hide an HIV-positive diagnosis. Because HIV has a long incubation period, identifying someone as HIV-positive amounts to an accusation that he or she had (in all likelihood) spread the disease to past and present sexual partners, and was therefore culpable of having caused their impending deaths. Such culpability may be exceptionally hard to bear. In the past, accusations about being HIV-positive have been a bitter

7 De Heusch (1980) shows that Tsonga people draw an analogy between birth and the baking and firing of clay pots.

8 Churches constructed AIDS as a new kind of leprosy: as an expression of God's wrath in a world gone astray and as a horribly deforming disease whose sufferers were maximally ravaged and horribly contagious persons, who bore an anomalous mixture of living and dead tissue. There is a vast discrepancy between Biblical and clinical leprosy, which is also known as Hansen's disease. The latter is more benign, curable, and less contagious than popular images thereof suggest (Lewis 1987; Douglas 1991; Barrett 2005). Isolated instances of clinical leprosy occurred in Bushbuckridge until the 1970s, but few villagers were acquainted with the disease.

source of conflict between husbands and wives; on at least one occasion such an accusation was the pretext for homicide (McNeill and Niehaus 2009: 20–2).

By seeing witchcraft where others saw AIDS, Jimmy was going against the drift of blaming the victim. He was also subverting the authority of elders such as his own father, who attributed the deaths of younger people to their own irresponsible sexual conduct. By regarding Rebecca and Andrew as undeserving victims of malevolent forces, he entertained a measure of hope. Whereas persons with AIDS were destined to die, the victims of witchcraft might still be saved by diviners, who could retrieve them from the witches. Witchcraft also made sense, given the long history of suspicion of his father. Important effects of witchcraft accusations are the 'cutting of networks' and construction of social boundaries (Strathern 1996: 523). At the same time, Jimmy's assertions about witchcraft affirmed the close bonds of kinship he sustained with his niece and half-brother. They also expressed – while half-obscuring – Jimmy's concerns about his own health.

Encountering Marashea's Witches

Jimmy's health – which had always appeared to be perfect – gradually began to deteriorate. His friend Patrick Monna told me that Jimmy had contracted a sexually transmitted disease in 1999, allegedly from having engaged in sexual intercourse with a woman who had had a backstreet abortion. Jimmy took three days' sick leave and consulted a well-known diviner, who administered an effective herbal concoction.

The next time that Jimmy became ill was when he resided in the noisy neighbourhood of Marashea's tavern in 2003. One evening Iris woke Jimmy and asked him to accompany her to the outside pit latrine. Whilst keeping guard, Jimmy saw and heard figures that might have been zombies. Later, during the course of the week, Jimmy suffered an attack either of severe flu, or maybe even of pneumonia:

For more than two weeks I was very sick. I coughed. I felt weak. I had a lack of appetite and also constipation. I went to a diviner. He threw his lots and said that my girlfriend's neighbours had set a trap for me. They laid a potion [xifulane] *on my path and I stepped on it. They actually wanted to kill me. The neighbours are very dangerous: they did not confront me with words, but with [witch] familiars. I only survived because another diviner from Thulamahashe had fortified me.*

The reason for this intentional harm, according to Jimmy, was that Iris's neighbours incorrectly and enviously believed that, as a teacher, he had been supporting his paramour's mother. It was this envy that had provoked their attempt on his life. This incident prompted Jimmy and Iris temporarily to hire their own room in Acornhoek, away from the noise and witches of Marashea, and even farther away from his father.

In the time that we were out of touch, my colleague, Jonathan Stadler, who was doing ethnographic fieldwork on the impact of AIDS in another village of Bushbuckridge, and his wife, Conny Mathebula, first suggested to me that Jimmy might be displaying the initial symptoms of AIDS. Jonathan noticed that Jimmy had lost weight, his glands were swollen to the size of golf balls, and there were sores on his face, which could not possibly have been the result of a shaving accident. Further confirming this possibility, Conny had met Jimmy at the Tintswalo Hospital where he had been treated for diarrhoea and dehydration. (Jimmy acknowledged this, but shrugged it off as being of minor importance.) She also recalls having met him at a supermarket, and having sparked his interest when she mentioned the name of a diviner who claimed to be able to cure AIDS.

Ace Ubisi, Jimmy's drinking partner, shared these perceptions. He told me that some of Jimmy's former sexual partners were known to have contracted HIV. Sheila Malatsi was critically ill and Patricia Biya had died of an AIDS-related illness during 2003. Ace commented that Jimmy was losing weight, but had initially assumed that his marriage problems might be to blame.

Iris's Sickness

Immediately after Jimmy's recovery from his first pneumonia attack, his girlfriend, Iris, also became ill. She suffered from endless menstruation (*ngobe*) and her condition became so serious that she and Jimmy had to return to the neighbourhood at Marashea's tavern:

When Iris became sick I had to take her back to her mother. I was in a great predicament. I had not paid bridewealth and therefore I had no right to keep her. Had she died I would have been in great shit. Now we were back to square one. Iris was too sick to work. We first took her to the hospital and then to a diviner. After about a year, she recovered. We thought that the diviner had cured her.

In 2004 Iris's cousin, Tulip Maatsie, recruited her at very short notice to work at a prestigious tourist lodge. The lodge is located in the savannah outside Impalahoek and its clientele are mainly wealthy European and American tourists. Iris was initially employed as a temporary worker, but the manager was so impressed by her work performance – the manner in which she cleaned, cooked, presented the menus, and beat the drums before meal times – that he asked her to stay on as an extra helping hand.

Iris was surprised to learn from the other employees that Tulip had spoken to them about her in the most unflattering terms, warning them that Iris's mother and Iris herself were witches. Worst of all, Tulip had promised the other employees that she planned to take revenge, and would hire a powerful Mozambican diviner to strike them down:

One day I arrived at the lodge and found that Iris was tired and very quiet. After a while she confided in me and told me what Tulip had gossiped about her to the other workers. Iris said that she no longer felt comfortable at the tourist lodge. Once they repaired the electricity and Iris had to sleep in Tulip's room. That evening she could not sleep. This young woman, Tulip, used potions for everything – she even put potions in her body lotion. She obtained these from diviners so that she could attract men. Iris also found ancestral cloths in Tulip's wardrobe and could not understand why a young woman would keep these things. Her mind is screwed. . . . Iris once saw how Tulip poured potions into the chocolate mousse she made for her boyfriend.[9] *He ate the potions there in Iris's presence, but she was too scared to make any comments.*

Tulip began to envy Iris because the manager liked her. Once Tulip came home and told her mother, 'I want Iris fired or I want her dead!' A few days later, Iris found a snake in her bed. This was very mysterious. Iris did not know where the snake came from because all the windows were closed. Now Iris's sickness reappeared. She complained to me about headaches, tiredness, and about an upset stomach. She cried when speaking to me on the phone. The manager wanted to take her to hospital, but Iris wanted to come home.

I took Iris to a local doctor and he gave her tablets. But I could see that Western medicine was not taking her anywhere. Iris then went to the ZCC [Zion Christian Church]. Here the prophets told her that some of her neighbours had put potions at her place of residence, and the prophets prescribed tea, coffee, Vicks, Vaseline, and Coke for Iris. The prophets instructed Iris to take the Coke bottle outside at midnight and smash it against a stone.

Since witches were plaguing Iris's workplace, Jimmy advised her to quit her job. Iris resigned at the end of May 2005 to begin working as a hairdresser from home and also from a salon in the town of Hoedspruit. This meant a considerable loss of income: Iris earned about R1,200 per month at the lodge in basic salary, plus free board and lodging, and in addition to this, she received about R200 in tips. But she found the more flexible schedules of hairdressing more amenable to her sickness.

[9] Jimmy possibly referred to *korobela*, a kind of potion used by women to win men's affection, to manipulate men by mystical means, and to bring them under a woman's control. Once doctored with *korobela*, a man would not display interest in any other woman (Niehaus 2002b: 5).

Jimmy's Second Pneumonia Attack?

I managed to do only a short bout of fieldwork during the winter vacation of 2005. Upon my arrival in Impalahoek, I immediately heard that Jimmy was seriously ill and was recuperating at the home of his sister, Jessie. On 20 June I found Jimmy, Iris, and his brothers seated in his sister's lounge, watching replays of European football matches on television. Jimmy was draped in a blanket. Although he was notably ill, Jimmy was very happy to see me, and said that he had recovered sufficiently to help me complete his biography. Jimmy insisted that I should interview him at my home at the Wits Rural Facility. This is where we spent the next four days. Here he felt safe from his father's witchcraft, could bathe in hot water, and enjoy the energy drinks, fish, and vegetarian meals that my colleague prepared. For the first time I noticed what others had seen much earlier: there were sores on Jimmy's lips and the skin on his forehead was badly discoloured.

We first went over the script I had written previously, and Jimmy proceeded to give me a day-by-day account of how his sickness had progressed:

On Friday, 10 June, I went to school as usual and I taught. But I had a premonition that something was wrong with my body. I came from my class and went to sleep in Thabo's car. When I woke up my whole body ached: my eyes itched, my throat was sore, and I had a headache and a swollen stomach. At one [pm] Thabo and I left for Banda's tavern. Thabo bought beers and invited me to join in, but I said, 'No! I can't drink beer today! I'm not feeling myself. Rather get me a can of soda water!' I thought that it might help my stomach.

Thabo then dropped me off at home. When I alighted from the vehicle I felt as if something had sat upon me. I went into the house and could not even climb onto the bed. I had no power. My legs were dangling in front of me and I felt terribly cold. I also had palpitations and I found it difficult to breathe. This was no ordinary sickness. As I lay on the bed my body went numb. It felt as if my lower torso was paralysed. I could not feel anything. I had never experienced such pain in my entire life – it was far worse than when they cut off my foreskin without an anaesthetic during my initiation.

Iris did not know what to do. I told her that I did not want anything to eat and that she should not tell my mother about my ailments. I did not want her to scare my mother. Iris left me on the bed, sat on the sofa, and cried. She asked the rhetorical question: 'Are you feeling better?' Actually, I felt worse. I wanted to die. I could no longer endure the pain. My whole body was dead. I cannot even give you a true description of what I felt. Whatever I will say would be an understatement. I was in pain and my eyes were closed. I could not even see. I also struggled to speak. I opened my mouth, but could not hear myself.

The people who came to see me did not have the guts to look at me. They did not think I would even make four hours.

On the weekend [11 and 12 June], I could not get out of bed and walk to the toilet [outside]. But I had diarrhoea. Iris would shift me onto a pot. To simplify things I stayed naked on the bed. I was very jittery and nervous. I could not sleep and I was sensitive to any movement. I did not like food and I did not like noise. I did not want to hear footsteps, cars driving, people talking, or radios playing.

On Monday 13 June I hired a car and asked Teddy Manzini [a neighbour] to drive me to a general practitioner in Dwarsloop. This guy [the doctor] was scared to see me. He took me into the consultation room for a check-up. I was in pain and I could not hear the things he said. He asked me whether I wanted an injection and I said, 'Yes.' I actually wanted it to make me sleep. My whole body was sore. I was on the [doctor's] bed for three minutes and I failed to climb off. The doctor said that I might have pneumonia and something like bronchitis. He gave me tablets and a bucket of syrup. This is because I coughed a lot. Then I went home. But the medicine was of no help. Not in any way! It worsened everything.

On Tuesday 14 June my mother came. She realised how bad things were, phoned my brothers, and told them to come back home. My mother also consulted a diviner called Monareng. That is how she discovered the witchcraft business. The diviner said that I had stepped on a very powerful potion [xifulane] *that witches had put at my gate. She also said that the witches had sent a* tokolotši *[ape] and other familiars to weaken me at night. She told my mother, 'If you don't pull up your socks your son won't live.' The diviner gave my mother some concoctions to burn in a clay pot and I had to inhale the smoke with a reed. Just imagine the pain I felt in my chest: the weak body of mine smoking heavy concoctions. The smoke made me cough like hell. I coughed until I lay without any feeling.*

Monareng, the diviner, came on Wednesday 15 June and she inquired about my welfare. I felt shit, but I lied to her and told her that I felt better. My head was sore and my breathing was very uneven. I could not eat, shit, get out of bed, or even put on my shoes. She asked me to come to her place, but I did not go. She was lucky. She would have been discredited if I had died at her place.

On Thursday [16 June] Jessie's boy [Jimmy's nephew] came early in the morning to see me. I thought I was going [dying]. The young boy just managed one glance. He could not tolerate a second one. Then he ran to my mother, saying, 'My uncle [malome] *is dying! Can't you do something?' As they conversed, Mrs Morema, a woman sitting next to my mother at the market, asked if she could help. She then accompanied my mother to my quarters. She [Mrs Morema] came into the bedroom, looked at me, and said, 'Yes. It is the potions* [xifulane] *witches are using these days to kill people.' She asked me how long I had been sick and then she said, 'It is late.' She then fetched a few things from her home and came back to me in no time. The woman quickly smeared potions on my head, legs, waist, breasts, and arms. Then she stretched me. She also took a brand new razor and cut incisions on my head, neck and arms. After that, I felt that a big load of weight had been taken off my shoulders. The pains were alleviated and for the first time I could sleep. I was grateful. But I could still not eat.*

On Friday [17 June] Mrs Morema made a concoction of tea, FG [coffee] and vinegar for my stomach. She also gave me a burning powder to stop my heart from palpitating. This powder was itchy and burnt my mouth. At eleven [am] she made an incision on the middle of my head.

Early in the morning my brothers, Moses, Kagišo, and Peter, went to a diviner and asked him to show them who is killing me. He took them into his divination hut [ndumba] *and asked them to drink a concoction from small glasses. Moses and Kagišo took the drug. They sat there and fell into a sort of a trance. The diviner then told Moses and Kagišo to stare at a white wall in front of them and call out the name of anyone whom they thought is a witch. The wall works like a sort of television.*[10] *They called our father and the guy immediately came out on the screen. Then they asked him, 'Go and call all your friends!' Then out came my father's brother, two of his cousins, his nephew, a ZCC minister, and Mahapa [one of Impalahoek's most notorious witches]. Moses and Kagišo also saw Kevin [their deceased brother], Duduzile, and Rebecca [Luckson's grand-daughters]. They were all alive.*[11] *These people all emerged from a two-roomed shanty. My brothers also saw my father's familiars – the snake* [mamlambo], *white woman* [missies], *and the* tokolotši *[ape] with which he screws men from behind.*

My brothers were angry and asked the diviner to help them kill our father. The diviner said, 'Give me a chance. I can kill him today! If you take me there I can kill him right now, even if he has a snake. I am more powerful than him.' My brothers even became scared listening to the diviner. The diviner did not see my father as a competitor. He spoke of my father as an ant that he could trample on. The diviner boasted that he had killed many other witches of my father's calibre. But he begged my brothers, 'Let's first focus on the person who is ill. I can see a sick man. He is bedridden.' The diviner gave my brothers

10 Delius (1996: 195–6) notes that during the witch-hunts conducted by the Comrades of Sekhukhuneland, some diviners hung white sheets on the wall of a darkened room and gave small groups green potions to drink. They would feel intoxicated, stare at the wall, and call out that those responsible for deaths should appear. The viewers would call out the names of individuals they knew. The screen was known as a 'video' or as 'African television'.

11 The first people to appear on the 'screen' were zombies and, thereafter, Luckson's accomplices in witchcraft. Generation is very significant here: the victims of witchcraft are seen to be youngsters, and the perpetrators thereof, elders.

prescriptions and asked them to bring me to his place in a week's time, so that he could make my father's witchcraft boomerang. For all this he did not even ask my brothers a cent.

Later that day my brothers told me that the diviner had revealed that my father was trying to change me into a zombie.

Kagišo found me in a terrible state. He hardly spent ten minutes with me. Then he became angry and he ran amok. As he walked to my parents' home, he saw my father seated next to the phone booth at the market. Kagišo whistled to my father, and signalled for my old man to come by hand.[12] *Kagišo then shouted at him, 'Let me tell you! You are a witch! I saw all the people you killed and I know all your friends! I give you two days to cure my brother. Otherwise, I am prepared to go to maximum [security] prison.' All the time my father pleaded, saying, 'I'm a Zionist. I know nothing about the things you say.'*

At five [pm] Kagišo again confronted my father. He said, 'You don't have to lock the gates of your home. We have hired Zulus from the hostels [migrant labour compounds] to kill you because you are so troublesome. I remind you, you have a day and a couple of hours to heal Jimmy.' My father pleaded with him to come into the home. But Kagišo refused. 'No,' he said 'you want to show me your snake and silence me!' That night the witch [Luckson] never slept. Each time that he heard a car pass, he jumped from bed to peep through the window to see if people were coming for him.

On Saturday evening [18 June] I began to show the first signs of life. That evening I moved to Jessie's [his sister's] home. The diviner told my brothers that he could not cure me at my own place because my father had planted things in the yard. Kagišo had fortified the room [at Jessie's home] on instructions from Moses. My brothers also followed the prescriptions of the diviner. They asked me to strip naked, made incisions on my joints, stretched my limbs, and asked me not to wash for two days. They also gave me a concoction for my breasts. My brothers don't allow people to see me. Whenever anyone comes, they will tell the person, 'Jimmy is not here!'

When I went to see Jimmy on Monday, 20 June, he felt a great deal better. A striking aspect of Jimmy's narrative was his present-orientated apprehension of pain (Wolff and Langley 1968). Jimmy was emotional and desired immediate relief from pain. He did not see his recovery as a long-term effect of the injection and tablets the doctor had provided a week earlier, but rather of the more recent interventions by the diviners

[12] Fairly elaborate rules of 'etiquette' and 'respect' (*hlompa*) that affirmed rank based on seniority, gender, and age marked everyday social intercourse in Bushbuckridge. Juniors and women were expected to acknowledge the seniority of any man by standing when he entered a room, offering him a seat, and holding both hands when greeting him. They also had to refrain from calling him by name or beckoning at him to come. By beckoning to his father, Kagišo showed insubordination and disrespect.

his brothers and mother consulted. Jimmy did not seem to fear the future recurrence of his symptoms. He was optimistic that he would make a complete recovery and that the diviner would soon defeat his father.

He [the diviner] assured us that in two days I would be on my feet again. Yesterday I walked to the toilet and relieved myself. The old people are surprised that I am not bedridden. Today was the first time that I could eat maize porridge. Sakkie, this is primary anthropology – living the facts of your research![13]

I don't know of any witch as intelligent as my father. Nobody informed him that I was ill, but he told my mother, 'I learn that my son is sick. He had sex with a woman who had committed an abortion. Get money so that Jimmy can see Timothy [another herbalist].' How did my father know that I am sick? From where does he get my symptoms? Does this not tell you that my father is a witch? Does this not show to you that this beast is intelligent? . . . But I am sure that the diviner can defeat him. The diviner cured me in two days. This shows you that he is more powerful than my father.

I did not share Jimmy's optimism. Despite his recovery from what I believed were some of the graver symptoms of pneumonia, Jimmy was still weak and coughed persistently. I also noticed him staring at the wounds on his mouth and at the discolouration on his forehead in my bathroom mirror. During my short stay in Bushbuckridge I had an earnest conversation with Jimmy. I told him that I believed his sickness might reappear and that he should not merely rely upon diviners, but that he should also consult a proper biomedical doctor. To be on the safe side, I advised Jimmy to undertake a test for HIV antibodies, and emphasised that even if he tested positive, he could control the condition with antiretroviral therapy. I also begged Jimmy to accompany me to Pretoria, which had better medical facilities than Bushbuckridge. Jimmy was adamant that he first wished to consult the diviner, and to ensure his father's final downfall. As a compromise, I gave Jimmy R1,000 and he promised me that he would use the money to consult the best available local doctor for a full medical check-up.

As puzzling to me as Jimmy's short-term apprehension of pain was his tendency to continue trusting in processes of divination, despite the fact that he often saw the interventions of particular diviners as unsuccessful. In retrospect, I have come to see his commitment to the paradigm subscribed to by diviners as an effect of diagnostic labelling and of the politics of culpability. From a pragmatic viewpoint which seeks to understand 'lived social processes' (Ortner 2006), the difference

[13] Here Jimmy referred to the numerous stories about witchcraft that we had listened to during the course of our research. We often listened to others recalling the misfortunes they had suffered at the hands of witches.

between Jimmy's and my perspectives involved more than a simple 'clash of values'. From Jimmy's position and perspective, accepting a diagnosis of witchcraft excused him from blame and provided greater hope of recovery. It also created the possibility of revenge against his father. A diagnosis of AIDS would have compelled Jimmy to confront the consequences of his sexual liaisons and to accept the possibility that he had spread the dreaded disease to his sexual partners. In short, this diagnosis and diagnostic paradigm would have undermined all claims to moral personhood. These factors did not apply to my own perspective, rooted in a position of relative detachment. Nonetheless, I cannot avoid the feeling that I made a serious mistake by not being more confrontational. In retrospect, I feel that I should have taken Jimmy to the Rixile clinic.

Luckson Attacked

The Mohale family planned to conduct the *hlobolo* ritual to formally close the period of bereavement for Andrew's death on Saturday 14 August. Without consulting their father, the Mohale siblings excluded him and started making preparations for the event by themselves. When Luckson visited the home of his second wife, *ngwa* Usinga, he was extremely surprised to find his sons busy erecting the tent. When he asked them where they had obtained the tent and chairs, Rodney Mohale (Andrew's younger brother) replied that they had borrowed it from the Wesleyan minister. Luckson became furious and immediately confronted the minister, who was also his neighbour, saying that he, as head of the family, should have borrowed these items. Luckson also accused the minister of gossiping about him with his sons. The minister then went to the home of the bereaved family to retrieve his tent and chairs. Rodney was extremely upset, saying that it would be impossible to host the ritual without shade and seats for the visitors. He pleaded with the minister, requesting him to leave the tent and chairs in place until the next day, when the ritual would have been completed.

Rodney then confronted Luckson, demanding an explanation for his interference. During the argument Luckson grabbed a broomstick and beat Rodney with it. But Rodney retaliated with his fists, and hit his father over the head with a brick. Luckson fell down, bleeding profusely from the wound. The minister came to Luckson's assistance and tried to calm Rodney.

A neighbour rushed Luckson to hospital, where nurses bandaged his head. The doctors asked him to file a claim of assault against Rodney at the police station. However, the police officers advised Luckson to resolve the dispute at home. Luckson invited his relatives to discuss the incident on the Sunday after the ritual. But they refused. Instead, the Mohale siblings congratulated Rodney for having beaten their father.

Our Last Meeting

On Thursday, 25 August, one of my other research assistants phoned my office in Pretoria from Bushbuckridge. He told me that Jimmy was seriously ill and said that he was concerned that Jimmy was not receiving appropriate biomedical care. Unfortunately, having health problems myself, I was unable to drive to Bushbuckridge that weekend. Only once a scan had revealed a growth on my pancreas to be a cyst rather than a tumour was I able to drive the necessary 480 kilometres.

On Saturday morning, 3 September, I knocked at the door of Jimmy's two-roomed house. Jimmy was guarded by his brothers, Moses and Kagišo, and also by his sister, Jessie, and was seated on a sofa, eating soft porridge. He looked like an old man. He was trembling, his eyes protruded, he was notably darker in complexion, and he had lost a great deal of weight.

Jimmy greeted me politely and invited me to sit next to him. I noticed that his demeanour had changed. Despite being able to speak only with great difficulty, and despite being characteristically sociable, his voice also had a new note of authority. It was, ironically, at the time of his greatest weakness and vulnerability that Jimmy assumed his most dominant persona. At times, he spoke as if he was issuing commands, and even when he did not, his words seemed to be especially thoughtful and profound. I immediately asked him whether there was anything that I could do for him. He looked me straight in the eyes, and said:

Sakkie, you cannot be both a player and a referee.

Jimmy had heard, via Moses, that I was concerned that he was not receiving appropriate biomedical care. He resented my attempts to interfere. He made it clear that he and his siblings were the players: they were in a better position to understand his illness and to seek a cure. As his biographer, I was a referee who merely had to observe the contest between them and his father.

I nonetheless drove to the nearest supermarket to purchase groceries, energy drinks, and fresh fruit and vegetables for the sick man. For that day and the next, I sat beside Jimmy's bed, chatting to him and recording his words. Jimmy's breathing was rushed and shallow, and when he asked to use the bucket, his urine was strikingly bright and orange in colour (possibly due to dehydration). Jimmy took great delight in eating the food I brought, especially the canned pears. He could no longer tolerate meat.

The following account of what had transpired in my absence is reconstructed from Jimmy's truncated speech, supplemented by interviews with his neighbour Ace Ubisi, who had visited him daily, and with his maternal cousin, Justice Monna. From these accounts, I learnt that Jimmy's siblings had constituted themselves as his 'therapy management group' (Janzen 1979). Together, Moses, Kagišo, Jessie, and Moses's son,

Mabetha, pooled their resources, cared for Jimmy's daily needs, arranged for his therapeutic consultations, administered the prescribed medications (described later), and evaluated the therapeutic outcomes. As precaution against the possibility that their father might send his agents of witchcraft to attack, Jimmy's siblings jealously guarded his home. They seldom allowed anyone to enter. I was a notable exception – not merely due to my friendship with Jimmy, but perhaps also because my status as a white person was so antithetical to the stereotypical image of a witch.

Iris no longer lived in the home that she once shared with Jimmy. Ace Ubisi told me that he heard from others that Jimmy's siblings had expelled her from the home. But he was of the opinion that Iris had actually abandoned Jimmy in his time of greatest need:

Iris did hairdressing in Hoedspruit and used to leave Jimmy alone at home, without food. She sometimes locked the door and took along the key. I once came to visit Jimmy and found his neighbours giving him soft porridge. She also did not wash his clothes or fetch water for him. Sometimes, when I visited him, he had not washed himself for two or three days. Jimmy once climbed through the window to go to the toilet. Other times he would shit and vomit in the bed. Iris now sleeps at her mother's place. She tells her friends that she won't bother helping Jimmy. When he dies, she says, she won't get a single cent. Jimmy's brothers also told Iris not to come there any longer. They said that he uses potions that won't work when a woman is near him. Kagišo came back from Johannesburg, where he was looking for work, and he took care of his brother. He washes Jimmy's blankets and trousers. Jessie also goes there.

It did not take me long to learn that Jimmy and his therapy management group had not used the money I gave him to consult a medical doctor. Ace emphasised:

Moses, Kagišo and George [Jimmy's cousin who is a lawyer] all say that Jimmy does not need a doctor. They say he needs a diviner.

During my two and a half months of absence, Jimmy had consulted an array of different diviners and Christian healers. Although Jimmy saw the sorts of therapies provided by diviners as his only option, he was critical of some of their interventions:

After you left here, the principal [of Tlasede High School, where Jimmy taught] recommended that I should go on leave. She instructed me to go home and listen to my body. I knew the magic had started and I knew the culprit. I went to an old Mogale man. He fortified me with powerful potions and I got better. He said that I was no longer sick, that I was safe, and that nothing could harm me. But I was only fine for a few weeks.

Then the illness started again. I was so sick. My whole body ached. I should have died. That is when I heard of another gentleman at Chavella Gaza.

He told me, 'This is nothing! I can help you.' The guy then started working on me. For three days I had to go there in the mornings and return in the evenings.

A certain woman took over from him and came here to smear my whole body with oils. This soothed me. With these oils, she removed all the familiars from my body. She took away the snakes. She also took away the antenna with which my father listened to all my conversations. But I did not like some of the things she did. She expected me to walk when I was unable to do so. I was dead and I was not fit to walk.

Jimmy also mentioned consulting a diviner who made him inhale the smoke of burning herbs, and Rampiri, a prophet from the Paradise Church, who treated his body with steaming:

The diviner said that I suffered from mafulara *[meaning that he had broken a funeral taboo by engaging in sex during the period of mourning]. After I inhaled his concoctions, I felt better. But now I'm suffering. My lungs are tired. My lungs are torn.*

I have faith in Rampiri, but I am angry with the boys who helped him. They put me in a small shanty where they steamed me. The boys had to pour water and put leaves on the burning coals, and then carefully move my feet over the coals. This is supposed to have a healing effect. But the boys burnt my feet. [At this point Jimmy asked me to remove his socks so that I could see the huge blisters on the soles of his feet.] I have faith in Rampiri. Mahapa [a most notorious witch] is dead. Rampiri killed him. Rampiri can also kill my father.

Jimmy still perceived diviners and Christian healers as preferable to biomedical doctors. The diviners and prophets whom Jimmy consulted operated within a paradigm that acknowledged the reality of witchcraft, and they impressed Jimmy with the confidence they expressed in the efficacy of their own therapies. Given a more present-time orientation towards pain, he was extremely attentive to minor improvements that occurred, despite his steadily worsening condition. Had it not been for these healers, Jimmy argued, he would have died a long time ago. Jimmy was also dead set against being admitted to the under-resourced Tintswalo Hospital:

Sakkie, Western medication is very good. But the Western doctors cannot diagnose what I have. Sakkie, witchcraft is there. . . . Let's not talk about the hospital. What do they give you at Tintswalo? Medicine? What else? Tablets? They only come to your bed at ten [am], twelve [noon], three and six [pm]. If they find that you are asleep, they just leave you. There is no nursing. When I am here I can drink Bioplus [an energy drink] and eat bananas. Those hospitals are horrible. Tintswalo is bad. Go to the TB ward today. Horrible things happen there. Julius Mashego went there with a very small disease and in three days he was diagnosed with typhoid. The hospital compounds your problems. Not too long ago the sewerage pipes burst and nobody attended to it.

Although the local hospital has suffered from severe financial cutbacks, Jimmy exaggerated its state of decay. Thom (2004) reports that health-care expenditure 'limped behind' in Limpopo (previously Northern) Province. The province spent only 16 per cent of its budget on health. This is in contrast to an average of 22 per cent in other provinces. One doctor in the public sector had to serve a population of 8,544, while a professional nurse had to serve 1,001 people.

Jimmy vehemently denied any possibility that he might be suffering from AIDS-related symptoms. He told me that when Lerato gave birth to their son Klatego at the Hoedspruit military hospital in 1999, the doctors screened Lerato's blood for HIV antibodies. This, however, had been almost six years before he became seriously ill; and the form of screening was probably sentinel surveillance testing, conducted purely for the purpose of generating statistical knowledge about the epidemiological distribution of HIV. Physicians do not communicate the results of these tests to their patients, unless explicitly requested to so. Further testimony to Jimmy's disinclination to engage with biomedical diagnosis was the fact that when his friend, Ronald Mokoena, visited him and advised him to get tested for HIV antibodies, Jimmy refused.

It is hard to assess the consistency and sincerity with which Jimmy held these views. At times Jimmy's claims about witchcraft sounded very much like veiled speech: they seemed to amount to an attempt to express that which he could not say directly. Jimmy seemed to have located his very persona in the liminal domain, betwixt and between life and death. He emphasised that his body was losing its normal functions – of speech, sight, and hearing – as well as its ability to breathe, walk, eat, and defecate properly. He was also concerned about the reactions of others towards him. As Jimmy's illness progressed, he increasingly described himself as a living corpse, who was socially dead yet physically still alive.[14] During our meeting he told me:

The Jimmy that you did research with had only half a life and it came from my maternal family. I only have ancestors on my maternal side. I am dead on my paternal side. . . . People around here know me as being dead. That is why I don't have to be seen. You are interviewing a dead person.

[14] Hertz (1960) observed that death is frequently conceptualised as a process in which the deceased is slowly transferred from the land of the living to the land of the dead, rather than as a single event. In this process, he argues, biological death that ends the human organism and social death that extinguishes a person's social identity need not coincide. Biological death usually precedes the social death in many African contexts where the person remains present in the lives of his or her kin as an ancestor. But there are also cases in which social death can precede biological death – for example, where persons are confined to institutions, such as hospices, for the rest of their lives (Helman 2000).

This statement points to the significance of engagement of social relations in the constitution of personhood. Jimmy did not merely see himself as wasting away physically. He was also concerned about the disrupted nature of his social relationships. He acknowledged the extreme importance of patrilineal kinship networks in providing protection against the witchcraft of outsiders and therapeutic assistance. He acknowledged the fragmentary and disrupted nature of these networks, and the 'malfunctioning' of his paternal ancestors, largely through the failure of his father as mediator.

This view was certainly shared by others, including his maternal cousin, Justice Monna:

Jimmy actually died before the real death. Everything in him changed. The texture of his skin changed and his hair became greyish rather than fuzzy. It also became very patchy. To disguise this he once shaved his hair. The right side of his face was swollen and the other side of his face was dark. But you could still see it was him. He also had no power. He could not move or pick up things. Everywhere people heard that Jimmy was dead.

At times, Jimmy's description of himself seemed to have drawn on discourses both of witchcraft and of AIDS. He sometimes presented his symptoms as indices that he was being turned into a zombie, partially located in the parallel world of witches, and anomalous to the categories of life and death. Jimmy also spoke of sexual entrapment through witchcraft:

After I was born my father instructed his snake [mamlambo] *and his* tokolotši *[ape] to lick me. . . . My father killed a woman and he lets this woman's ghost sleep with me. Each and every night it comes to me. It is like* likubalo *[a potion used to trap illicit lovers]. This thing is difficult to explain.*

As we have seen in the introduction, both the snake-like *mamlambo* and ape-like *tokolotši* have sexual connotations. The *mamlambo* could assume the form of a white lover with shiny silver hair, who satisfies the witch's hedonistic desire for sexual pleasure, but demands regular sacrifices of blood. The *tokolotši*, in turn, perpetrates violent sexual attacks. *Likubalo* can be described as a sort of mystical 'chastity belt'. Adults are said to treat their partners with *likubalo* to prevent them from cheating. One of the ingredients of this potion is a dog's penis, and it allegedly causes illicit lovers to become stuck, like mating dogs, or else to be discovered (Niehaus 2002b: 279).

I again pleaded with Jimmy to use clinical medicine. I argued that even when consulting diviners and prophets, he should not neglect biomedical doctors. As in the case of most things in life, I said, true strength and healing come from a combination of 'tradition' (*setšo*) and 'things of the whites' (*sekgowa*). Clinical medicine was powerful and, even if he was dying, it could alleviate his pains. Moses agreed, but said that he would first take Jimmy to Polokwane, where his brother, Henry, had arranged for him to consult yet another powerful diviner. Jimmy, however, stated his intention to remain in Polokwane only for four days, preferring to return to Impalahoek to see the Christian prophet, Rampiri. He was convinced that Rampiri would save him and 'take out' his father. Nonetheless, I left Jimmy money with which he could seek clinical care.

Before I left, Jimmy called together all the members of his therapy management group, and told them always to regard me as their brother. He cried as I walked out of the door. I felt extremely humbled and distressed, but only cried late that evening. Despite our very intimate social ties, I could not share the conviction of witchcraft that united Jimmy and his siblings. My suspicion of AIDS seemed to have confirmed my status as a perennial outsider.

9 (Re)constructing an Ideal Life

Henry Mohale phoned my office in Pretoria on Friday morning, 16 September. When I returned the call, he informed me that Jimmy had died at six o'clock on Thursday morning at the Mankweng hospital in Polokwane, only eleven days after I had last seen him. Henry said I was one of the first people to be informed and that he expected me to make a speech at Jimmy's funeral on Saturday 24 September. It was not clear precisely what had happened in Polokwane. Jimmy's siblings were secretive about his therapeutic consultations because they feared that their father might use such information to cause him further harm. Before Jimmy died, he reportedly said that their father had finally defeated him, and warned that Henry might become their father's next victim. I felt shocked, but thanked Henry for having taken Jimmy to hospital so that he could receive good palliative care during the last days of his life.

Most people in Impalahoek heard about Jimmy's death through rumours. The first person to break the news was a petrol pump attendant at a local filling station, whose relatives had phoned him from Polokwane. Ace Ubisi heard about Jimmy's death at the sports field, and was surprised that Jimmy's parents were still going about their usual chores. His father was reading his Bible and polishing his shoes on the veranda of their home; and his mother was selling fruit and vegetables at the market. Only at noon on Friday did one of Jimmy's cousins relay the terrible news of his death to them.

By sunset on Friday many people had congregated at Luckson's home. They included Henry, who had driven down from Turfloop, and two of Jimmy's cousins, who had come all the way from Johannesburg. Luckson sat quietly in a corner, accompanied by two Zionist ministers. Jimmy's siblings were very despondent. Rodney said that no single diviner had managed to counter Luckson's power, and that even the most powerful diviners from Venda were too scared to enter his yard. He also complained that it was impossible to hire 'hit men' to assassinate Luckson.

Moses then took out his pistol and breeched it, Rodney produced a knife, George fetched an axe, and Henry picked up a rake to confront Luckson. Ace Ubisi recalled:

They acted as if they were mad. They were making a great noise and were shouting at Luckson, saying, 'You killed our brothers and our sisters! We'll kill you before we bury Jimmy!' One of them shouted, 'No! We'll kill you today!' Luckson ran and locked himself in his own room. The two ZCC ministers sat on the veranda, but they were too scared to speak.

Stephen Ndlovu [a neighbour who was a policeman] and I pleaded with Jimmy's brothers and I asked them to go to the car. We said, 'Guys. Don't make noise! Don't kill your father!' But they said, 'Ace! Shut up! He is not bewitching you.' We replied, 'We don't say that he is not a witch. But don't kill him now! Kill him after Jimmy is buried. You'll all be arrested and then there will be nobody left to bury your brother. Hire a tent, point out where we must dig the grave, phone the family, and welcome the mourners!' We finally managed to calm them down. Only Rodney did not want to listen.

Whilst Stephen Ndlovu, the policeman, guarded Moses and Rodney, Henry, George, and Ace set off to the home of Jimmy's girlfriend, Iris, to ask for his belongings, so that they could cleanse these with holy water.[1] Iris invited George and Ace to enter, but wanted nothing to do with Henry, with whom she had clashed in the past. She was extremely angry. She had heard about Jimmy's death from her friends in Polokwane. On phoning Kagišo to ask him whether the news was correct, she had been fobbed off. Ace recalled a tense exchange of words:

We introduced ourselves and we said that the Mohale family had sent us to tell her that her boyfriend had passed away. Iris just said, 'So! What must I do?' There were no tears. We said, 'They ask for their son's belongings. You know the procedure. The belongings must be cleansed. We'll return them on Sunday after the funeral.' She replied, 'I can hear what you say. But why did they not inform me when they took Jimmy to Polokwane? Why did they not send you sooner to tell me that Jimmy is late [dead]? Why did I have to hear about it on the streets? Only now, when you want his belongings, do you tell me that he is late.'

She also asked, 'What belongings?' I saw only a sofa in the room. The fridge, television, microwave oven, and video machine were all gone. Iris asked us to follow her into the bedroom. She gave us a plastic bag containing a blanket, electric cable, and some of Jimmy's clothes. There were also fifteen bottles of potions – all of different colours. She said, 'Here are all his belongings! He had nothing else!' We asked her, 'Did Jimmy never have a cup, a spoon, or a plate?' She said, 'No! These all belong to me.' Iris insisted that the fridge, television,

[1] In the case of death, the breath (*moya*) and aura (*seriti*) are believed to separate from the corporeal body and to pollute any object, item, or person with whom the deceased had come into contact whilst he or she was still alive. Such pollution is recognised as dangerous and all utensils and belongings of the deceased have to be cleansed thoroughly to 'tie' his or her 'breath' (*hlema moya*) (Niehaus 2002a: 201, 203).

microwave oven, and video machine belonged to her. She said that Jimmy had bought the fridge, but that she paid the instalments. She was very aggressive.

Iris's statement contained some truth but was not completely correct: the microwave oven had been bought by Jimmy with money he earned from his work as a research assistant. Ace recalled that Jimmy's siblings became furious when they heard that his girlfriend refused to part with his belongings:

Moses was very angry. He said that he needed the furniture, and also the keys for Jimmy's car. By now the car had been standing [stationary] in the backyard of his home for almost two years. Peter took a knife and ran down the street, shouting, 'I'm going to kill that whore [sefebe]*!' But the policeman [Stephen] grabbed Peter and brought him back to the car.*

On Saturday the Mohale siblings sent Jimmy's cousin, Meriam Ngobeni, to inform Jimmy's wife, Lerato, about his death. They gave Meriam R200 and asked her to give this to Lerato so that she could purchase mourning clothes. This encounter was equally tense. Lerato reportedly told Meriam that she wished to bury Jimmy at her own home, and that she refused to mourn at his parents' place.

Henry later met with Lerato and her brothers at a local football field, and pleaded with them not to fight over the corpse, but rather to assist them in burying Jimmy at his parents' home. He promised Lerato that he, himself, would pay for the entire funeral, that all money recovered from Jimmy's accounts would go to their children, and that the house in White River would be hers. Lerato's brothers, nonetheless, proceeded to pitch a second funeral tent at her home, and said that Lerato would attend Jimmy's funeral service only if Iris was absent.

Jimmy's siblings then set off to inform more distant kin about his death. They asked Father Mnisi for permission to use the very large hall of the Pentecostal Crusade Church for Jimmy's funeral service. Father Mnisi consented, but only on condition that the mourners refrained from wearing hair-dos, jewellery, or silver Zion Christian Church badges. He said that the church council had imposed these restrictions. Henry and Lerato then went to draw money from a bank in Nelspruit, and arranged for the Elite Funeral Parlour to fetch Jimmy's corpse from Polokwane, keep it in a mortuary nearby, and undertake the necessary funeral arrangements.

On Wednesday 21 September, Jimmy's siblings asked Ace to organise a team of young men to dig a grave in the local burial ground, at a site indicated by Jimmy's oldest son, born from his first extramarital relationship. Giving Ace some money, they instructed him to purchase cannabis, Boxer tobacco, Peter Stuyvesant cigarettes, and home-brewed sorghum beer for the gravediggers. Smoking and drinking reportedly enable men to cope with drudgery in the polluted graveyard. They also, perhaps, generate an experience of altered consciousness. Villagers perceive graveyards as dangerous spaces, polluted by the breath (*moya*) and aura (*seriti*) of the deceased, especially of those who have died unexpectedly – such as the victims of murder, witchcraft, or motor vehicle accidents. Children below the age of 16 and persons in a dangerous state of heat, such as widows and pregnant women, may not enter, as it is feared that they might become sick from inhaling the aura of the deceased.

Preparations for the funeral suggested that it would be no less conflictual than others described in this account. Moses purchased an ox, which men slaughtered, roasting the liver in the flames of the funeral fire. However, nearly all those who ate the meat developed diarrhoea. Some youngsters claimed that Luckson had bewitched the beast, and changed its liver into a snake liver. But elders blamed the slaughterers for being negligent: to avoid diarrhoea, they said, one should always tie the ox's tail into a knot before slaughtering it.

Further tensions arose at the home of the bereaved family, when people complained that Jimmy's oldest daughter, Kgopotšo, had not attended a single prayer meeting. Kgopotšo said that she was acting under instruction from her mother. But the Mohale siblings reprimanded her, saying that her non-attendance would result in their refusal, as her paternal kin, to assist her in the event of her marriage. In an attempt to keep some tensions at bay, the siblings undertook to maintain cordial relations with Luckson throughout the funeral period.

On the same day that Ace and his men began digging the grave, teachers of the Tlasede High School and the entire Mohale family attended a memorial service for Jimmy at the Impalahoek Community Hall. Only Jimmy's wife, Lerato, was absent, perhaps in order to avoid encountering Jimmy's girlfriend, Iris. But Iris did not attend either.

The Night Vigil and Funeral

I arrived at the Mohale home from Pretoria on the afternoon of Friday 23 September. After making a financial contribution to assist Henry with meeting the enormous expenses that he was likely to incur, I joined the other mourners.

At sunset a cavalcade of motor vehicles left Impalahoek to fetch Jimmy's corpse from the Elite mortuary (about five kilometres away). The casket lay open and Jimmy's corpse was dressed in a dark suit, surrounded by yellow flowers. Pastor Monareng of the Hope Fellowship read a passage from the Bible describing how Moses had commanded the Israelites to exhume his corpse and take his bones to Canaan. The pastor said we should all be buried at the place of our ancestors, and that like the Israelites, we were now taking Jimmy to his home. We must thank God for the time we spent with Jimmy, and there must be peace in his family during this difficult time. Mourners then closed the lid of his coffin and loaded it into a large white Mercedes Benz. The cavalcade moved slowly towards Impalahoek.

The hearse stopped in front of the main gate of Jimmy's parents' home. In the case of violent deaths, suicide, and AIDS coffins are sometimes left in the hearse, outside the gate. But young men carried Jimmy's coffin into the home and placed it in the room that he and Lerato had shared for so many years. The (re)location of the deceased back into the social space of the patrilineage is an extremely important aspect of funerals, in Bushbuckridge and elsewhere in Africa (Smith 2004). This act provoked strong emotions. I felt tearful as I recalled the happy times that Jimmy had spent at this home: the times when we ate watermelon and watched football matches in the dining room, played with his children, and slept on reed mats in the shade of an apricot tree instead of doing a social survey as we'd intended. But I also recalled how Jimmy had later avoided his father at all costs, refusing even to walk past the home. I had often wished that Jimmy would return to the room with his wife and children and reconcile with his father. Ironically, this was possible only after his death.

Pastor Monareng proclaimed that Jimmy's corpse would wait in this room until the next morning, when we would take it to its final resting place. Hereafter, the men loudly prayed individual prayers, screaming out the words in a cacophony of sound, and women relatives laid bright flowers in the room. Henry asked me if I wished to see Jimmy for the last time, but I declined, saying that I preferred to remember him as he had been while alive.

The night vigil started at 10 pm and was an extremely dignified event. Mourners sang hymns and prayed in a large tent that was pitched in the yard. The Mohale siblings succeeded in suppressing almost all tensions from public view. The evening was marred by only one incident. One of Jimmy's cousins refused to shake hands with Luckson and said, straight to his face, 'You fucking witch! You killed Jimmy!' But the other mourners calmed the young man down, and ministers from several churches protected Luckson from potential harm throughout the night. The vigil, as observed by Klaits (2010: 72–4), consoles the bereaved kin by means of word and prayer, and also strengthens them for ensuing events, particularly at the dangerous graveyard.

The next morning, men again loaded Jimmy's coffin into the Mercedes Benz. Schoolgirls dressed in the orange skirts of Tlasede High School marched in two lanes, alongside the hearse. Nearly 2,000 mourners gathered in the enormous Pentecostal Crusade Church hall to attend the funeral service. This was an exceptionally large turnout: the funeral of a shop owner, held on the same day, drew only a hundred mourners. The hall was decorated with flowers and with two large graduation photographs of Jimmy. There was also a banner at the back of the stage, proclaiming in black letters on a golden background, 'REST IN PEACE JIMMY'. Men placed the coffin in front of the elevated centre stage, where all close kin and speakers sat. A two-man band, playing an electronic keyboard and electric guitar, provided the music.

In social contexts where the relational attributes of personhood are repeatedly emphasised, death is often portrayed as a diffuse process, in which multiple social relations that constitute the person are terminated or reconfigured (Bloch 1988). Funerals in Bushbuckridge dramatised this process. Different speakers were called upon to represent the therapy management group, paternal kin, maternal kin, and affines of the deceased; as well as the professional bodies, community organisations, and churches to which the deceased belonged. Jimmy's funeral service was exceptional: not only because there were as many as nineteen different speakers, but also because at least eight of us were Jimmy's professional colleagues. All speakers were dressed in a manner befitting members of the educated middle class.

Pastor Monareng started with Bible reading and prayer, thereby sacralising the procedures. He said that we as neighbours and friends had come to pay our last tributes to Jimmy and celebrate the last chapter of his life. The pastor prayed for the master of ceremonies and for all participants, mentioning the speakers, the learners who had come to sing and console the family, and also the pastors who had come to deliver the word of God. He concluded by saying that we had to accept what had happened, be courageous, and be strong.

Ripho Mokoena, a director of the Limpopo Department of Education, acted as master of ceremonies. I had never met Ripho on any previous occasion, but was told that he had studied with Jimmy at Turfloop. Ripho commanded everyone to switch off their mobile phones:

I have switched off my three phones. Even if you have an appointment to speak with the President of South Africa: put your phone on silent.

As elder brother, **Moses Mohale** had the unenviable task of describing the circumstances surrounding Jimmy's death. Moses adopted a minimalist approach, giving only the barest details. He said that Jimmy was ill for only a short period, recovered, but again became terminally ill. This statement can be read as a denial that Jimmy might have died from any AIDS-related disease. In a context where people used a limited vocabulary of disease, AIDS is usually described as a 'long' or 'protracted' illness (LeClerc-Madlala 2000). Moses emphasised that they had done everything they could, and took Jimmy to healers in Polokwane, where he finally passed away. (He used the Northern Sotho word *ngaka*, which can either mean diviner or biomedical doctor.)

Jimmy's daughters, **Kgopotšo and Thandi Mohale**, then ascended the podium. They wore black and white dresses, with black shawls covering their shoulders, and held flowers in their hands. Kgopotšo spoke, saying that they would miss Jimmy and that he was one of the very best fathers children could have.

You were so strong, father! You were a leader to us! You taught us to be strategic and to do things in a good way. We as your daughters and as your son say we are proud of you. We will always remember you. May your soul rest in peace!

Wearing a fashionable ear-ring and dark suit which belied his image as an ordinary mineworker, **Patrick Monna** represented Jimmy's friends. Patrick remarked:

We lost a great friend and mentor, who always joked and made people laugh. Nobody ever saw Jimmy being angry. Jimmy left good memories and we as Jimmy's friends should maintain the ties of friendship between us.

Stephen Ndlovu, the police lieutenant, spoke on behalf of Jimmy's neighbours:

Jimmy's death bit us. He was our brother and our neighbour. He was not only a teacher at school. He was also a teacher at home. He always told us to go to school and to read books. He also asked, 'What are you doing now?' I have progressed as a policeman because I started reading books. Jimmy used to say to me, 'One day I want to hear that you are the station commander.'

Cain Ngobeni – Jimmy's maternal uncle (*malome*), a school principal – represented Jimmy's maternal kin. He described Jimmy as a nephew, son, and friend. Cain recalled that he once advised Jimmy about his marital problems and that Jimmy heeded the advice:

Jimmy was an angel. He was also a negotiator. Whenever people were angry we sent him to calm them down. . . . I say this to Mohale. When a son is born we open the door. When a child is born it is registered that he or she will die one day. Don't worry about Jimmy's death. His job is done. I want to tell you something. Death opens two gates. Death opens a gate of hopelessness that destroys everything. It can cause problems that make families separate. But death also opens a gate of strength and of power. When you decide which gate to use, press the button for the gate of happiness and unity. In the beginning you, my sister, said that you loved [Luckson] Mohale. We would still love to see you love Mohale. The same applies to you, Luckson. We want to see you take good care of our sister. We also want you, as parents, to love your children. Children! We as uncles love to see you respect your parents. Rebuild the unity and be together as a large family.

Selina Mohale – Jimmy's father's classificatory sister (*rakgadi*) – spoke on behalf of his paternal family:

When Jimmy was young we referred to him as a small branch. Small branches need support. We wanted Jimmy to become a large branch, who developed many smaller branches of the family. But Jimmy's life was cut short. We must now accept God's will.

Meriam Mashile – another teacher – represented Lerato's kin. She described Jimmy as their only son-in-law and as a very good father:

Even if he is late, we will love him in all directions. He always greeted people and we loved his professionalism. He would always help you if you wanted additional education. He was a good brother-in-law who listened. His death hurt us. We do not know where to go when God takes people we love. But Mohale's children are still alive. Jimmy's death must not make his children uncontrollable and end their future. They need a father figure. We must take care of Jimmy's leaves [his progeny]. Lerato does not know what to do now, but God will advise her.

Jimmy's professional colleagues included two school principals, a university professor, the chief's older sister, as well as representatives of the Tlasede school governing body, and of the South African Democratic Teachers' Union (SADTU).

B. R. Chiloane, a school principal who lived within 200 metres of Jimmy's parents, emphasised Jimmy's commitment to schooling, saying that he first completed all grades before attending the circumcision lodge. Few learners would do so today:

Jimmy was a good listener and congratulated you when you did good things. When I came from Phalaborwa I saw seven people who had died in a car accident. The people who came to look cried. Should Jimmy have been there they would not have cried. He would have comforted them. The Mohale family lost a member and we don't know how to replace him. Jimmy was our prodigal son.

The master of ceremonies then read out a letter written by **Prudence Mashile**, the chief's sister. Unfortunately, she was too ill to attend Jimmy's funeral. In the letter, Prudence gave her condolences and mentioned that she was always close to Jimmy and to the Mohale family. She met Jimmy in 1981, when they were in the same class at high school, and recalls that he was fairly reserved. In 1985 they again met at the University of the North, where Jimmy studied difficult subjects. She also recalled that Jimmy had invited her to his graduation. She then acknowledged Jimmy's contribution to organising a series of winter schools as part of the Progress Education Project in 1996.

I spoke as Professor of Anthropology at the University of Pretoria. In my speech I said that I was blessed to have known Jimmy and that working with him was one of the highlights of my life. I remarked that through the research we did we sought to promote better understanding between different sections of South Africa's population. Jimmy admired Nelson Mandela, and like his political idol, he worked for peace and reconciliation, if only in some small way. I said that Jimmy visited me in Johannesburg, Durban, Cape Town, and in Pretoria where he met numerous anthropologists and historians, both from South Africa and abroad. My parents and academics in countries such as Uganda, the Netherlands, Australia, the United Kingdom, and the United States were shocked to hear about Jimmy's death and asked me to relay their condolences. We should remember Jimmy, perhaps by instituting a book prize in his honour. Moreover, I remarked that I was always impressed with Jimmy's intelligence and kindness, and recalled that he once bought his unemployed cousin a personal computer, thereby enabling him to set up a small business.

Joyce Modike, principal of the Tlasede High School, where Jimmy taught, said that she never realised Jimmy was so popular, nor that he had collaborated on the production of important academic texts. She, nonetheless, described Jimmy as an excellent teacher, who played a major role in helping to raise Tlasede's matriculation pass rate from 20 to 69 per cent. Joyce said that she resisted all attempts by the Department of Education to send Jimmy to another school during the redeployment of teachers:

We as educators and as learners were shocked to hear of Jimmy's death. We did not believe that he would die. He was always strong and reliable. He was a role model who always stood up against things that were wrong.... Even though our school is in a poor neighbourhood, Jimmy would say that things would be all right. After a staff meeting he once wrote a letter to the MEC [Member of the Executive Council] for Education at Limpopo to request equipment. Jimmy said that he was not scared of the MEC – who is a person just like him. Jimmy will leave an enormous gap. We don't know why God took him.

Rapule Segodi spoke as Jimmy's colleague. He recalled that when they were in high school the teachers wished to let Jimmy skip a grade because he attained such good marks. Even though Jimmy was from a poor background he proceeded to study at university, join the ANC, and become a teacher. Jimmy always approached difficulties with a sense of humour. But he became angry when learners returned late after break time. Because Jimmy loved his own children, he sent them to a well-disciplined school in Middelburg. Jimmy was a leader, who was not given the chance to test his full potential.

OBITUARY

This is to certify that I, Jimmy 'Lepara' Mohale of Stand No. 2, Impalahoek village was born on 9 June 1964. I am the third-born child of Mr Luckson and Mrs Selina Mohale.

I received my primary education from Impalahoek School between 1971 and 1977, and went further to receive my secondary education from Mashile High School between 1978 and 1982. When I could not further my studies at tertiary institutions in 1983, I was appointed as a casual teacher at Impalahoek Primary School.

After having saved enough, I then enrolled for BA (ED) with the University of the North, currently known as the University of Limpopo, which I completed in 1989. In 1990, I enrolled for the BA (ED) Hons as a part-time student whilst teaching at the Moletele High School. Due to the fact that the degree to me was not challenging, I then enrolled for my BA Hons in Science of Mission and Religion and the title of the dissertation was *The Concept of Salvation in Black Theology: A Critical Study* and I obtained Cum Laude.

Allow me to be brief and say that I worked at Tlasede High School from 1999 until I took ill and later my untimely demise on the 15 September 2005. I guess now you want to know about my leadership and community involvement roles.

Please be advised that I acted as

- Founder member and Headmaster of the Progress Education Project in 1996
- Executive Member of the Bushbuckridge Rural Resource Centre
- Secretary of the School Governing Body
- Member of the African National Congress

And my achievements?

- Best History student in the former Mapulaneng Circuit in 1981.
- The most important highlight of my life is when I met Prof Sakkie Niehaus in 1990 and became his research assistant; as a result of the academic relationship we published two books together.

I am survived by my beloved wife Lerato Mashile, my beloved children, my parents, and five siblings.

To all my relatives, friends, colleagues, it is time to leave. Please be strong and may the almighty answer your prayers. Till we meet again.

Dated at Pentecostal Crusade Church on this 24th day of September 2005

Figure 9.1. Jimmy Mohale's obituary, September 2005

Justice Kgwedi praised Jimmy's contribution to the School Governing Body, asked everyone to stand up, and read out Jimmy's obituary, which had already been distributed to all mourners (see Figure 9.1).

Thereafter the master of ceremonies, **Ripho Mokoena**, gave a lengthy oration on behalf of the Limpopo Department of Education. He acknowledged that he had known Jimmy from university, and had also met him at SADTU (South African Democratic Teachers' Union) meetings:

I read about death each time I open the newspapers, but I was shaken when I heard about Jimmy's death. Jimmy was disciplined and educated. He was also courageous. . . . Jimmy was part of a delegation who came to speak to me about the conditions in their school. Once Mr. Mabuza and I stopped a driver and told him that he drove so badly that he would kill people. Jimmy was like this. He would tell people when they were wrong. If we were all like Jimmy things would be fine. He was a role model. Like a Mandela, he would say, 'Calm down! Don't fight!

We should emerge strong after his death. South Africa almost came to a standstill in 1993. Chris Hani was murdered and Oliver Tambo died one month later.[2] *People responded by going in their millions to vote ANC and to make Hani and Tambo proud. I do not say, 'Vote ANC'. Vote for the party of your choice. But we must also respond to Jimmy's death. Learners! Pass your exams with flying colours! Jimmy will only rest in peace if you do well. Show that you remember him! Perhaps we should name a block at the school after him.*

Tom Mzimba spoke on behalf of SADTU:

VIVA SADTU! LONG LIVE SADTU! VIVA! VIVA! A hero fell. . . . Only the good people go. Today we lost a peacemaker. We lost an adviser. I don't know how to explain precisely who Jimmy was. He could see danger ahead. School kids, honour Jimmy by passing his favourite subject, history, but not only history.

Towards the end of the funeral service, Lerato's sisters laid wreaths of flowers on the coffin, and read messages of condolence from various close kin and from the learners of Tlasedi. The message from Lerato read:

My dearest husband. We've had our ups and downs. My love persists.

Pastor Nxumalo of the Jubilee Church gave the final sermon. He read from Acts 13: 30–1 and reminded people that Jimmy loved God and had chosen to study Science of Mission and Religion. In the energetic oratory

[2] Chris Hani was leader of the South African Communist Party and chief of staff of Umkhonto We Sizwe, the armed wing of the ANC. Right-wing extremists assassinated Hani outside his home in Boksburg on 10 April 1993. Oliver Tambo served as national chairperson of the ANC from 1967 until his death on 24 April 1993. Tambo died due to complications following a stroke.

style of a seasoned charismatic American evangelist, the pastor warned all mourners of the dangers of hell, and pleaded with us to commit our lives to Jesus, so that we could be saved and enter the Kingdom of God. His sermon provoked a great deal of laughter, undercutting his seriousness:[3]

God bless you! I greet you in the name of Jesus! To all in church, God can help us. Lift your eyes and look! He is the one to give us strength! Believe in God and in Jesus! See the body of Jimmy. We will also die. Thanks God! It is time to get closer to God. Rise up! It is time to change! Jesus can change your life! Accept Jesus as your personal saviour! Tell the Lord that you are sick and tired of the life you are living, that you are in pain, that you have lost a relative. Only the Lord can help!

Jimmy's coffin then left the hall, carried by his kin and followed by his affines. The pallbearers loaded it into the back of the Elite Funeral Parlour hearse, which transported the coffin to one of Impalahoek's six graveyards, almost two kilometres away. A procession of sedans and a discordant variety of vans followed the hearse, directed by the local traffic police.

The Graveyard

Apart from the hearse, which drove right up to Jimmy's grave, all cars parked outside the graveyard fence. At each graveyard, local headmen and their assistants enforce strict rules. Upon entering the yard, men must wear jackets and women must cover their heads with headscarves and their shoulders with shawls. Men should always enter first and women should follow them. The mourners must switch off their mobile phones, are not allowed to visit other graves, and may not leave the graveyard whilst the funeral is in progress. In this manner they show respect to the deceased.

The pallbearers placed Jimmy's coffin on a small scaffold above the grave, suspended on electronic belts. Ministers and pastors surrounded the grave, whilst men stood on their right and women on their left. **Pastor Sibotse**, who had not spoken before, opened the proceedings with a prayer and blessed the grave until the time of resurrection should come. He spoke only a few words, largely aimed at consoling the bereaved family.

Kin placed a reed mat on the floor of the grave and draped the coffin in a clean blanket, reinforcing the symbolic association of death with sleeping. An undertaker from the Elite Funeral Parlour then lowered the coffin

[3] Karp (1987) sees laughter as a form of subversion in performance. He shows that whereas brides display anxiety and tension at wedding rituals among the Iteso of Kenya, women spectators treat these as an occasion for laughter and joking. Through laughter the 'unofficial' gains a momentary triumph over the 'official' and women seem to enjoy the problems they represent both to men and also to themselves.

electronically, and once he had removed the belts, men immediately set to work. They filled the bottom half of the grave with wet cement, making it impossible for robbers to disturb the deceased.[4] The men then filled the remainder of the grave with soil, using spades for this purpose. The men took turns: each scooped and threw soil only a few times, before placing the shovel on the ground, waiting for the next man to pick it up. They explicitly refrained from handing the spades directly to each other. This act possibly alludes to the dangerous power of the graveyard soil. The sharing of work dramatised masculine cooperation and marked the masculine role as being that of labourer and breadwinner. Some of the poorer men were dressed in overall tops, perfectly acceptable dress for the graveyard. At the same time as the men worked, women sang hymns and church songs. It was noteworthy that the men buried all funeral programmes in the grave. They swept the last bits of soil and dust onto the mound with green branches, buried the branches in the soil, and laid a ring of bricks around the mound.

In sharp contrast to the proceedings at the church hall, only elderly men spoke at the graveside. They included representatives of the local branch of the South African National Civics Association, the local headman, and the Elite Funeral Parlour.

Elmon Mashile spoke on behalf of the headman, thanking the ministers and pastors, the gravediggers, and everyone who had come to pray for the bereaved family each afternoon during the preceding week. But Elmon also expressed some anger:

We must not repeat the same mistake as the Mohale family. They only came to the graveyard at eleven [am]. Here we must bury people by eight [am]. The Mohale people are lucky because we sometimes allow teachers and policemen to take longer. The programme is too long when we bury important people. The master of ceremonies and the ministers must now be brief.

At this point Ripho Mokoena told Elmon Mashile that he had no right to tell people what to do. Several onlookers laughed at the nature of the power play that disrupted the proceedings. Some noted that the headman's representative was not supposed to usurp Ripho's role as master of ceremonies.

Harry Maluleke from the Elite Funeral Parlour had the final word, explaining what procedures people should follow to join the Elite burial society. He also warned people to take care of their cards and wallets,

[4] Grave robberies have occasionally been a source of serious concern in Bushbuckridge. The robbers reportedly stole coffins from the graves for resale, or cut parts of flesh or organs from the corpses to sell to diviners residing in Venda and even closer to home, who allegedly used these as potions for attaining wealth and power. Human flesh obtained in this manner is used for the same purpose as in the notorious *diretlo* murders in Lesotho (Murray and Sanders 2005).

noting that a woman had been robbed whilst she withdrew money from an automatic teller machine in Bushbuckridge.

The procession then left for the home of the bereaved family, where women served everyone an elaborate funeral meal. The mourners took great care to avoid any form of pollution from the graveyard. My companions told me that everything that belongs to the graveyard, such as the soil and programmes, should remain there, and should not be taken home. Moreover, before entering the yard, each mourner had to be cooled and cleansed. Men sprinkled us with water, both the front and rear of our bodies. We also had to kneel to drink water from a cup, and wash our hands in a large basin. At the same time ministers thoroughly cleansed the polluted spades with holy water, outside the gates of the family home.

On the Real and the Ideal

The funeral carefully choreographed a biography that was at odds, sometimes starkly so, with the manner in which Jimmy had told his own life story to me. The organisers of Jimmy's funeral did not simply represent, but selectively (re)constructed Jimmy's biography and social relations. In line with Bloch's (1974) more general comments about ritual, the funeral concealed as much as it revealed. In this respect, Handelman's (2009) suggestion that it might be fruitful to imagine ritual through film seems appropriate. Handelman remarks that film shares with ritual non-linear dynamics, and is:

> hyper visual, magnifying, reducing, changing proportions, giving shape to the seemingly shapeless, speeding up, slowing down, superimposing, fading and zooming, reversing time, inverting space through shot, cut and montage. (Handelman 2004: 149)

The images and oratorical statements at the funeral portrayed Jimmy as a highly successful professional, a member of a stable middle class, and as an exemplary colleague, kinsman, affine, husband, and father. These images and statements zoomed in and magnified Jimmy's achievement as a student, teacher, and research assistant. There were also ample indices of middle-class status. The respectable Elite Funeral Parlour organised Jimmy's funeral. His corpse lay in a beautiful coffin costing R14,000 and travelled in a Mercedes-Benz. There were also Pentecostal preachers, electronic keyboards, and an ostentatious funeral meal with a choice of different kinds of meat and vegetables. The orators referred to multiple mobile phones, newspapers, and fears of having one's credit cards and watches stolen. In the funeral ritual these items appeared as a taken-for-granted part of everyday life.

Moreover, the ritual portrayed Jimmy as a man with a broad circle of kin, colleagues, and friends, including men and women of status.

The alternate use of Northern Sotho, Tsonga, and English hinted at Jimmy's cosmopolitanism. There were references to 'the President of South Africa', to Chris Hani, Oliver Tambo, and Nelson Mandela. The orators described Jimmy as a good father and mentor who motivated and advised people, calmed and reconciled them, and who was also courageous and unafraid of speaking out against forms of injustice. The speakers readily described Jimmy as a man who loved God, was loved by his wife, and belonged to community organisations and to the ANC. Jimmy received in death the wealth and harmony he could never attain in life.

The mourners enacted a situation of harmonious cooperation. The funeral programme created space for all to speak. Tasks were divided clearly by gender: men shared the work of digging and filling the grave, and women sang collectively.[5] Ideologically, gender is the most crucial axis of social life in Bushbuckridge, with men being identified as wage earners and women as child bearers. But in an era of de-industrialisation these distinctions are rapidly being eroded. At Jimmy's funeral the division of tasks by gender symbolically reasserted this boundary.

The funeral ritual carefully edited out, faded out, or concealed the less palatable aspects of Jimmy's biography. There were no references to Jimmy's hardships, desperate struggles and disappointments, or to the enmities and violent conflict that characterised his social world. In contrast to the images conveyed by the funeral, Jimmy died as a virtual pauper, who earned no more than R650 per month after deductions. He had accumulated hardly any property, apart from a stationary Corsa sedan, and an incomplete house in White River. There was also no mention of the fact that Jimmy resented the modernist Pentecostal churches because of their restrictive puritan ethics. In conversation with me he frequently criticised their noisiness, and remarked that they mistakenly believed 'God is deaf'. Neither was there any mention of the fact that Jimmy had been threatened with expulsion at high school, or that the University of the North was barely functioning during the 1980s. The orators carefully refrained from mentioning that Jimmy had stopped working as my research assistant for almost two years, was unable to secure a promotion as a teacher for more than thirteen years, regularly fought with many of his colleagues, and often desperately wished to leave his profession.

The organisers and orators at Jimmy's funeral effectively concealed that he had separated from his wife and deserted his children; that his

[5] A social survey of 89 households in Impalahoek shows that whereas the numbers of unemployed women had remained constant at about 60 per cent between 1991 and 2004, the numbers of unemployed men had increased from 16 to 47 per cent (see Appendices 1 and 2). The greatest job losses occurred in mining, Pretoria's steel factories, and the military. On average girls attained better grades than boys at school, and women dominated white-collar professions such as teaching. Divorce and separations also increased.

relations with his affines were disharmonious and bitter; and that he had accused his father of witchcraft, no longer visited his parental home, and described the paternal side of his social relations as 'dead'. There were no references to Jimmy's short temper towards the end of his life, his very opportunistic reasons for supporting the ANC, or to his loneliness when he was terminally ill. Nobody dwelt on the nature of Jimmy's illness: it was simply described as a sudden, unanticipated interruption, bringing a premature end to an otherwise brilliant career. Rumours about his bewitchment or about the possibility that Jimmy might have died from an AIDS-related illness were carefully suppressed in public discourse.

The oratorical statements of speakers at the funeral bear striking resemblances to praise singing for high office, a very common and widespread practice in Southern Africa. Apter (2007a) observes that though cast in the language of praise, such singing is actually a complex form of poetry, which sometimes contains veiled allusions to less palatable realities beneath the surface. These allusions were evident in a number of statements. Jimmy's paternal aunt (*rakgadi*) Selina Mohale expressed regret that Jimmy failed to beget smaller branches of the family. His maternal uncle (*malome*) went to lengths to warn of possible divisions and discord amongst Jimmy's parents and immediate kin. The school principal B. T. Chiloane bluntly described Jimmy as a 'prodigal son'. The principal at Tlasede announced her surprise at Jimmy's popularity, and his colleague Rapule Segodi remarked that much of Jimmy's potential had remained untested. In her letter that accompanied the flowers Lerato placed on his coffin she wrote that their marriage 'had its ups and downs'. Further discord was evident in the fact that a policeman refused to pour soil into Jimmy's grave. Such avoidance was explained to me with reference to the fact that a man who has shared a female sexual partner with the deceased might also die if he poured soil into this man's grave.[6]

But how, then, do we account for the divergence between the virtual, edited, realities of the funeral, and the actual realities of Jimmy's life, and for the great lengths and enormous expense to which people go to maintain this divergence? I can think of three possible answers, none of them mutually exclusive.

As Durham and Klaits (2002) show for Botswana, funerals have become one of the most significant public spaces where issues of citizenship are debated. It is through joint participation at funerals that

[6] In Bushbuckridge sexual intercourse is believed to be extremely contaminating, because it transfers fluids between the bodies of partners. Should a woman make love to several men, her lovers would absorb fluids from each other's bodies, through her. Their blood would pollute each other, and their auras would cling to each others' bodies. It could thus be fatal to attend a funeral of your partner's lover. An informant explained this conception to me as follows. 'There is dirt. He is in you and dies in you. Naturally you also die. You are in him and you die in him' (Niehaus 2002a: 199).

individuals engage in the well-being and suffering of others, that households engage in broader circles of cooperation, and that communities take shape. But contra Habermas's (1989) depiction of the public sphere, the mutuality constructed at funerals is based upon sentiment rather than discursive rationality. The disclosure of sympathetic concern militates against harm otherwise caused (Durham and Klaits 2002; Durham 2002). For example, residents of Botswana seldom announce AIDS as a cause of death. This is because the stigma of AIDS casts aspersions on individual character, and because attributions of AIDS amount to a curse. They imply, or prophesise, the imminent death of the widow. Here concealment avoids creating long-standing antagonisms and feelings of anger: an explanation equally plausible in the case of suspected witchcraft.

Some of my informants gave another, very different reason for the disjunction between the 'actual' of everyday life and the 'virtual' of funerals. They observed that mourners were fearful of the 'breath' (*moya*) and 'aura' (*seriti*) of the deceased. In cases of sudden death these substances might be restless, might haunt the living at the place of death, and might cause others to die in a similar manner. For this reason, they said, people did their utmost not to speak ill of the deceased at any stage of the funeral. One of Jimmy's maternal cousins, who also attended his funeral, presented me with the following argument:

There can be great trouble when a spirit does not come to rest and moves about. The spirit can cause deaths of the same kind. It can also cause other kinds of trouble. It can make the hearse to break down and the coffin not to move. Even if a man was a thug or a drunkard people will lie at his funeral to give a better picture. The pastors will say that he was a good guy and a churchgoer. People are scared of death. Death is a big monster. But people want to change it and make it good. They might even give the minister R3,000 to say that he [the deceased] was a hero.

Even though Jimmy was deceased, there was a sense that the invisible components of his body lingered and sought not to be offended. The funeral programme intimated that it was Jimmy, himself, who had called people to speak and written his own obituary. This reinforced the impression of his abiding presence.

The third reason for the disjuncture between Jimmy's life story as told by himself, and the biography that mourners crafted for him at the funeral, is that the organisers purposefully aimed to construct a contrived reality: not a 'representational model' of what Jimmy's life actually was, but rather an 'operational model' stating what his life should have been (Handelman 1998). The funeral did not relay the life of a man who endured endless misfortune: it choreographed an ideal life course of a respectable middle-class person. It portrayed a world in which a combination of education and merit was the most legitimate route to prosperity and success. It enacted an ideal state of *communitas*: disclosing solidarity and the things that people share, and concealing conflict and divisions amongst them (Turner 1969). In Handelman's (1998) terms, the ritual served as a 'model', not a 'mirror', of social life.

From these perspectives, the silences in public discourses at funerals are as important as those things that are spoken. They exist as a 'subtext' or as 'deep knowledge' that exists in hidden, safeguarded places, where formal orthodoxies can be re-evaluated, subverted, and contested (Apter 2007b: 101–2). Witchcraft is often absent from public events and from spaces of public political debate (Niehaus 2010a). This is not only due to silencing or to censorship by a modernist state, but is also to some extent intrinsic to discourses of witchcraft. Although these are open-ended and have an endless capacity to incorporate new themes, accusations of witchcraft largely occur among insiders, such as kin and neighbours. Indeed, Geschiere (1997: 25) calls witchcraft 'the flip side of kinship'. Hence, discussions of witchcraft are deemed more appropriate to private domestic spaces than to public political spheres. But there is a second, perhaps more crucial factor: namely the ontological status of witchcraft as a mystical reality that transcends ordinary perception. Ordinary villagers know only too well that accusations of witchcraft cannot meet the standards of evidence demanded by formal courts of law.

However, things left unsaid on the 'front stage' of the funeral ritual became a prominent topic of 'backstage' gossip (Goffman 1971). In the weeks after Jimmy's funeral there was intense speculation throughout Impalahoek about the actual causes of his death. Many villagers had heard about the accusations of witchcraft he made against his father. I also heard people talking about the possibility that Jimmy had died from an AIDS-related illness, as well as allegations that Jimmy was really the victim of his girlfriend, who used potions to win his affection.

In addition, some elders said that Jimmy had transgressed a taboo (*diila*) because he had refused to abstain from sexual intercourse during the mourning period following the death of one of his relatives. Hence Jimmy was afflicted with *mafulara* – a sickness marked by endless coughing. Yet another opinion was that Jimmy had weakened his own body by using too many different potions from too many different diviners. To cite some of Jimmy's friends and colleagues:

I think the old man bewitched him. Luckson has a big snake. He saw Jimmy as a pillar of the Mohale family. Jimmy helped them when they were sick and he made the work of his father very difficult.

This comment insinuates that Jimmy was bewitched precisely because he had obstructed his father's attempts to kill other family members.

One cannot say that it was the dreaded disease [AIDS] without doctors having done the tests. I don't have a good history because I did not grow up with Jimmy. I can't say whether it is true or not. It can only be a speculation. Jimmy was okay. He was only coughing. But then he went to different diviners and mixed their potions. Some of these potions cannot combine. Perhaps this killed him.

I think Iris bewitched Jimmy. She was not working when he met her. To make ends meet she lured someone with a steady job and with a steady salary. At one stage we phoned Iris. Then she was with a prophet. After meeting this prophet her life began to improve. This showed that she used potions.

This contrast between the manner in which things 'should have been' and the manner in which 'they actually were' generates reflective thought and criticism both about the social structures that constrain people, and also about the moral failings of persons. In this respect, the construction of a contrived ideal world through elaborate ritual procedures may well be seen as a form of protest, or at least a form of cultural critique. Such protest often focuses on personal conduct and on social relations. This is especially important in places such as Bushbuckridge, where kinship, neighbourliness, and collegiality are extremely important social resources that are often vital to people's survival (Sharp and Spiegel 1985).

10 Last Words

During an interview with me, weak-voiced eleven days before his death, Jimmy Mohale offered a number of comments that he regarded as 'last words', words that summarise the central themes and implications of his life story. Jimmy told me that he had suffered from tuberculosis as a child, but he described the six months he spent in hospital as amongst the most relaxed times of his life. He then proceeded to highlight the terrible insecurity that he and others experienced in everyday life, outside such comforting institutional frameworks. He saw insecurity as a common denominator of the misfortune and witchcraft that he personally encountered, and described it as the most important issue any future South African government needs to address.

When I was only seven years old I spent six months in the TB room at the Ethel Lucas Memorial Hospital.[1] *This was in 1971. This hospital was good when those whites were still there. They took good care of us. For me it was nice to be hospitalised. The white American nurses at the hospital were friendly, gave us tablets and sweets, and taught us to say the Lord's Prayer each evening. At the hospital we ate meat, and this was not something we had at home. We slept on beds, and this was also something we never had at home. There was food and security. I did not want to go home. Imagine taking a child from Diepsloot ['Deep Ravine', a shanty town] to such a place, where he ate sandwiches, used large towels, could shower, got a good breakfast and lunch, and was well cared for. Do you think he would like to go back to Diepsloot?*

Sakkie, many whites [makgowa] *don't understand the plight of the black people. You whites eat ice cream. We don't want to be rich. We want security. This is where this government fails. It will fail for a very long time. In this country there will still be civil war. [Jacob] Zuma steals money and [Terror]*

[1] The International Holiness Mission (IHM) established the Ethel Memorial Hospital in Acornhoek in 1937, when its main source of income derived from fund-raising campaigns in Britain. In 1952 the IHM fused with the Nazarene Church. American medical officers, medical students, and finances then streamed in. By the 1970s, however, the hospital had been transferred to the South African government (Nkuna 1986: 141–59).

Lekota steals money.[2] *But nobody does anything about it. People want security. These volatile facts will spark a civil war.*

This childhood memory leads Jimmy well beyond any preoccupation with his own medical condition.[3] It also highlights themes that are central to the life story that he narrated. Along with the material presented in the different chapters of this biography, Jimmy's 'last words' will enable us to reflect upon key anthropological assumptions about witchcraft, paternity, and cultural relativism.

Witchcraft and Post-Apartheid

Biographical narratives offer a valuable tool to a pragmatic perspective that seeks to transcend the binary oppositions between social structure and individual agency, and also between historical processes and specific events (Ortner 2006). This perspective recognises that 'individuals are neither speaking cultural truths, nor are they entirely free from them' (Hastrup 2005: 138). Biographical narrative also attends to once-occurring events in the lives of persons that are the product not of systemic processes but rather of 'conjunctive agency' (Sahlins 2004). In this manner they enable the social analyst to access the 'processes by which the social emerged as an objective force' (Hastrup 2005: 139).

Jimmy's life story and last words illuminate the immensely complex relationship of witchcraft beliefs with the contexts in which they occur. They suggest a less deterministic reading than previous ones of the connections between witchcraft and post-apartheid (Ashforth 1999; 2005; Comaroff and Comaroff 1999b; 2000). Far from being a response to this specific political situation, witchcraft appears as a much more fluid and shifting, but nonetheless ever-present language or discourse. It is constantly being redeployed, reinterpreted, and reconfigured. Evidence from Bushbuckridge does not lend unequivocal support to the

2 This is a direct reference to the South African arms procurement scandal. In 2003 the South African Auditor General found a litany of irregularities in a fifty-billion-rand arms deal. Key players had clear conflicts of interest, government excluded deal-making costs in the award of the most lucrative contracts, and there were allegations that bidders donated R5 million to the ANC veterans' association and at least R10 million to South Africa's Minister of Defence, Joe Modise (Feinstein 2007: 150–5). In June 2005 Judge Hilary Squires found Schabir Shaik, a businessman who had acted as Zuma's financial adviser, guilty of bribery, and sentenced him to 15 years' imprisonment. In the aftermath of the trial the National Prosecuting Authority formally charged Zuma with corruption. No allegations of impropriety have been made against Terror Lekota, who served as Defence Minister.

3 Childhood exposure to tuberculosis does not provide immunity to the onset of the disease later in life, especially not if the immune system has been compromised (Dr Martin Lacque, personal communication).

suggestion that witchcraft accusations have increased significantly in the post-apartheid era. On the contrary, it was the apartheid years, marked by villagisation, the destruction of the last remnants of subsistence agriculture, and people's dependence upon oscillating labour migration, that saw the advent of new witch-familiars, metaphors, and technologies of witchcraft. Large-scale witch-hunts instigated by Comrades were a hallmark of the national liberation struggle at the dawn of the post-apartheid period (Niehaus 2001: 130).

Jimmy's life story also shows the role played by unprecedented incidents of misfortune in structuring his fears of witchcraft. The accusation that Jimmy made against his father, Luckson, was not a simple response to a stressful relationship between son and father. In fact, the suspicions that Luckson practised witchcraft had arisen much earlier, amongst his own siblings. Such suspicions stemmed from competition over the inheritance of cattle and were reinforced by the conjunction between Luckson's retirement and an uncanny series of deaths amongst his patrilineal kin. Other factors, too, lent an 'aura of factuality' (Geertz 1973a) to suspicions of witchcraft. These include the reputation that Luckson's mother had of practising witchcraft; the fact that Luckson fainted precisely when Zionist ministers cleansed his home of malevolent substances; Luckson's peculiar, unbecoming conduct during the deaths and funerals of his close kin; and also the revelations of several diviners and Christian healers.

Purely structural and historical accounts of witchcraft fail to capture the significance of such unprecedented and singular events for the way specific social actors experience witchcraft. Jimmy had assisted me in seeking sociological explanations for the sorts of violence and misery that people encounter in Bushbuckridge. For more than 15 years, we had explored the impact of racial discrimination, the failure of certain post-apartheid policies, and diseases of inequality such as AIDS upon people's lives. But Jimmy saw the limitations of these models in explaining 'particularities of misfortune' (Evans-Pritchard 1937: 69) that are products of 'conjunctive agency' (Sahlins 2004: 155). He recognised a difference between 'doing anthropology' and 'living the realities of your research'.

Jimmy's life story does show, however, how the broader contexts of apartheid and post-apartheid have shaped his encounters with misfortune and witchcraft. It is not so much abstract beliefs in witchcraft as the actual fear of destructive mystical forces that is a prominent theme in his life story. Jimmy's last words to me virtually echo Ashforth's (2005) depiction of the post-apartheid situation as one of social and spiritual insecurity in South Africa, marked by an ethos of anxiety. Thus, although there is no causal relationship between insecurity and witchcraft, there certainly does appear to be a relationship of 'elective affinity'[4] between them. Such insecurity is rooted in Jimmy's encounters with 'structural' and 'interpersonal' violence during the apartheid era. The concept of 'structural violence' refers to 'sustained' and 'insidious . . . assaults on dignity', as represented by social inequality and institutionalised racism (Farmer 1997: 261). Of particular relevance to his life story were the location of black South Africans in marginal and overcrowded reserves, spartan conditions in under-resourced schools and universities, political repression, and the system of labour migration that separated fathers from mothers and children. Jimmy's life story also captures the impact of more insidious forms of violence at home, on village streets, and in public institutions such as schools and universities. As I argued in Chapter 2, if one were to view witchcraft in terms of the metaphor of a mirror, then what the mirror reflects are various forms of everyday violence. There is continuity between the violence of mystical and social realms.

The depiction of the post-apartheid situation by Ashforth (2005) and by Comaroff and Comaroff (1999b; 2000) is, however, relevant for an understanding of other important themes in Jimmy's life story. The concept of 'occult economies' (Comaroff and Comaroff 1999b) provides a rare attempt at theoretical generalisation. Critics have found the concept unhelpfully broad, and argue that the notion of 'the occult' is foreign to African cosmologies (Ranger 2007; Ter Haar and Ellis 2009). Yet the concept does capture anxieties aroused by the paradoxical emergence of new opportunities and expectations, at the same time as new forms of exclusion. Like many young South African men, Jimmy failed to realise promises of postcolonial prosperity. He felt deeply frustrated when his investment in education and his dedicated hard work as a teacher failed to pay dividends. Given his intelligence and qualifications, Jimmy felt that he should have been better off. He perceived the fulfilment of his ambitions as a rational goal beset by a violent and unremitting storm of mishaps and ill-will. In particular, the venality of South Africa's political system and nepotistic practices at his school thwarted the triumph of his personal abilities. And likewise, he had come to see witchcraft as blocking his progress in life.

But witchcraft in the post-apartheid era deals with issues other than thwarted desires for wealth. Jimmy's life story highlights the impact of sickness and successive deaths among kin in structuring perceptions of witchcraft. Stephen (1999) suggests that psychoanalytic theories of the ambivalent emotions of bereavement can shed light on this topic. She refers to Klein's (1988) observation that subjects often evoke persecutory

4 Weber (1905) uses the idea of 'elective affinity' to refer to the contingent connections between phenomena – such as those between the Protestant religion and the capitalist economic order.

fears during the initial stages of grief and mourning, following death. In the unconscious fantasy system, Klein argues, bereaved persons equate the loss of loved ones with the painful loss of 'inner objects'. This effect is enhanced in contexts where the self is viewed socio-centrically, and is invested in social relations with others (Stephen 1999: 713). At a young age Jimmy was overwhelmed by the death of his brother. This death seems to have provoked such anxiety that as an adult he could no longer tolerate attending funerals, even those of close kin.

Blaming the Father

Jimmy's biography casts important light on the emergence of the father as suspected witch. In the accusations of witchcraft that I recorded in Impalahoek, between 1996 and 2008, 17 per cent (34) of all accused were fathers of their victims. This trend is very significant, given that more households are now female-headed, with fathers completely absent.[5] The enmities that existed between Jimmy and his father, Luckson Mohale, succeeded rather than preceded accusations of witchcraft. Although Jimmy deeply resented his father's foul temper and his failure to provide adequately for his mother, he greatly admired his father's cleanliness, knowledge of tradition, and even his strictness as head of his family.

Anthropological literature provides little insight into the reasons for these accusations. Existing studies on the Gisu of Uganda by La Fontaine (1967) and Heald (1986), and on the Zambian Tonga by Colson (2000), give accounts of situations where sons accuse their fathers of witchcraft. These authors relate this to paternal control of inheritance in the land and the cattle on which youth rely for subsistence and marriage. By withholding the inheritance from their children, they argue, fathers pervert their sons' life course, creating enormous tensions. But this explanation does not apply to Bushbuckridge today, where the rural resource base has collapsed, where there is hardly any land or cattle to inherit,[6] and where unwritten rules specify, and amicable arrangements ensure the inheritance of parents' domestic property by their youngest son.

Psychoanalytic models offer another potential explanation. The Oedipus complex denotes a situation in which sons become attached to their mother as the first love object, and develop feelings of homicidal rage towards the father upon recognising him as mate of the mother. However, in fear of castration boys renounce the mother as love object, instead

[5] Female-headed households in the Agincourt district of Bushbuckridge increased significantly from 27.6 per cent in 1992 to 35.9 per cent in 2003 (Madhavan and Schatz 2007: 91).

[6] Even in the past when the inheritance of cattle was a major cause of strife, the tensions only emerged after the death of the father, and it was siblings who accused each other of witchcraft.

coming to identify with and admire the father. Early hatreds nonetheless remain unresolved and the father remains as a figure of fundamental ambiguity (Freud 1905). Post-Freudian relationship theories emphasise identity rather than sexuality. Theorists working in this vein contend that, like girls, boys establish the primary sense of identity with their mother as nurturing parent. But, for boys, the individuation involves the acquisition of a different gender identity, which is the opposite of hers. This was apparent in my discussion of the circumcision ritual, where boys renounce the bond with the mother. A subconscious desire to regress nonetheless persists (Gilmore 1990).

Whilst we cannot discount these deep psychic processes, they do not explain variations in the frequency of witchcraft accusations against the father. Fatherhood is less natural than psychoanalytic theory assumes (Malinowski 1937; Hiatt 1994; Gutmann 1996). In the particular context of domestic organisation in Bushbuckridge, the absence of the father as oscillating labour migrant makes dis-identification from the mother problematic. But again, psychoanalytic theory associates the renunciation of maternal bonds with misogynistic violence towards the mother, rather than hatred or violence towards the father (Cameron and Frazer 1987; Gilmore 2001: 151–68).

A more fruitful line of enquiry is to view discourses about the father as witch in the particular contexts of history, de-industrialisation, generation, and gender. In local cosmologies witchcraft is believed to be perpetrated by deprived, envious, and resentful insiders, who strike out to 'level' inequalities. They include neighbours who struggle to make ends meet, wives who feel deprived of remittances and cheated by their husbands, as well as neglected kin. Witches are also imagined to be elders who have lost their virility and vitality.

The status of fathers is extremely ambivalent. Ideologies of kinship and domesticity construct fathers as pre-eminent and authoritative persons, who represent their households to the outside world (Simpson 2005). But discourses about lineal progress, as in ideologies of development and modernisation propagated by Pentecostal churches and by movements of national liberation, marginalise the paternal generation. These discourses construct children as an improved version of their parents – more sophisticated and cosmopolitan, better educated, and entitled to enjoy greater prosperity. Yet people's experiences of de-industrialisation and of the AIDS pandemic contradict these discourses (Cole and Durham 2007: 1–28). Older men like Luckson Mohale, although poorly educated and coming of age in a time of greater political repression, in fact experienced far greater work security than their sons. Luckson worked in the centres of South African industry for 46 years, both as a highly skilled driver and as a foreman. At home Luckson displayed unrivalled authority, married two wives, and established paternity over thirteen children. He also enjoyed good health. Though in his seventies, Luckson only occasionally complained of neck pains.

Despite their better education, Luckson's sons faced greater insecurity. Moses, Peter and Kagišo were consistently unemployed, whilst Jimmy and Henry failed to secure promotion. Luckson's sons worked in service economies with an increasingly feminised workforce, removed from South Africa's centres of wealth and power. They seldom visited the cities about which Luckson spoke with intimate knowledge. Luckson's sons also experienced less authority than their father in the domestic domain. Moses was twice divorced, Peter once, whilst Henry and Kagišo were unwilling or unable to pay bridewealth. Whether initially residing with his wife's kin, eventually separating from her, or losing touch with his children, Jimmy felt equally emasculated. Luckson outlived three of his sons. Kevin (who died at the age of 13), Andrew (at 35), and Jimmy (at 41), as well as his grandchildren Duduzile and Rebecca, all predeceased him. Whereas Luckson was able to support his children, his sons were unable to assist him financially, once they had left home.

All these factors, in combination, lent credibility to suspicions that fathers secured their authority by mystical means. In local belief, fathers purchased potions and the snake-like *mamlambo* on the urban markets to ensure promotion at work. Once they had retired, these creatures returned home with their purchasers to torment their kin. Hence, fathers were seen as sacrificing the futures of their descendants for the relative prosperity that they themselves had enjoyed in the past.[7] In Jimmy's opinion,

My father's generation was more successful. There was unemployment then, but not like now. The elders had snakes [mmamokebe] *that gave them money and they used potions* [muti] *to get ahead. Our fathers had to be fortified with snakes when they worked on the mines. They fortified themselves because the work was so tedious. They wanted to be elevated and to do light work. When they had snakes the whites would recognise them. They also used potions so that they could screw other men. Else it would be painful. . . .*[8] *Now when they are retired 80 per cent of miners have had quarrels with their families. This is connected with witchcraft. Here at home their snakes and their potions eat their families. They cause misery and create feuds.*

Unsuccessful men blame their fathers for obstructing their path to progress. But accusations of witchcraft also enable sons to opt out of redistributive networks and obligations and keep their income to

[7] This situation bears great resemblance to perceptions in the United Kingdom that members of the so-called 'baby-boom' generation experiences greater prosperity than their children, and monopolises valuable social and economic resources (Willetts 2010).

[8] Here Jimmy refers to the common practice of male-to-male sex in the South African gold mining compounds (Moodie 1988; Harries 1990).

themselves, or at least to spend it on their own nuclear families. Meyer (1998) has pointed to a similar process in Ghana, where younger people often experience their extended kinship networks as a burden that drains their resources. Through converting to Pentecostalism young professionals are able to make a complete break with the past, which they now see as a diabolical domain of witchcraft. Such a motive was also apparent in Jimmy's biography as when, to escape from his cognates, he sought to build a new home in a middle-class residential suburb in White River.

As pre-eminent kinsman, the father is expected to provide for household members and represent the household to the outside world. It is he who names the children and supports them through remittances. His sister (*rakgadi*) conducts sacrifices to invoke and placate the ancestors on their behalf (Hammond-Tooke 1981: 86–95). Hence, it is logical for the father to be held accountable when there is trouble and grave misfortune within the household. When things fall apart, the suggestion that one might be the victim of someone as close and as authoritative as one's father seems uniquely plausible. Mothers take care of the day-to-day running of the home, but, ultimately, the father is held accountable for its welfare.

The father is also the judge and punisher, responsible for disciplining children (Last 2000; Simpson 2005: 576–9). The Northern Sotho word *kgoro* denotes both the male space in the household, near the gate, and also a court. This theme of punishment is a central component of witchcraft. In an extremely perceptive essay, Bercovitch (1989) has argued that, like the notion of conscience and guilt, witchcraft confronts individuals with the moral significance of their actions. He maintains that among the Nalumin of Papua New Guinea the theory of witchcraft reveals the wrongs individuals have done, and people's failure to act according to their own ideals.

> The witch reminds people of how they have wronged others. But the witch reminds people that they have done wrong in a manner different from how conscience is said to work: as an external threat of vengeance rather than an internal sense of guilt. (Bercovitch 1989: 155)

It is possible to see Jimmy's awareness of his own moral shortcomings as accentuating fears of his father. Jimmy was well aware that his wife, Lerato, frequently complained to his father about his extramarital liaisons, excessive drinking, absence from home, and failure to support his dependents. Jimmy could sense Luckson's terrible disappointment and anger. Jimmy found it extremely hard to justify (to me) his decision to abandon Lerato and his three children:

> *The last time I saw Kgopotšo was a month ago, Thandi about four months ago, and Katlego more than eight months ago. This does not only upset me, Sakkie.*

It haunts me. Who does not want to bring up your children? I am the one who was responsible for the plan of taking them to good schools. I do not know if a woman can raise the kids without a father figure. I dream about them and I love them because they are my kids. I am also worried that they would be told lies about me. Sometimes things happen that make you develop a second skin. You say that there is nothing that you can do. You say that it was destiny and a fact.

Processes of projection might also be involved in witchcraft at a deep, subconscious, level (Kluckhohn 1962: 88–95; Lambek 2003). The subject expels from the self qualities, feelings, and wishes that he refuses to recognise in himself, and locates these in another person: in this case the witch (Lambek 2003: 199). These qualities, feelings, and wishes are often aggressive, anti-social ones. The process of projection is non-discursive, and therefore exceedingly hard to demonstrate. Yet it is striking that it was at the same time as Jimmy abandoned his own dependents that he started accusing his father of bewitching his mother, his siblings, and himself. This conjunction appears to be more than coincidental. In South African rural areas, the accusation of fathers as witches by men might well be intricately connected to issues of paternity that they, themselves, experience. Richter and Morrell (2006: 6–7) draw attention to a South African 'crisis of fatherhood'. This is evident in high rates of child sexual abuse, and in the fact that 42 per cent of children lived only with their mothers.

The concept of projection helps us understand how Jimmy shifted culpability from himself. Jimmy and Luckson experienced fatherhood very differently, and Jimmy may well have projected his own failure to act responsibly towards his children onto his father.

Relativism and Critical Engagement

The story of Jimmy's life and death raises a number of uncomfortable questions about the relativist orientation of anthropology.

The relativist goal, most clearly formulated by Boas and his followers, challenges the ethnocentric, often racist, use of Western values and concepts as a yardstick for human behaviour. Culture, the Boasians assert, must be understood and evaluated in its own terms (Stocking 1968: 233–333). The relativist orientation is also apparent in the works of interpretative anthropologists such as Geertz (1973b), who argue that culture should be treated as a system of symbols or as a text, the message of which has to be grasped. A more recent version of this orientation characterises the postmodern concern to represent indigenous voices without imposing editorial censorship. Although the political implications of this approach are unclear, postmodern anthropologists invite us to pay particular attention to 'social criticism made from socially subordinate positions' (Rosaldo 1989: 195). There appears to be an affinity between postmodernism and the argument that it 'takes a Serb to know a Serb' (van de Port 1999), and that outsiders cannot grasp the inwardness of native culture (Kuper 1992).

The goal of allowing ethnographic subjects to speak for themselves is indispensable for anthropological understanding. Yet the experience of writing this biography has underlined the pitfalls of treating the evocation of local symbolic meanings as the sole anthropological aim. As Hastrup (1995: 148) argues, 'to assimilate interpretation with the adoption of the agent's point of view is crippling to theory'. This is particularly pertinent to the cases of witchcraft and divination, and of local responses to HIV/AIDS.

There has been a long history of exceedingly 'generous' or 'charitable' anthropological treatment of witchcraft and of divination – a separate but, as we have seen, intrinsically linked phenomenon. Whilst generally accepting that witchcraft beliefs were based upon 'mistaken premises' (Evans-Pritchard 1937), British anthropologists asserted, nonetheless, that they had positive social functions. Witchcraft was logical and had lubricating social effects: it allowed hidden tensions to be articulated and social relationships to be readjusted, and promoted charitable behaviour (Evans-Pritchard 1937; Marwick 1965; V. Turner 1967b; Middleton 1964). Divination sessions enabled the formation of social consensus (Peters 1972).

Interpretive anthropologists have gone further, rejecting the claim that witchcraft and divination are based upon erroneous ontological assumptions. For example, Jackson (1989) examines the grounds on which Karanko believe that certain persons can predict the future and change themselves into animals. He sees these beliefs as grounded in personal experiences and argues that their truth is defined in the context of their use. He treats the reality of these beliefs as immaterial or unknowable.

Stoller and Olkes (1987), Favret-Saada (1980), E. Turner (1992), and Willis (1999) write about witchcraft and divinatory truths as objectively real – even if inexplicable in terms of scientific knowledge – and celebrate the existence of alternative realities. Van Binsbergen (2003: 135–298) sees African divination as a valid form of knowledge production and therapy that works beyond the cultural context in which he initially encountered it. Divination, he argues, should be appreciated as a valid form of extrasensory knowledge.

A recent volume of the journal *Social Dynamics* discusses the role of diviners in treating AIDS-related diseases. Most contributors accept the spiritual authority of diviners, and agree that they are motivated by a calling from the ancestors rather than by questions of money. They portray diviners as having popular appeal, being accessible, and providing services that are psychologically soothing, culturally appropriate, and shift blame from the victim. Different contributors also assert that the medication diviners provide can suppress the effects of the virus and prolong life. Moreover, they see collaboration with biomedicine as both possible and desirable (Devenish 2005; Henderson 2005; Wreford 2005a; 2005b).

I see as laudable the aims of debunking Western claims to superiority in thought processes; of capturing the dehumanising power relations enshrined in medical science; and of exposing exploitative aspects of biomedicine. Yet anthropological studies can ill afford to adopt an uncritical, purely interpretive, stance towards witchcraft and divination. Lett (1991: 313) suggests that an anthropological account based solely upon the explication of meaning can lead to absurd conclusions, endorsing claims that certain people can really turn themselves into elephants, or predict the future. Also, he argues, it is a 'cop out' to treat the ontological reality of mystical entities as immaterial. If certain people can actually turn themselves into elephants, then it is ridiculous to examine the grounds on which Karanko accept this belief as true.

Witchcraft may have the potential to serve positive psychological and social functions. But, for the most part, the material presented in this biography concurs with Ashforth's claim (2005: 69) that witchcraft enhances fears, anxieties, and spiritual insecurities. 'Life in a world of witchcraft', he writes, 'is lived in the light of the presumption of malice: one must assume that anyone with the motive to harm has access to the means and that people will cause harm because they can.' To paraphrase Geertz's more general comments about religion (1973a: 103), witchcraft disturbed rather than cheered Jimmy, and forced him 'into a head-on, unblinking confrontation of the fact that' he 'was born to trouble'. Jimmy's last words echo Ashforth's comments about spiritual insecurity. The belief in witchcraft accentuated his distrust of the most intimate relationships in his life.

There is also good reason to pose critical questions about the therapeutic role of diviners, particularly in treating AIDS-related diseases. As anthropologists we should not lightly endorse claims that diviners possess powers of extrasensory perception. An insufficiently critical stance leads us to ignore the problematic role of diviners in fomenting anxiety, and in authenticating accusations that have led to brutal killings, in South Africa and also in Tanzania.[9] By diagnosing what might well be AIDS-related diseases as symptoms of bewitchment, diviners discourage people from testing for HIV antibodies, and may even actively discourage their clients from using antiretroviral drugs (Wreford 2005b).

[9] No fewer than 3,072 witch-killings occurred in Sakumaland, Tanzania, between 1970 and 1988 (Mesaki 1994: 52). Sungusungu vigilante groups often undertake responsibility for administering justice (Bukurura 1994).

The practices of diviners are not always those of the subaltern. During Thabo Mbeki's presidency, diviners received ideological support from the state. President Mbeki and South Africa's health minister rejected the conventional biomedical theory that AIDS is transmitted by sexual intercourse, appointed dissident scientists to advisory panels on AIDS, and curtailed the use of antiretroviral drugs (van der Vliet 2004). Government formed an alliance with the Traditional Healers' Organisation and encouraged the use of alternative remedies, outside the remit of scientific regulation (Geffin 2005).

The diviners and Christian healers whom Jimmy consulted made their diagnoses almost exclusively in terms of witchcraft. Their revelations first accentuated his anxieties, before they prescribed remedies. Zionist prophets revealed that there was a pool of human blood in the centre of his parental homestead, Dr Sugar that his father kept a snake and numerous zombies, and the prophet in Phalaborwa that witches had placed a ghost on Jimmy's body to make other people hate him. The thousands of hard-earned rands that Jimmy spent did not enable him to regain his health. The attempts by prophets and diviners to fortify his family members; make his father's witchcraft rebound; and to retrieve Andrew's aura from the witches met with little success, by Jimmy's own admission. Remedies such as making Jimmy inhale smoke from concoctions burnt in a clay pot, smearing his body with oil, stretching his limbs, moving his feet over burning coals, and feeding him tea, coffee, and other liquids had little effect in improving his condition. Jimmy consistently ignored pleas from others that he should undertake a test for HIV antibodies, and use antiretroviral drugs should he test positive.

Jimmy accepted the powers of witchcraft as real. For him witchcraft was not simply an explanation of misfortune; it was a crucial part of the misfortunes that bedevilled his life. Jimmy would have preferred to live in a world without witches. But in an environment beset by envy, inequality, and insecurity this remained a utopian ideal, perhaps attainable by whites. Jimmy seldom disputed divinatory revelations, and argued that if it had not been for the numerous diviners and prophets whom he had consulted, he would have died long before he actually did.

According to many anthropologists, consultations with diviners attain value in situations of dialogue and of medical pluralism, in which people seek the best from different worlds in their quest for therapy (Janzen 1979; Mills 2005). Peek (1991) argues that divinatory consultations are motivated by an intense desire to know the real reasons for the occurrence of events. In times of crisis, diviners generate a temporary shift to a contrary, non-rational, non-normal (perhaps paranormal is a better word) mode of cognition. Because the language of divination is cryptic and ambiguous, all revelations have to be translated and discussed. During the dialogue there is a transference and counter-transference of information. Known facts are scrutinised in the light of a different perspective and old elements are reorganised into new arrangements (ibid.: 202).[10]

In the latter stages of Jimmy's life divination lost these dialogical properties, and attained theoretical closure. The circularity of witchcraft made it all-encompassing. Witchcraft virtually became a world to itself: a totalising and all-consuming world of zombies, of snake- and ape-like witch-familiars, and of potions. It resembled what Kapferer (2003) calls a 'phantasmagoric space'. These spaces exist apart from ordinary life; have a reality and inner praxis of their own, and no necessary symbolic connection to realities outside of them. As an 'imaginal field' such a space has a force that derives not from what it represents external to itself, but from the potentialities, generative forces, linkages, and redirections that it opens up within itself (Kapferer 2003: 22). The spaces stand on their own, outside reason, with their own truth that is not subject to any kind of external falsification.

The pervasiveness of misfortune helps to explain the all-consuming nature of witchcraft, but there might well be other reasons for Jimmy's reluctance to seek alternative explanations and therapies, including the stigma of AIDS. Such a stigma does not necessarily arise from the association of AIDS with sexual promiscuity. Jimmy readily spoke to me about his sexual liaisons and extramarital affairs. The perception of a person afflicted with AIDS as a living corpse, tainted by the pollution of death, seems a more likely cause (Niehaus 2007). An admission to being HIV-positive would have made Jimmy culpable, not only of his own disease, but also of the deaths of others, whom he might have infected through unprotected sexual intercourse. Being a victim of the witchcraft of envious others was more congruent with the perception of himself as a morally responsible person. There are more unanswered questions. We cannot exclude the operation of what Freud (1989: 55–8, 102–6) identified as *thanatos* or the 'death wish', at a deep subconscious level. At times, Jimmy seemed more concerned with revenge than with regaining his health. These are pieces in the puzzle that assist us in gaining insight into Jimmy's complex and at times contradictory intentions, but they are not all the pieces.

Though indispensable, any anthropological account based purely upon the explication of meaning, and any engagement based purely upon listening, is perennially incomplete. Critical empathy seems to be a more appropriate intellectual and ethical stance. I cannot escape feeling that I should have been more assertive in helping Jimmy. I recorded details of

10 Heald (1991) shows that scepticism about diviners is endemic among the Gisu of Uganda. This is because Gisu diviners are socially marginal, and because clients have greater knowledge of their own immediate social environments than the diviners whom they consult.

his life and his beliefs, I offered advice, and I gave him money to consult biomedical doctors; but, more actively, I should have arranged therapeutic consultations and endeavoured to ensure that they took place. The relevance of anthropology lies in inter-subjective encounters, open-ended conversations, and dialogue between ethnographers and research participants (Gudeman and Rivera 1990). The interpretation of meaning remains a crucial anthropological task. But we also need to consider more objective factors (Weber 1949) and seek comparative, inter-contextual, understanding (Hahn 1995). Anthropology is not a nativist project, but a cosmopolitan enterprise (Kuper 1992). For these reasons anthropology is difficult, hard, and exhausting human science.

Appendices

1: The Employment Status of Adults in Sampled Households by Gender, Impalahoek, 1990/1

Employment Status	Men	Women	Total
Self employed	7 (4%)	12 (7%)	19 (6%)
Locally employed	55 (34%)	36 (22%)	91 (28%)
Migrant labourers	76 (46%)	11 (7%)	87 (26%)
Not working	26 (16%)	108 (65%)	134 (40%)
Total	164	167	331

2: The Employment Status of Adults in Sampled Households by Gender, Impalahoek, 2003/4

Employment Status	Men	Women	Total
Self employed	13 (6%)	12 (5%)	25 (5%)
Locally employed	50 (22%)	52 (25%)	102 (24%)
Migrant labourers	53 (24%)	20 (8%)	73 (15%)
Not working	107 (47%)	161 (62%)	268 (56%)
Total	223	245	468

3: The Relationship between Those Accused of Witchcraft and their Assumed Victims, Impalahoek, 1960–95 and 1995–2008

	1960–95	1995–2008
Non-kin	130 (47%)	44 (22%)
Affines	43 (15%)	34 (17%)
Related by polygamous marriage	17 (6%)	3 (2%)
Spouses	23 (8%)	24 (12%)
Cognates	66 (24%)	93 (47%)
Total accusations	279	198

References

Abu-Lughod, L. 2005. *Dramas of Nationhood: the politics of television in Egypt*. Chicago IL and London: University of Chicago Press.

Anderson, J. A. 2002. 'Sorcery in the era of "Henry IV": kinship, mobility and morality in Buhera District, Zimbabwe', *Journal of the Royal Anthropological Institute* 8 (3): 425–99.

Apter, A. 2007a. 'The politics of panegyric' in *Beyond Words: discourse and critical agency in Africa*. Chicago IL: University of Chicago Press.

______ 2007b. 'Griaule's legacy' in *Beyond Words: discourse and critical agency in Africa*. Chicago IL: University of Chicago Press.

Ardener, E. 1970. 'Witchcraft, economics and the continuity of belief' in M. Douglas (ed.), *Witchcraft Confessions and Accusations*. London: Routledge.

Ashforth, A. 1999. *Madumo: a man bewitched*. Chicago IL: University of Chicago Press.

______ 2002. 'An epidemic of witchcraft? Implications of AIDS for the post-apartheid state', *African Studies* 61 (1): 121–44.

______ 2005. *Witchcraft, Violence and Democracy in South Africa*. Chicago IL: University of Chicago Press.

Ashley, M. 1989. *Ideologies and Schooling in South Africa*. Cape Town: SATA.

Auslander, M. 1993. 'Open the wombs! The symbolic politics of modern Ngoni witchfinding' in J. Comaroff and J. L. Comaroff (eds), *Modernity and Its Malcontents: ritual and power in postcolonial Africa*. Chicago IL: University of Chicago Press.

Badat, S. 1999. *Black Student Politics, Higher Education and Apartheid: from SASO to SANSCO, 1968–1991*. Pretoria: Human Sciences Research Council.

Badstuebner, J. 2003. '"Drinking the hot blood of humans": witchcraft confessions in a South African Pentecostal church', *Anthropology and Humanism* 28 (1): 8–22.

Bähre, E. 2007. *Money and Violence: financial self-help groups in a South African township*. Leiden: Brill.

Bailey, F. G. 1998. *Witch Hunt in an Indian Village, or the Triumph of Morality*. Ithaca NY and London: Cornell University Press.

Barrett, R. 2005. 'Self-mortification and the stigma of leprosy in northern India', *Medical Anthropology Quarterly* 19 (2): 216–30.

Bercovitch, E. 1989. 'Moral insights: victim and witch in the Nalumin imagination' in G. Herdt and M. Stephen (eds), *The Religious Imagination in New Guinea*. New Brunswick NJ: Rutgers University Press.

Bertaux, D. 1981. 'Introduction' in D. Bertaux (ed.), *Biography and Society: the life history approach in the social sciences*. Berkeley Hills CA: Sage.

Bloch, M. 1974. 'Symbols, song, dance, and features of articulation', *European Journal of Sociology* 15 (1): 55–81.

______ 1988. 'Death and the concept of a person' in C. Cederroth, C. Corlin, and J. Lundstrom (eds), *On the Meanings of Death: essays on mortuary rituals and eschatological beliefs*. Stockholm: Almqvist and Wicksell International.

Bonner, P. and K. Shapiro. 1993. 'Company town, company estate: Pilgrim's Rest, 1910–1932', *Journal of Southern African Studies* 19 (2): 171–200.

Boonzaier, E., P. Skalnik, R. Thornton, M. West, and R. Gordon. 1990. 'Review Discussion of *Waiting: the whites of South Africa* by Vincient Crapanzano' in P. Hugo (ed.), *Truth Be in the Field: social research in Southern Africa*. Pretoria: University of South Africa Press.

Bothma, C. V. 1978. 'Sosiologiese teenoor biologiese vaderskap in 'n Noord-Sothostam', *Suid-Afrikaanse Tydskrif vir Etnologie* 1: 11–13.

Brown, K. M. 2001. *Mama Lola: a vodou priestess in Brooklyn*. Berkeley CA: University of California Press.

Bukurura, S. 1994. 'Sungusungu and the banishment of suspected witches in Kahama' in R. Abrahams (ed.), *Witchcraft in Contemporary Tanzania*. University of Cambridge: African Studies Centre.

Burgos-Debray, E. 1996 (1984). *I, Rigoberta Menchú: an Indian woman in Guatemala*. London: Verso.

Burns, C. 2000. 'Censorship and affection: South African women's letters during World War Two', unpublished paper, History and African Studies Series, University of KwaZulu-Natal, Durban.

Cameron, E. 2005. *Witness to AIDS*. Cape Town: Tafelberg.

Cameron, D. and E. Frazer. 1987. *The Lust to Kill: a feminist investigation of sexual murder*. Cambridge: Polity Press.

Campbell, C. 2003 (1997). *Letting Them Die: why HIV/AIDS prevention programmes fail*. Oxford: James Currey.

Caplan, P. 2004. 'Terror, witchcraft and risk', unpublished paper, New Social Formations Seminar Series, University of Stellenbosch.

Carruthers, J. 1995. *The Kruger National Park: a social and political history*. Pietermaritzburg: University of Natal Press.

Chernoff, J. 2003. *Hustling Is Not Stealing: stories of an African bar girl*. Chicago IL: University of Chicago Press.

Ciekawy, D. and P. Geschiere. 1998. 'Containing witchcraft: conflicting scenarios in postcolonial Africa', *African Studies Review* 41 (3): 1–14.

Clifford, J. 1988. *The Predicament of Culture: twentieth-century ethnography, literature, and art*. Cambridge MA: Harvard University Press.

Clifford, J. and G. Marcus (eds). 1986. *Writing Culture: the poetics and the politics of ethnography*. Berkeley CA: University of California Press.

Cole, J. and D. Durham. 2007. 'Introduction: age, generation and the intimate politics of globalization' in J. Cole and D. Durham (eds), *Generations and Globalization: youth, age, and family in the new world*. Bloomington IN: Indiana University Press.

Colson, E. 2000. 'The father as witch', *Africa* 70 (3): 333–58.

Comaroff, Jean. 1985. *Body of Power, Spirit of Resistance: the culture and history of a South African people*. Chicago IL: University of Chicago Press.

Comaroff, Jean and John Comaroff. 1999a. 'Occult economies and the violence of abstraction: notes from the South African postcolony', *American Ethnologist* 26 (4): 279–303.

______ 1999b. 'Alien-nation: zombies, immigrants and millennial capitalism', *Codesria Bulletin* 3 (4): 17–28.

______ 2000. 'Millenial capitalism: first thoughts on a Second Coming' in Jean and John L. Comaroff (eds), *Millenial Capitalism and the Culture of Neoliberalism*, Special Edition, *Public Culture* 12 (2): 1–31.

Coplan, D. 1998. 'Fieldsights: the anthropological narration of post-apartheid South Africa', *African Studies* 57 (2): 133–45.

Crapanzano, V. 1980. *Tuhami: portrait of a Moroccan*. Chicago IL: University of Chicago Press.

______ 1985. *Waiting: the whites of South Africa*. New York NY: Random House.

Crehan, K. 1997. *The Fractured Community: landscapes of power and gender in rural Zambia*. Berkeley CA: University of California Press.

de Boeck, F. 2005. 'The divine seed: children, gift and witchcraft in the Democratic Republic of Congo', in A. Honwana and F. De Boeck (eds), *Makers and Breakers: children and youth in postcolonial Africa*. Oxford: James Currey.

de Heusch, L. 1980. 'Heat, physiology, and cosmogony: *rites de passage* among the Thonga' in I. Karp and C. S. Bird (eds), *Explorations in African Systems of Thought*. Bloomington IN: Indiana University Press.

Delius, P. 1996. *A Lion amongst the Cattle: reconstruction and resistance in the northern Transvaal*. Johannesburg: Ravan Press.

______ 2001. 'Witches and missionaries in nineteenth-century Transvaal', *Journal of Southern African Studies* 27 (3): 429–43.

Delius, P. and C. Glaser. 2004. 'The myths of polygamy: a history of extra-marital and multi-partnership sex in South Africa', *South African Historical Journal* 50 (1): 84–104.

Devenish, A. 2005. 'Negotiating healing: understanding the dynamics amongst traditional healers in KwaZulu Natal as they engage with professionalisation', *Social Dynamics* 31 (2): 243–84.

Donham, D. 1999. *Marxist Modern: an ethnographic history of the Ethiopian revolution*. Berkeley CA: University of California Press.

Dostoyevsky, F. 1990. *The Brothers Karamazov* (translated by R. Pevear and L. Volokhonsky). New York NY: Farrar, Strauss, and Giroux.

Douglas, M. 1970. 'Introduction: Thirty years after witchcraft, oracles and magic' in M. Douglas (ed.), *Witchcraft Confessions and Accusations*. London: Tavistock.

______ 1991. 'Witchcraft and leprosy: two strategies of exclusion', *Man (New Series)* 26 (4): 723–36.

Dumont, L. 1965. 'The modern conception of the individual', *Contributions to Indian Sociology* 8: 13–61.

Durham, D. 2002. 'Love and jealousy in the space of death', *Ethnos* 67 (2): 155–79.

Durham, D. and F. Klaits. 2002. 'Funerals and the public space of sentiments in Botswana', *Journal of Southern African Studies* 28 (4): 777–95.

Ellis, S. 1989. 'Tuning in to pavement radio', *African Affairs* 88 (352): 321–30.

Epstein, H. 2008. *The Invisible Cure: Africa, the West and the fight against AIDS*. London: Penguin.

Evans-Pritchard, E. 1937. *Witchcraft, Oracles and Magic among the Azande of Anglo-Egyptian Sudan*. Oxford: Oxford University Press.

Farmer, P. 1997. 'On suffering and structural violence: a view from below' in A. Kleinman, V. Das and M. Lock (eds), *Social Suffering*. Berkeley CA: University of California Press.

Fassin, D. 2007. *When Bodies Remember: experiences and politics of AIDS in South Africa*. Berkeley CA: University of California Press.

Favret-Saada, J. 1980. *Deadly Words: witchcraft in Brocage*. Cambridge: Cambridge University Press.

______ 1989. 'Unbewitching as therapy', *American Ethnologist* 16 (1): 40–56.

Feinstein, A. 2007. *After the Party: a personal and political journey inside the ANC*. Johannesburg: Jonathan Ball Publishers.

Ferguson, J. 1999. *Expectations of Modernity: myths and meanings on the Zambian Copperbelt*. Berkeley CA: University of California Press.

______ 2006. 'Decomposing modernity: history and hierarchy after development' in James Ferguson (ed.), *Global Shadows: Africa in the neoliberal world order*. Durham NC: Duke University Press.

Ferrarotti, F. 1981. 'On the autonomy of the biographical method' in D. Bertaux (ed.), *Biography and Society: the life history approach in the social sciences*. Berkeley Hills CA: Sage.

Foster, G. 1965. 'Peasant society and the image of limited good', *American Anthropologist* 67 (2): 293–315.

Freud, S. 1962 (1905). *Three Essays on the Theory of Sexuality*, translated by J. Strachey. New York NY: Basic Books.

______ 1989 (1929). *Civilization and Its Discontents*, translated by J. Strachey. New York NY: W. W. Norton.

Gear, S. 2005. 'Rules of engagement: structuring sex and damage in men's prisons and beyond' in G. Reid and L. Walker (eds), *Men Behaving Differently: South African men since 1994*. Cape Town: Double Storey.

Geertz, C. 1973a. 'Religion as a cultural system' in *The Interpretation of Cultures*. New York NY: Basic Books.

______ 1973b. 'Thick description: toward an interpretive theory of culture' in *The Interpretation of Cultures*. New York NY: Basic Books.

Geffin, N. 2005. 'Echoes of Lysenko: state-sponsored pseudoscience in South Africa', *Social Dynamics* 31 (2): 183–210.

Geschiere, P. 1997. *The Modernity of Witchcraft: politics of the occult in postcolonial Africa*. Charlottesville VA: University of Virginia Press.

Gilmore, D. 1990. *Manhood in the Making: cultural concepts of masculinity*. New Haven CT and London: Yale University Press.

______ 2001. *Misogyny: the male malady*. Philadelphia PA: University of Pennsylvania Press.

Gluckman, M. 1962. 'Les rites de passage' in Max Gluckman (ed.), *Essays on the Ritual of Social Relations*. Manchester: Manchester University Press.

Goffman, E. 1961. *Asylums: essays on the social situation of mental patients and other inmates*. Harmondsworth: Penguin.

______ 1971. *The Presentation of Self in Everyday Life*. Harmondsworth: Penguin.

Goldstein, D. 2003. *Laughter out of Place: race, class, violence and sexuality in a Rio shantytown*. Berkeley CA: University of California Press.

Green, M. 1994. 'Shaving witchcraft in Ulanga: Kunyulewa and the Catholic Church' in Ray Abrahams (ed.), *Witchcraft in Contemporary Tanzania*. Cambridge: African Studies Centre.

Green, M. and S. Mesaki. 2005. 'The birth of the salon: poverty, modernisation and dealing with witchcraft in southern Tanzania', *American Ethnologist* 32 (3): 371–88.

Gudeman, S. 2006. 'Sacred cows and critics: what's in a controversy', unpublished paper presented at the European Association of Social Anthropologists (EASA) Biennnial Conference, Bristol.

Gudeman, S. and A. Rivera. 1990. *Conversations in Colombia: the domestic economy in life and text.* Cambridge: Cambridge University Press.

Gutmann, M. 1996. *The Meanings of Macho: being a man in Mexico City.* Berkeley CA: University of California Press.

Habermas, J. 1989. *The Structural Transformation of the Public Sphere: an enquiry into a category of bourgeois society.* Cambridge MA: MIT Press.

Hahn, R. 1995. 'Three theories of sickness and healing' in *Sickness and Healing: an anthropological perspective*, New Haven CT: Yale University Press.

Hammond-Tooke, W. D. 1981. *Boundaries and Belief: the structure of a Sotho worldview.* Johannesburg: Witwatersrand University Press.

——— 1989. *Rituals and Medicines: indigenous healing in South Africa.* Johannesburg: Ad Donker.

Handelman, D. 1998. *Models and Mirrors: towards an anthropology of public events.* New York NY: Berghahn Books.

——— 2009. 'Thinking Moëbiusly: can we learn about ritual from cinema in *Mulholland Drive*?' in A. Hobart and B. Kapferer (eds), *Human Interface between Ritual, Theatre and Film.* Oxford: Berghahn Books.

Harries, P. 1981. 'The anthropologist as historian and as liberal: H.-A. Junod and the Thonga', *Journal of Southern African Studies* 8 (1): 37–50.

——— 1989. 'Exclusion, classification and internal colonialism: the emergence of ethnicity among Tsonga-speakers of South Africa' in L. Vail (ed.), *The Creation of Tribalism in Southern Africa.* London and Berkeley CA: James Currey.

——— 1990. 'Symbols and sexuality: culture and sexuality on the early Witwatersrand gold mines', *Gender and History* 2 (3): 318–36.

——— 1994. *Work, Culture and Identity: migrant labourers in Mozambique and in Southern Africa.* Portsmouth NH: Heinemann.

Hastrup, K. 1995. *A Passage to Anthropology: between experience and theory.* London: Routledge.

——— 2005. 'Social anthropology: towards a pragmatic enlightenment', *Social Anthropology* 13 (2): 133–49.

Heald, S. 1986. 'Witches and thieves: deviant motivations in Gisu society', *Man* 21 (1): 65–78.

——— 1991. 'Divinatory failure: the religious and social role of Gisu diviners', *Africa* 61 (3): 299–317.

——— 1996. 'The ritual use of violence' in *Manhood and Morality: sex, violence and ritual in Gisu society.* London: Routledge.

Helman, C. 2000. *Culture, Health and Illness* (fourth edition). London: Heinemann.

Henderson, P. 2005. 'A gift without shortcomings: healers negotiating the intersection of the local and the global in the context of HIV/AIDS', *Social Dynamics* 31 (2): 24–54.

Hertz, R. 1960 (1907). *Death and the Right Hand.* London: Cohen and West.

Hiatt, L. 1994. 'Indulgent fathers and collective male violence' in S. Heald and A. Deluz (eds), *Anthropology and Psychoanalysis; an encounter through culture.* London: Routledge.

Hirst, M. 1993. 'The healer's art: Cape Nguni diviners in the townships of Grahamstown, Eastern Cape, South Africa', *Curare* 16 (1): 97–114.

Holdstock, T. 1990. 'Violence in schools: discipline' in B. McKendrick and W. Hoffman (eds), *People and Violence in South Africa.* Cape Town: Oxford University Press.

Honwana, A. 2003. 'Undying past: spirit possession and the memory of war in southern Mozambique' in B. Meyer and P. Pels (eds), *Magic and Modernity: interfaces of revelation and concealment.* Stanford CA: Stanford University Press.

Hoskins, J. 1998. *Biographical Objects: how things tell the stories of people's lives.* New York NY and London: Routledge.

Hugo, P. 1990. '*Waiting: the Whites of South Africa* by Vincent Crapanzano: a review focus' in P. Hugo (ed.), *Truth Be in the Field: social research in Southern Africa.* Pretoria: University of South Africa Press.

Hunter, M. 2002. 'The materiality of everyday sex: thinking beyond "prostitution"', *African Studies* 61 (1): 99–120.

______ 2010. *Love in the Time of AIDS: inequality, gender and rights in South Africa.* Bloomington IN: Indiana University Press.

Iliffe, J. 2006. *The African AIDS Epidemic: a history.* Oxford: James Currey.

Jackson, M. 1989. *Paths towards a Clearing: radical empiricism and ethnographic enquiry.* Bloomington IN: Indiana University Press.

James, D. 1988. 'Land shortage and inheritance in a Lebowa village', *Social Dynamics* 14 (2): 36–51.

Janzen, J. 1979. *The Quest for Therapy in Lower Zaire* (in collaboration with W. Arkinstall). Berkeley CA: University of California Press.

Jedrej, C. and R. Shaw. 1992. 'Introduction' in C. Jedrej and R. Shaw (eds), *Dreaming, Religion and Society in Africa.* Leiden: E. J. Brill.

Jewkes, R. and N. Abrahams. 2002. 'The epidemiology of rape and sexual coercion in South Africa: an overview', *Social Science and Medicine* 55: 1231–44.

Jewkes, R., J. Levin, N. Mbananga, and D. Bradshaw. 2002. 'Rape of girls in South Africa', *The Lancet* 359: 319–20.

Junod, H.-A. 1966 (1913). *The Life of a South African Tribe. Volume 1: Social Life.* New York NY: University Books.

Junod, H.-A. and A. Jaques. 1939. *The Wisdom of the Tsonga-Shangaan People.* Cleveland, Transvaal: Central Mission Press.

Kahn, K., M. Garenne, M. Collinson, and S. Tollman. 2007. 'Mortality rates in the new South Africa: hard to make a fresh start', *Scandinavian Journal of Public Health* 35 (69): 29–34.

Kapferer, B. 2003. 'Introduction: Outside all reason – magic, sorcery and epistemology in anthropology' in B. Kapferer (ed.), *Beyond Rationalism: rethinking magic, witchcraft and sorcery.* New York NY and Oxford: Berghahn Books.

Karp, I. 1987. 'Laughter at marriage: subversion in performance' in D. Parkin and D. Nyamwaya (eds), *Transformations of African Marriage.* Manchester: Manchester University Press.

Kiernan, J. 1990. *The Production and Management of Therapeutic Power in Zionist Churches within a Zulu City.* Lewiston NY: Edwin Mellen Press.

______ 1997. 'Images of rejection in the construction of morality: Satan and the sorcerer as moral signposts in the social landscape of urban Zionists', *Social Anthropology* 5 (2): 243–54.

Kirkaldy, A. 2006. 'Vhuloi and witch-hunting in late nineteenth-century Vendaland' in B. Nicolini (ed.), *Studies in Witchcraft, Magic, War and Peace in Africa: nineteenth and twentieth centuries*. Lewiston NY: Edwin Mellin Press.

Klaits, F. 2010. *Death in a Church of Life: moral passion during Botswana's time of AIDS*. Berkeley CA: University of California Press.

Klein, M. 1988. *Love, Guilt and Reparation, and Other Works 1921–1945*. London: Virago Press.

Kluckhohn, C. 1962 (1944). *Navaho Witchcraft*. Boston MA: Beacon Press.

Kotzé, J. C. 1986. 'Levels of domination and a point of convergence in Gazankulu', unpublished paper presented to the Department of Social Anthropology, University of Cape Town.

Kuckertz, H. 1997. '*Ukuhlonipha* as idiom of moral reasoning in Mpondo' in P. McAllister (ed.), *Culture and the Commonplace: anthropological essays in honour of David Hammond-Tooke*. Johannesburg: Witwatersrand University Press.

Kuper, A. 1987. 'The magician and the missionary' in *South Africa and the Anthropologist*. London: Routledge and Kegan Paul.

______ 1992. 'Culture, identity, and the project of a cosmopolitan anthropology', *Man* 29 (3): 537–54.

______ 1999. '*"Culture": the anthropologists' account*. Cambridge MA: Harvard University Press.

La Fontaine, J. 1967. 'Parricide in Bugisu: a study in intergenerational conflict', *Man* (New Series) 2 (2): 249–59.

Lambek, M. 2003. 'Fantasy in practice: projection and introjection, or the witch and the spirit-medium' in B. Kapferer (ed.), *Beyond Rationalism: rethinking magic, witchcraft and sorcery*. Oxford: Berghahn Books.

Lan, D. 1993. 'Resistance to the present by the past: mediums and money in Zimbabwe' in J. Parry and M. Bloch (eds), *Money and the Morality of Exchange*. Cambridge: Cambridge University Press.

Last, M. 2000. 'Children and the experience of violence: contrasting cultures of punishment in northern Nigeria', *Africa* 70 (3): 359–93.

Lategan, Z. 2006. 'Learning through Sickness: an ethnographic study of children in Bushbuckridge, South Africa'. BA (Honours) dissertation, Department of Anthropology and Archaeology, University of Pretoria.

Leach, E. 1966. 'Virgin birth', *Proceedings of the Royal Anthropological Institute of Great Britain and Ireland* (1966): 39–49.

Leclerc-Madlala, S. 2001. 'Science, AIDS and sexual culture in Africa', *Women's International Network News* 27 (1): 20–2, <http://www.looksmartsavings.com/p/articles/mi_m2872/is_1_27/ai_71563341>, accessed 25 August 2010.

______ 2005, 'Popular responses to HIV/AIDS and policy', *Journal of Southern African Studies* 31 (4): 845–56.

Leggett, T., A. Louw, M. Schönteich, and M. Sekhonyane. 2003. *Criminal Justice in Review 2001/2002*, Monograph No. 88. Pretoria: Institute of Security Studies.

Lett, J. 1991. 'Interpretive anthropology, metaphysics and the paranormal', *Journal of Anthropological Research* 47 (2): 305–29.

Lewis, G. 1987. 'A lesson from Leviticus: leprosy', *Man* 22 (4): 593–612.

LiPuma, E. 1998. 'Modernity and forms of personhood in Melanesia' in M. Lambek and A. Strathern (eds), *Bodies and Persons: comparative perspectives from Africa and Melanesia.* Cambridge: Cambridge University Press.

Littlewood, R. and M. Lipsedge. 1987. 'The butterfly and the serpent: culture, psychopathology and biomedicine', *Culture, Medicine and Psychiatry* 11: 289–335.

Lodge, T. 1991. 'Rebellion: the turning of the tide' in T. Lodge and B. Nasson *et al.* (eds), *All Here and Now: Black Politics in South Africa in the 1980s.* New York NY: Foundation and Foreign Policy Association.

Lurie, M. 2000. 'Migration and AIDS in Southern Africa: a review', *South African Journal of Science* 97: 343–47.

MacFarlane, A. 1970. *Witchcraft in Tudor and Stuart England.* London: Routledge and Kegan Paul.

MacPherson, P., M. Moshabela, N. Martinson, and P. Pronyk. 2008. 'Mortality and loss to follow-up among HAART initiators in rural South Africa', *Transactions of the Royal Society of Tropical Medicine and Hygiene* 103 (6): 588–93.

Madhavan, S. and E. Schatz. 2007. 'Coping with change: household structure and composition in rural South Africa, 1992–2003', *Scandinavian Journal of Public Health* 35 (69): 85–93.

Malinowski, B. 1955 [1927]. *The Father in Primitive Psychology.* New York NY: The Norton Library.

______ 1937. *Sex and Repression in Savage Society.* London: Kegan Paul.

Malkki, L. 1997. 'News and culture: transitory phenomena and the fieldwork tradition' in A. Gupta and J. Ferguson (eds), *Anthropological Locations: boundaries and grounds of a field science.* Berkeley CA: University of California Press.

Mandela, N. 1995. *Long Walk to Freedom: the autobiography of Nelson Mandela.* New York NY: Little, Brown, and Company.

Marriot, M. 1976. 'Hindu transactions: diversity without dualism' in B. Kapferer (ed.), *Transaction and Meaning: directions in the anthropology of exchange and symbolic behaviour.* Philadelphia PA: Institute for the Study of Human Issues.

Marwick, M. 1965. *Sorcery in Its Social Setting: a study of the Northern Rhodesian Cewa.* Manchester: Manchester University Press.

______ 1970 (1964). 'Witchcraft as a social strain-gauge' in M. Marwick (ed.), *Witchcraft and Sorcery: selected readings.* Harmondsworth: Penguin Books.

Marx, K. 1959. *Economic and Philosophical Manuscripts of 1844.* Moscow: Progress Press.

Mayer, P. 1954. 'Witches', Inaugural Lecture delivered at Rhodes University, Grahamstown.

Mayer, P. and I. Mayer. 1970. 'Socialisation by peers: the youth organisation of the Red Xhosa' in P. Mayer (ed.), *Socialization: the approach from Social Anthropology.* London: Tavistock.

Mbali, M. 2004. 'AIDS discourses and the South African state: government denialism and post-apartheid policy making', *Transformations* 54: 115–16.

Mbeki, T. 2008. 'The African Renaissance, South Africa and the world' in P. Geschiere, B. Meyer and P. Pels (eds), *Readings in Modernity in Africa.* Bloomington IN: Indiana University Press.

McCaskie, T. C. 2000. *Asante Identities: history and modernity in an African village, 1850–1950.* London: Edinburgh University Press and the International African Institute.

McNeill, F. 2011. *AIDS, Politics and Music in South Africa*. Cambridge and New York NY: Cambridge University Press and the International African Institute.

McNeill, F. and I. Niehaus. 2010. *Magic: AIDS Review 2009*. Pretoria: Centre for the Study of AIDS, University of Pretoria.

Mesaki, S. 1994. 'Witch-killing in Sakumuland' in R. Abrahams (ed.), *Witchcraft in Contemporary Tanzania*. Cambridge: Cambridge University Press.

Meyer, B. 1998. '"Make a complete break with the past": memory and postcolonial modernity in Ghanaian Pentecostal discourse', *Journal of Religion in Africa* 27 (3): 931–44.

______ 2009. 'Response to Ter Haar and Ellis', *Africa* 79 (3): 413–15.

Mfecane, S. 2010. 'Exploring Masculinities in the Context of ARV Use: a study of men living with HIV in a South African village'. Unpublished PhD thesis, University of the Witwatersrand.

Middleton, J. 1964. *Lugbara Religion: ritual and authority among an East African people*. Oxford: Oxford University Press.

Mills, C. W. 1975. *The Sociological Imagination*. Harmondsworth: Penguin.

Mills, E. 2005. 'HIV illness meanings and collaborative healing strategies in South Africa', *Social Dynamics* 31 (2): 126–60.

Mintz, S. 1972. *Worker in the Cain: a Puerto Rican life history*. New York NY: W.W. Norton and Company Inc.

Mönnig, H. O. 1988. *The Pedi*. Pretoria: van Schaik.

Moodie, D. 1988. 'Migrancy and male sexuality on the South African gold mines', *Journal of Southern African Studies* 14 (2): 228–56.

Moore, H. and T. Sanders (eds). 2001. *Magical Interpretations, Material Realities: modernity, witchcraft and the occult in postcolonial Africa*. London and New York NY: Routledge.

Morrell, R. 1998. 'Of boys and men: masculinity and gender in Southern African Studies', *Journal of Southern African Studies* 24 (4): 605–30.

Murray, C. 1975. 'Sex, smoking and the shades: a Sotho symbolic idiom' in M. Whisson and M. West (eds), *Religion and Social Change in Southern Africa: anthropological essays in honour of Monica Wilson*. Cape Town: David Philip.

Murray, C. and P. Sanders. 2005. *Medicine Murder in Colonial Lesotho: the anatomy of a moral crisis*. Edinburgh: Edinburgh University Press and the International African Institute.

Niehaus, I. 1994. 'Disharmonious spouses and harmonious siblings: conceptualising household formation amongst urban residents in Qwaqwa', *African Studies* 53 (1): 115–35.

______ 2000a. 'Coins for blood and blood for coins: from sacrifice to ritual murder in the South African Lowveld, 1930–2000', *Etnofoor* 13 (2): 31–54.

______ 2000b. 'Towards a dubious liberation: masculinity, sexuality and power in South African Lowveld Schools, 1953–1999', *Journal of Southern African Studies* 26 (3): 387–407.

______ (with E. Mohlala and K. Shokane). 2001. *Witchcraft, Power and Politics: exploring the occult in the South African Lowveld*. London and Sterling VA: Pluto Press.

______ 2002a. 'Bodies, heat and taboos: conceptualising "modern personhood" in the South African Lowveld', *Ethnology* 41 (3): 189–207.

______ 2002b. 'Perversions of power: witchcraft and the sexuality of evil in the South African Lowveld', *Journal of Religion in Africa* 32 (3): 1–31.

______ 2002c. 'Renegotiating masculinity in the South African Lowveld: narratives of male–male sex in labour compounds and in prisons', *African Studies* 61 (1): 77–97.

______ 2005a. 'Witches and zombies in the South African Lowveld: discourses, accusations and subjective reality', *Journal of the Royal Anthropological Institute* 11 (2): 191–210.

______ (with G. Jonsson). 2005b. 'Dr Wouter Basson, Americans and wild beasts: men's conspiracy theories of HIV/AIDS in the South African Lowveld', *Medical Anthropology* 24 (2): 177–206.

______ 2006a. 'Biographical lessons: life stories, sex and culture in Bushbuckridge, South Africa', *Cahiers d'Etudes Africaines* XLVI, 1 (181): 51–73.

______ 2006b. 'Doing politics in Bushbuckridge: work, welfare and the South African elections of 2004', *Africa* 76 (4): 521–48.

______ 2007. 'Death before dying: understanding AIDS stigma in the South African Lowveld', *Journal of Southern African Studies* 33 (4): 845–60.

______ 2009. 'Beyond the instrumentality of violence: five homicides in the South African Lowveld', *Focaal* 54: 16–32.

______ 2010a. 'Witchcraft as sub-text: deep knowledge and the South African public sphere', *Social Dynamics* 36 (1): 65–77.

______ 2010b. 'Maternal incest as moral panic: envisioning futures without fathers in South Africa', *Journal of Southern African Studies* 36 (4): 833–49.

Niehaus, I. and J. Stadler. 2004. '*Muchongolo* dance contests: deep play in the South African Lowveld', *Ethnology* 43 (4): 363–80.

Nkuna, W. 1986. 'The Contribution and Influence of the Holiness Mission Churches in the Acornhoek-Bushbuckridge Area, 1930–1970'. MA Dissertation, Department of History, University of South Africa.

Odendaal, W. 1988. 'Agter die yesterhekke van "Turf"', *Die Suid-Afrikaan* (April/May): 12–16.

Ortner, S. 1984. 'Theory in anthropology since the Sixties', *Comparative Studies in Society and History* 26 (1): 126–66.

______ 1996. *Making Gender: the politics and erotics of culture*. Boston MA: Beacon Press.

______ 2006. *Anthropology and Social Theory: culture, power and the acting subject*. Durham NC: Duke University Press.

Orwell, G. 1945. *Animal Farm*. London: Secker and Warburg.

Oxlund, B. 2010. 'Responding to university reform in South Africa: student activism at the University of Limpopo', *Social Anthropology* 8 (1): 30–43.

Pawninski, R. and U. Lalloo. 2001. 'Community attitudes to HIV/AIDS'. *South African Medical Journal* 91: 448–53.

Peek, P. 1991. 'African divination systems: non-normal modes of cognition' in P. M. Peek (ed.), *African Divination Systems: ways of knowing*. Bloomington IN: Indiana University Press.

Pels, P. 1992. 'Mumiani: the white vampire: a neo-diffusionist analysis of rumour', *Etnofoor* 5 (1/2): 165–87.

Peters, E. 1972. 'Aspects of the control of moral ambiguities: a comparative analysis of two culturally disparate modes of social control' in M. Gluckman (ed.), *The Allocation of Responsibility*. Manchester: Manchester University Press.

Philips, H. 2001. 'AIDS in the context of South Africa's epidemic history', *South African Historical Journal* 45: 11–26.

Piot, C. 1999. *Remotely Global: village modernity in West Africa*. Chicago IL: University of Chicago Press.

Posel, D. 2005. 'Sex, death and the fate of the nation: reflections on the politicization of sexuality in post-apartheid South Africa', *Africa* 75 (2): 125–53.

Posel, D. and R. Devey. 2006. 'The demographics of fatherhood in South Africa: 1993–2002' in L. Richter and R. Morell (eds), *Baba: men and fatherhood in South Africa*. Pretoria: Human Sciences Research Council (HSRC) Press.

Probst, P. 1999. 'Mchape '95, or, the sudden fame of Billy Goodson Chisupe: healing, social memory and the enigma of the public sphere in post-Banda Malawi', *Africa* 69 (1): 108–37.

Pronyk, P. 2003. 'Assessing health seeking behaviour among tuberculosis patients in rural South Africa', *International Journal of Tuberculosis and Lung Disease* 5 (7): 619–27.

Rabinow, P. 1977. *Reflections on Fieldwork in Morocco*. Berkeley CA: University of California Press.

Radcliffe-Brown, A. 1965 (1924). 'The mother's brother in South Africa' in *Structure and Function in Primitive Society*. London: Cohen and West.

Rakitzis, A. 1987. 'A Cross-Cultural Study of the Educative Use of Corporal Punishment'. Unpublished BA (Honours) dissertation, Department of Psychology, University of the Witwatersrand.

Ranger, T. 2007. 'Scotland Yard in the bush: medicine murders, child witches and the construction of the occult: a literature review', *Africa* 77 (2): 272–83.

Richter, L. and R. Morrell. 2006. 'Introduction' in L. Richter and R. Morrell (eds), *Baba: Men and Fatherhood in South Africa*. Cape Town: HSRC Press.

Ritchken, E. 1990. *Learning in Limbo, Part II: experiences of secondary schooling in the Mapulaneng District, Lebowa*. Johannesburg: Education Policy Unit, University of the Witwatersrand.

——— 1995. 'Leadership and Conflict in Bushbuckridge: the struggle to define moral economies in the context of rapidly transforming political economies'. Unpublished PhD thesis, Department of Political Studies, University of the Witwatersrand.

Robinson, V. 2004. 'Changing workforce erodes skills plan', *Mail and Guardian*, 30 April to 6 May.

Rodgers, G. 1993. 'Therapeutic Power: a comparison of Christian and ancestral healers in Acornhoek'. Unpublished BA (Hons) thesis, Department of Anthropology, University of the Witwatersrand.

Rosaldo, R. 1989. *Culture and Truth: the remaking of social analysis*. Boston MA: Beacon Press.

Sahlins, M. 2004. 'Culture and agency in history' in *Apologies to Thucydides: understanding history as culture and vice versa*. Chicago IL and London: University of Chicago Press.

SAIRR (South African Institute of Race Relations). 1980. *Race Relations Survey, 1979*. Johannesburg: South African Institute of Race Relations.

——— 1988. *Race Relations Survey, 1987*. Johannesburg: South African Institute of Race Relations.

——— 1989. *Race Relations Survey, 1988*. Johannesburg: South African Institute of Race Relations.

——— 1994. *Race Relations Survey 1993/1994*. Johannesburg: South African Institute of Race Relations.

______ 2002. *South Africa Survey 2001–2002*. Johannesburg: South African Institute of Race Relations.

Saloojee, H. and K. Kahn, 2005. 'INDEPTH Verbal Autopsy Causes of Death MONOGRAPH: Data Template for Agincourt' (July 2005) available at <http://www.samclark.net/Files/Chapters/Samuel-Clark_INDEPTH-Agincourt-COD.pdf>, accessed 20 June 2007.

Sanday, P. 1990. *Fraternity Gang Rape: sex, brotherhood and privilege on campus*. New York NY: New York University Press.

Schatzberg, M. 1993. 'Power, legitimacy and "democratisation" in Africa', *Africa* 63 (4): 444–61.

Scheper-Hughes, N. 2000. 'Ire in Ireland', *Ethnography* 1 (1): 117–40.

______ 2001. *Saints, Scholars and Schizophrenics: mental illness in rural Ireland*. Berkeley CA: University of California Press.

Schoepf, B. 1988. 'Women, AIDS and economic crisis in Central Africa', *Canadian Journal of African Studies* 22 (3): 625–44.

______ 2001. 'International AIDS research in anthropology: taking a critical perspective on the crisis', *Annual Review of Anthropology* 61: 335–61.

Sharp, J. and A. Spiegel. 1985. 'Vulnerability to impoverishment in South African rural areas: the erosion of kinship and neighbourhood as social resources', *Africa* 55 (2): 133–52.

Sideris, T. 2005. '"You have to change and you don't know how": contesting what it means to be a man in a rural area of South Africa' in G. Reid and L. Walker (eds), *Men Behaving Differently: South African men after 1994*. Cape Town: Double Storey.

Siegel, J. 2006. *Naming the Witch*. Stanford CA: Stanford University Press.

Simpson, A. 2005. 'Sons and fathers/boys to men in the time of AIDS: learning masculinity in Zambia', *Journal of Southern African Studies* 31 (3): 569–89.

Smith, D. 2004. 'Burials and belonging in Nigeria: rural–urban relations and social inequality in a contemporary African ritual', *American Anthropologist* 106 (3): 569–79.

Smith, J. 2008. *Bewitching Development: witchcraft and the reinvention of development in neoliberal Kenya*. Chicago IL: University of Chicago Press.

Solway, J. 1990. 'Affines and spouses, friends and lovers: the passing of polygyny in Botswana', *Journal of Anthropological Research* 46 (1): 41–66.

Spiegel, A. 1986. 'Dispersing dependants: a response to the exigencies of labour migration in rural Transkei' in J. Eades (ed.), *Migrants, Workers and the Social Order*. London: Tavistock.

______ 1991. 'Polygyny as myth: towards understanding extramarital relations in Lesotho' in A. D. Spiegel and P. A. McAllister (eds), *Tradition and Transition in Southern Africa*. Johannesburg: Witwatersrand University Press.

Stadler, J. 2003a. '"The young, the rich and the beautiful": secrecy, superstition and discourses of AIDS in the South African Lowveld', *African Journal of AIDS Research* 2 (2): 123–35.

______ 2003b. 'Rumour, gossip and blame: implications for HIV/AIDS prevention in the South African Lowveld', *AIDS Education and Prevention* 15 (4): 357–68.

Statistics South Africa. 2000. *October Household Survey 1999*. Pretoria: Statistics South Africa.

Stephen, M. 1999. 'Witchcraft, grief, and the ambivalence of emotions', *American Ethnologist* 26 (3): 711–37.

Steward, P. and A. Strathern. 2004. *Witchcraft, Sorcery, Rumours and Gossip*. Cambridge: Cambridge University Press.

Stocking, G. 1968. *Race, Culture and Evolution: essays on the history of anthropology*. New York NY: The Free Press.

Stoll, D. 1999. *Rigoberta Menchú and the Story of All Poor Guatemalans*. Boulder CO: Westview Press.

Stoller, P. and C. Olkes. 1987. *In Sorcery's Shadow: a memoir of apprenticeship among the Songhay of Niger*. Chicago IL: University of Chicago Press.

Strathern, M. 1988. *Gender of the Gift: problems with women and problems with society in Melanesia*. Berkeley CA: University of California Press.

______ 1996. 'Cutting the network', *Journal of the Royal Anthropological Institute* 2 (3): 517–35.

Taylor, C. 1990. 'Condoms and cosmology: the "fractual" person and sexual risk in Rwanda', *Social Science and Medicine* 31 (9): 1023–38.

______ 1992. *Milk, Honey and Money: changing concepts of Rwandan healing*. Washington DC: Smithsonian Institution.

Taylor, J. 1979. *Eva Peron: myths of a woman*. Chicago IL: University of Chicago Press.

Ter Haar, G. and S. Ellis. 2009. 'The occult does not exist: a response to Terence Ranger', *Africa* 79 (3): 399–412.

Thom, A. 2004. 'Limping behind in health care', *Mail and Guardian*, 26 March to 1 April.

______ 2006. 'ARVs vital in the battle against AIDS', *The Star*, 4 September.

Thornton, R. 2008. *Unimagined Community: sex, networks, and AIDS in Uganda and South Africa*. Berkeley CA: University of California Press.

Turner, E. (with W. Blodgett, S. Kahona, and F. Benwa). 1992. *Experiencing Ritual: a new interpretation of African healing*. Philadelphia PA: University of Pennsylvania Press.

Turner, V. 1967a. 'Betwixt and between: the liminal period in *rites de passage*' in *The Forest of Symbols*. Ithaca NY: Cornell University Press.

______ 1967b. 'A Ndembu doctor in practice' in *The Forest of Symbols*. Ithaca NY: Cornell University Press.

______ 1969. *The Ritual Process: structure and anti-structure*. Ithaca NY: Cornell University Press.

van Binsbergen, W. 2001. 'Witchcraft in Africa as virtualized boundary conditions of the kinship order' in George C. Bond and Dianne Ciekawy (eds), *Witchcraft Dialogues: anthropological and philosophical exchanges*. Athens OH: Centre for International Studies.

______ 2003. *Intercultural Encounters: African and anthropological lessons towards a philosophy of interculturality*. Műnster: Lit Verlag.

van de Port, M. 1999. 'It takes a Serb to know a Serb: uncovering the roots of obstinate otherness in Serbia', *Critique of Anthropology* 19 (1): 7–30.

van der Vliet, V. 1991. 'Traditional husband, modern wives? Constructing marriage in a South African township' in P. A. McAllister and A. D. Spiegel (eds), *Tradition and Transition in Southern Africa*. Johannesburg: Witwatersrand University Press.

______ 2004. 'South Africa divided against AIDS: a crisis of leadership' in K. Kauffman and D. Lindauer (eds), *AIDS and South Africa: the social expression of a pandemic*. New York NY: Palgrave.

van Gennep, A. 1961. *The Rites of Passage*. London: Routledge and Kegan Paul.

van Kessel, I. 1993. '"From confusion to Lusaka": the youth revolt in Sekhukhuneland', *Journal of Southern African Studies* 19 (4), 593–614.

______ 2000. *'Beyond Our Wildest Dreams': the United Democratic Front and the transformation of South Africa*. Charlottesville VA: University of Virginia Press.

van Onselen, C. 1984. *The Small Matter of a Horse: the life of 'Nongoloza' Mathebula, 1867–1945*. Johannesburg: Ravan Press.

______ 1993. 'The reconstruction of a rural life from oral testimony: critical notes on the methodology employed in the study of a black South African sharecropper', *Journal of Peasant Studies* 20 (3): 494–514.

______ 1996. *The Seed Is Mine: the life of Kas Maine, a South African sharecropper, 1894–1985*. Cape Town: David Philip.

______ 2007. *The Fox and the Flies: the world of Joseph Silver, racketeer and psychopath*. London: Jonathan Cape.

Wagner, R. 1986. *Symbols That Stand for Themselves*. Chicago IL: University of Chicago Press.

Wahlstrộm, Å. 2002. 'The Old Digging Graves for the Young: the cultural construction of AIDS among youth in the South African Lowveld'. BSc Thesis, Brunel University, London.

Walker, L., G. Reid, and M. Cornell. 2004. *Waiting to Happen: HIV/AIDS in South Africa*. Cape Town: Double Storey Books.

Weber, M. 1985 (1905). *The Protestant Ethic and the Spirit of Capitalism*. London: Unwin Paperbacks.

______ 1949. 'Objectivity in social science and in social policy' in *The Methodology of the Social Sciences*. Glencoe: Free Press.

Webster, D. 1977. 'Spreading the risk: the principle of laterality in Chopi society', *Africa* 47 (1): 192–207.

______ 1991. '"*Abafazi bathonga bafihlakala*": ethnicity and gender in a KwaZulu border community' in P. A. McAllister and A. D. Spiegel (eds), *Tradition and Transition in Southern Africa*. Johannesburg: Witwatersrand University Press.

Werbner, R. 1991. *Tears of the Dead: the social biography of an African family*. Edinburgh: Edinburgh University Press and the International African Institute.

West, H. 2006. 'Working the borders to beneficial effect: the not-so-indigenous knowledge of not-so-traditional healers in Mozambique' in H. West and T. Luedke (eds), *Borders and Healers: brokering therapeutic resources in southeast Africa*. Bloomington IN: Indiana University Press.

______ 2007. *Ethnographic Sorcery*. Chicago IL: University of Chicago Press.

West, H. and T. Luedke. 2006. 'Introduction: Healing divides: therapeutic border work in southeast Africa' in H. West and T. Luedke (eds), *Borders and Healers: brokering therapeutic resources in southeast Africa*. Bloomington IN: Indiana University Press.

Whisson, M. 1990. 'Review of *Waiting: the whites of South Africa* by Vincent Crapanzano' in P. Hugo (ed.), *Truth Be in the Field: social research in Southern Africa*. Pretoria: University of South Africa Press.

White, L. 1994. 'Between Gluckman and Foucault: historicizing rumour and gossip', *Social Dynamics* 20 (1): 75–92.

______ 2000. *Speaking with Vampires: rumour and history in colonial Africa*. Berkeley CA: University of California Press.

Wilkens, I. and H. Strydom. 1980. *The Super Afrikaners: inside the Afrikaner Broederbond*. Johannesburg: Jonathan Ball Publishers.

Willetts, D. 2010. *The Pinch: how baby-boomers took their children's future – and why they should give it back*. London: Atlantic Books.

Willis, P. 1977. *Learning to Labour: how working-class kids get working-class jobs*. Farnborough: Saxon House.

Willis, R. 1999. *Some Spirits Heal, Others Only Dance: a journey into human selfhood in an African village*. Oxford: Berg.

Wilson P., G. McCall, W. R. Geddes, A. K. Mark, J. Pfeiffer, J. Boskey, and C. Turnbull. 1975. 'More thoughts on the Ik and anthropology', *Current Anthropology* 16 (2): 343–58.

Wojcicki, J. 2002. '"She drank his money": survival sex and the problem of violence in taverns in Gauteng Province, South Africa', *Medical Anthropology Quarterly* 16 (3): 267–93.

Wolff, B. and S. Langley. 1968. 'Cultural factors and the response to pain: a review', *American Anthropologist* 70 (3): 494–501.

Worobec, C. 1995. 'Witchcraft beliefs and practices in pre-revolutionary Russian and Ukranian villages', *The Russian Review* 54 (April): 165–87.

Wreford, J. 2005a. 'Missing each other: problems and potentials of collaborative efforts between biomedicine and traditional healers in South Africa in the time of AIDS', *Social Dynamics* 31 (2): 55–89.

______ 2005b. 'Sincedisa – We can help! A literature review of current practice involving traditional African healers in biomedical HIV/AIDS intervetions in South Africa', *Social Dynamics* 31 (2): 90–117.

Yamba, C. B. 1997. 'Cosmologies in turmoil: witchfinding and AIDS in Chiawa, Zambia', *Africa* 67 (2): 200–23.

Ziervogel, D. 1954. *The Eastern Sotho*. Pretoria: van Schaik.

Index

TITLES IN THE SERIES

42 Fraser G. McNeill
AIDS, Politics, and Music in South Africa
41 Krijn Peters
War and the Crisis of Youth in Sierra Leone
40 Insa Nolte
Obafemi Awolowo and the Making of Remo: the local politics of a Nigerian nationalist
39 Ben Jones
Beyond the State in Rural Uganda
38 Ramon Sarró
The Politics of Religious Change on the Upper Guinea Coast: iconoclasm done and undone
37 Charles Gore
Art, Performance and Ritual in Benin City
36 Ferdinand de Jong
Masquerades of Modernity: power and secrecy in Casamance, Senegal
35 Kai Kresse
Philosophising in Mombasa: knowledge, Islam and intellectual practice on the Swahili coast
34 David Pratten
The Man-Leopard Murders: history and society in colonial Nigeria
33 Carola Lentz
Ethnicity and the Making of History in Northern Ghana
32 Benjamin F. Soares
Islam and the Prayer Economy: history and authority in a Malian town
31 Colin Murray and Peter Sanders
Medicine Murder in Colonial Lesotho: the anatomy of a moral crisis
30 R. M. Dilley
Islamic and Caste Knowledge Practices among Haalpulaar'en in Senegal: between mosque and termite mound
29 Belinda Bozzoli
Theatres of Struggle and the End of Apartheid
28 Elisha Reene
Population and Progress in a Yoruba Town
27 Anthony Simpson
'Half-London' in Zambia: contested identities in a Catholic mission school
26 Harri Englund
From War to Peace on the Mozambique–Malawi Borderland
25 T. C. McCaskie
Asante Identities: history and modernity in an African village 1850–1950
24 Janet Bujra
Serving Class: masculinity and the feminisation of domestic service in Tanzania
23 Christopher O. David
Death in Abeyance: illness and therapy among the Tabwa of Central Africa
22 Deborah James
Songs of the Women Migrants: performance and identity in South Africa

21 BIRGIT MEYER
Translating the Devil: religion and modernity among the Ewe in Ghana
20 DAVID MAXWELL
Christians and Chiefs in Zimbabwe: a social history of the Hwesa people c. 1870s–1990s
19 A. FIONA D. MACKENZIE
Land, Ecology and Resistance in Kenya, 1880–1952
18 JANE I. GUYER
An African Niche Economy: farming to feed Ibadan, 1968–88
17 PHILIP BURNHAM
The Politics of Cultural Difference in Northern Cameroon
16 GRAHAM FURNISS
Poetry, Prose and Popular Culture in Hausa
15 C. BAWA YAMBA
Permanent Pilgrims: the role of pilgrimage in the lives of West African Muslims in Sudan
14 TOM FORREST
The Advance of African Capital: the growth of Nigerian private enterprise
13 MELISSA LEACH
Rainforest Relations: gender and resource use among the Mende of Gola, Sierra Leone
12 ISAAC NCUBE MAZONDE
Ranching and Enterprise in Eastern Botswana: a case study of black and white farmers
11 G. S. EADES
Strangers and Traders: Yoruba migrants, markets and the state in northern Ghana
10 COLIN MURRAY
Black Mountain: land, class and power in the eastern Orange Free State, 1880s to 1980s
9 RICHARD WERBNER
Tears of the Dead: the social biography of an African family
8 RICHARD FARDON
Between God, the Dead and the Wild: Chamba interpretations of religion and ritual
7 KARIN BARBER
I Could Speak Until Tomorrow: oriki, women and the past in a Yoruba town
6 SUZETTE HEALD
Controlling Anger: the sociology of Gisu violence
5 GUNTHER SCHLEE
Identities on the Move: clanship and pastoralism in northern Kenya
4 JOHAN POTTIER
Migrants No More: settlement and survival in Mambwe villages, Zambia
3 PAUL SPENCER
The Maasai of Matapato: a study of rituals of rebellion
2 JANE I. GUYER (ed.)
Feeding African Cities: essays in social history
1 SANDRA T. BARNES
Patrons and Power: creating a political community in metropolitan Lagos

Lightning Source UK Ltd.
Milton Keynes UK
UKOW04f1347201217
314800UK00001B/34/P

9 781108 442695